GOD AND EARTHLY POWER

THE UNIVERSITY OF
WINCHESTER

GOD AND EARTHLY POWER

AN OLD TESTAMENT POLITICAL THEOLOGY

GENESIS–KINGS

by

J. G. MCCONVILLE

t&t clark

Published by T&T Clark

A Continuum imprint

The Tower Building, 11 York Road, London SE1 7NX
80 Maiden Lane, Suite 1704, New York, NY 10038

www.continuumbooks.com

New Revised Standard Version Bible: Anglicized Edition, copyright 1989, 1995, Division of Christian Education of the National Council of the Churches of Christ in the United States of America. Used by Permission. All rights reserved.

J.G. McConville has asserted his right under the Copyright, Designs and Patents Act, 1988, to be identified as the Author of this work.

British Library Cataloguing-in-Publication Data
A catalogue record for this book is available from the British Library

Typeset by CA Typesetting Ltd, www.sheffieldtypesetting.com
Printed on acid-free paper in Great Britain by Biddles Ltd, King's Lynn, Norfolk

ISBN-10: HB: 0-567-04493-9
          PB: 0-567-04570-6
ISBN-13: HB: 978-0-567-04493-8
          PB: 978-0-567-04570-6

For Bishop Kenneth Cragg

On seventy years of ordination

(Deut. 26.9) ויבאנו אל־המקום הזה

CONTENTS

PREFACE

The present volume had its genesis in a Consultation in the Scripture and Hermeneutics Project series, held in Cheltenham in 2001. The topic was the use of the Bible in ethics and politics, and it took the form of a dialogue with Professor Oliver O'Donovan of Oxford University. I am indebted to Professor O'Donovan, not only for his published work which was the text for the Consultation (*The Desire of the Nations*), but also for his penetrating responses to the papers given there, including my own. (The papers and responses are in the volume entitled *A Royal Priesthood?*) Professor O'Donovan's proposal to build a political theology on the foundation of the Old and New Testaments was an indispensable stimulus to the thesis I offer here.

By the same token, I owe a debt of gratitude to my former colleague at the University of Gloucestershire, Professor Craig Bartholomew, now of Redeemer University College, Ancaster, Ontario. As the Director of the Scripture and Hermeneutics Project, and a visionary advocate of the importance of hermeneutics in theology and biblical studies, he bears some responsibility for my attempt to broaden my study into this area.

The topic addressed here stands at a place where Biblical Studies meets other disciplines in Theology, and I have benefited from the wisdom of many in attempting to understand broader issues, though none bear responsibility for the specific formulations in this thesis. Among them I would mention Professor Jonathan Chaplin of the Institute of Christian Studies, Toronto, an influential contributor to the Consultation and volume named above. And Professor Stephen Williams of Union Theological College and Queen's University, Belfast, proved a friend indeed by graciously undertaking a close reading of the manuscript at an advanced stage, and making many useful observations on both form and content, which have had an important effect on the final form.

I am grateful too to my colleagues in the Department of Humanities at the University of Gloucestershire for their friendly collegiality and encouragement, enabling me to find the time to complete the work.

The book is dedicated, however, to Bishop Kenneth Cragg, in gratitude for the kindness and wisdom of a senior friend who attains in 2006 the seventieth anniversary of his ordination to the priesthood, and from whom I have learnt immeasurably, not least of the entailments of 'earthly power'. It comes with the warmest respect and good wishes.

I am grateful also to the editors at T&T Clark International, who have been unfailingly patient and helpful. While on the subject of their patience, I should explain my approach to transliteration of Hebrew in this volume. I have normally followed the series practice of giving Hebrew in the unpointed original, but have used informal transliterations for words that recur frequently in the argument or in particular passages, in the hope that the book may not prove unintelligible to non-Hebraists. Where I have referred to standard translations of biblical texts, I have resorted most often, though not invariably, to NRSV.

ABBREVIATIONS

AB	Anchor Bible
ABRL	Anchor Bible Reference Library
ANE	Ancient Near East(ern)
ANET	James B. Pritchard (ed.), *Ancient Near Eastern Texts Relating to the Old Testament* (Princeton: Princeton University Press, 1954)
AOAT	Alter Orient und Altes Testament
AOTC	Apollos Old Testament Commentary
BBB	Bonner biblische Beiträge
BEATAJ	Beiträge zur Erforschung des Alten Testaments und des antiken Judentums
BHT	Beiträge zur historischen Theologie
BIS	Biblical Interpretation Series
BTAT	Beiträge zur Theologie des Alten Testaments
BWANT	Beiträge zur Wissenschaft vom Alten und Neuen Testament
BZ	*Biblische Zeitschrift*
BZAW	Beihefte zur *ZAW*
CBQ	*Catholic Biblical Quarterly*
ConBot	Coniectanea biblica, Old Testament
Dtr	The Deuteronomist, Deuteronomistic
ESV	English Standard Version
EUS	European University Studies
EVV	English language versions
FAT	Forschungen zum Alten Testament
HAT	Handbuch zum Alten Testament
HBS	Herders Biblische Studien
HSM	Harvard Semitic Monographs
IDB	George Arthur Buttrick (ed.), *The Interpreter's Dictionary of the Bible* (4 vols.; Nashville: Abingdon Press, 1962)
IDBSup	*IDB*, Supplementary Volume
JBL	*Journal of Biblical Literature*
JR	*Journal of Religion*
JSOT	*Journal for the Study of the Old Testament*
JSOTSup	*Journal for the Study of the Old Testament*, Supplement Series
KJV	King James Version
NAC	New American Commentary
NIBC	New International Biblical Commentary
NIV	New International Version
NRSV	New Revised Standard Version
OBO	Orbis biblicus et orientalis
ÖBS	Österreichische biblische Studien
OBT	Overtures to Biblical Theology
OTL	Old Testament Library
RSV	Revised Standard Version

SAA	State Archives of Assyria
SBAB	Stuttgarter Biblische Aufsatzbände
SBLSS	SBL Semeia Studies
SCI	*Studia Classica Israelica*
SCJ	*Sixteenth Century Journal*
SBTS	Sources for Biblical and Theological Study
SHS	Scripture and Hermeneutics Series
StudBib	*Studia Biblica*
TynBul	*Tyndale Bulletin*
TBü	Theologische Bücherei
ThPQ	*Theologisch-Praktische Quartalschrift*
TTod	*Theology Today*
VT	*Vetus Testamentum*
VTE	The Vassal Treaties of Esarhaddon
VTSup	*Vetus Testamentum*, Supplement Series
WBC	Word Biblical Commentary
WMANT	Wissenschaftliche Monographien zum Alten und Neuen Testament
ZAW	*Zeitschrift für die alttestamentliche Wissenschaft*

LXX	The Septuagint
MT	Masoretic Text
OG	Old Greek

Chapter 1

READING THE OLD TESTAMENT POLITICALLY

1. *The Old Testament in the Modern World*

The present volume aims to contribute to a discussion of how the Old Testament might be understood politically, both in its own terms and in relation to the modern world. Such a project is contentious from every conceivable angle. A secular world would banish the Bible from public discourse, and so if possible pre-empt the question. A suspicious world regards the Bible as serving the interests of those who promote it, powerful élites, insiders excluding outsiders, and so doubts its capacity to be the vehicle of radical critique. And an influential voice within biblical scholarship gives credence to this suspicious attitude, with its thesis that the Old Testament was born in an act of self-assertion by an élite group in post-exilic Judah, pressing its claim to land and status over against other contenders.

I introduce the present topic in this way, not to concede any of the above, but to declare the nature of the argument. The responses to the Old Testament that I have alluded to here (and which will be represented specifically as the argument proceeds) are not themselves value-free, but are part of the passionate discourse that the Bible provokes. For the Bible is of course contentious, with its claims about a world that is subject to the mercy and judgement of the one God, made known in the life and the Scriptures of Israel. Its message (in the course of its growth and development) ran counter to the interests of great powers from Assyria to Rome, as well as meeting resistance from many who called themselves 'Israel'. And this was so because by its nature it intruded upon public and private life, and compelled response.

The topic, therefore, demands attention, not avoidance. The Old Testament has exerted influence on political life in many ways over centuries, and even today it still does so, whether overtly, as in the politics that converge on Palestine, or somewhat tacitly, in the ways in which nations with Christian traditions have subtly drawn on it in support of national aspirations.[1] The Old Testament's presence in public life has not simply faded into the past, but is alive and well. It

1. Or not so subtly; see below, Chapter 5, for examples. See also Adrian Hastings, *The Construction of Nationhood: Ethnicity, Religion and Nationalism* (Cambridge: Cambridge University Press, 1997), pp. 185–209, especially pp. 195–8; and also Michael Burleigh, *Earthly Powers* (London: HarperCollins, 2005), for an account of the legacy of biblical and religious ideas in European politics since the French Revolution.

is also potentially dangerous, as many of its modern critics have quite rightly seen, for undeniably the name of God has been invoked in the interests of human power and ambition, and with violence. But it is for this reason that it needs to be heard and understood. It is open to abuse not only by those who would exploit it for their own purposes, but also by those who would reduce or dismiss it by casting it as the willing tool of such interests. Yet when carefully heard, it may prove the only bulwark against self-aggrandizement and idolatry.

2. *Reading the Old Testament*

If the Old Testament is contentious in the world at large it is no less so in the scholarship that is dedicated to it. For here as elsewhere the overarching commitments that are played out in contemporary hermeneutics are manifest. For classical critical scholarship, the issue confronted was the perceived hegemony of Christian theology in matters of biblical interpretation, and the aim was to preserve the Bible from misappropriation in the interests of dogma. As part of its reconstruction of Israelite history and religion, it sought to uncover the interests that lay behind texts. The surface biblical story of how God providentially delivered his chosen people Israel from captivity in Egypt gave way to a narrative in which the texts were found to lack fundamental unity, but rather expressed various aspirations. The 'J' document was propaganda for the Davidic Empire; the Priestly parts of the Pentateuch promoted the interests of the Aaronide priests; the deuteronomic literature promoted the reform of King Josiah, and thus the interests of the royal court of Judah.

In recent times, the debate about the Bible has taken on the hues of modern hermeneutical discourse, and the tendencies in classical criticism have been pursued in new ways. Here one sees quite distinct directions. In one important version, the suspicion implicit in the older scholarship has been taken to a new level. The search for underlying agendas is no longer perceived as a matter of judicious historical research, but is rather of the essence. Consequently, the Old Testament has been 'rumbled' by the alert critic. The Old Testament, as winners' history, may not be trusted in the matters about which it purports to speak. There was in reality no 'ancient Israel'; rather this is a construct of a powerful group that needed a sacred history in order to authenticate its political goals.[2]

The newness of this mood should not be underestimated. The older scholarship, though alert to various interests, largely supposed that the writers of the Old Testament preserved actual sources, to which they were in measure bound.[3] With

---

2.   Oliver O'Donovan, in his bid to restore biblical history to the discourse of political theology, begins his thesis with a chapter entitled 'Beyond Suspicion'; O'Donovan, *Desire of the Nations: Rediscovering the Roots of Political Theology* (Cambridge: Cambridge University Press, 1996), pp. 6–29.

3.   Martin Noth's analysis and explanation of the Deuteronomistic History is a case in point. Much of the work on DtrH since Noth shares his intention of reconstructing a history; e.g. G. N. Knoppers, *Two Nations Under God: the Deuteronomistic History of Solomon and the Dual Monarchies* (HSM, 52-53; 2 vols.; Atlanta: Scholars Press, 1993–94).

careful reading, a course of Israelite history and religion might still be discerned. Moreover, many of those who based their work on the critical reconstruction of Old Testament history did so in the hope of promoting a better understanding of theology.[4] The more suspicious modern readings, beginning roughly with Morton Smith and Joseph Blenkinsopp,[5] diverge in principle from this kind of interpretation. Adopting sociological models, they look deliberately to the period in which the books are thought to have been formed to discover ideological reasons for their composition. P. R. Davies has pursued the argument rigorously. For him, 'ancient Israel' is an invention of the religious élite in Persian Yehud, under the aegis of the Persian authorities and their policy of reorganizing the empire around temple administrations and law codes.[6] The Old Testament was written in scribal schools, to which are owed both its impression of unity and its apparent antiquity.[7] It is important to note that the accounts of Smith, Blenkinsopp and Davies all aim to explain the Old Testament as *canon*. Canon itself thus becomes a function of domination.

The renunciation of a history and religion of ancient Israel in this approach is overdrawn, there being little evidence that the kind of literary activity described by Davies happened in the manner or milieu he postulates. More important for our present interest, however, is the way in which the approach tends to disqualify the Old Testament from speaking, especially on political matters. The scribes could criticize their own régime, but did so circumspectly, '...so that no direct criticism of the current authorities is explicit'.[8]

Keith Whitelam, accepting Davies' analysis,[9] took forward the idea of domination. Not only was the Old Testament itself the product of an exclusive group's bid to protect its position, but biblical scholarship was affected more than it realized by the Old Testament's own account and interests. To the extent that the object of its interest was conceived as the 'history of Israel' it failed to be a history of the region and its peoples as such. Whitelam's sub-title, 'the silencing of Palestinian history', illustrates his thesis, that both the Old Testament itself and its interpreters have been guilty of an act of exclusion, an exclusion that

4. This point has been well made by John Barton, who disputes the explicit or implicit claims of the modern 'canonical approach' that historical criticism was anti-theological, and argues that many of its practitioners from early to recent times had religious beliefs and theological interests; John Barton, 'Canon and Old Testament Interpretation', in Edward Ball (ed.), *In Search of True Wisdom: Essays in Old Testament Interpretation in Honour of Ronald E. Clements* (JSOTSup, 300; Sheffield: Sheffield Academic Press, 1999), pp. 37–52 (39–43).

5. Morton Smith, *Palestinian Parties and Politics That Shaped the Old Testament* (New York: Columbia University Press, 1971; London: SCM Press, 2nd edn, 1987); J. Blenkinsopp, *Prophecy and Canon: A Contribution to the Study of Jewish Origins* (Notre Dame: University of Notre Dame Press, 1977), e.g. pp. 147–8.

6. P. R. Davies, *In Search of 'Ancient Israel'* (JSOTSup, 148; Sheffield: Sheffield Academic Press, 1992, repr. 1995), pp. 101–3, 111–12.

7. Davies, *'Ancient Israel'*, pp. 114–15, 124–5.

8. Davies, *'Ancient Israel'*, p. 103. As Davies' thesis depends on the assumption that texts ostensibly about the past are really about the present (see p. 118) this argument is rather weak.

9. Keith W. Whitelam, *The Invention of Ancient Israel: The Silencing of Palestinian History* (London: Routledge, 1996), p. 3.

applies both to ancient non-Israelite peoples, and to modern Palestinians. Citing
Edward Said's thesis regarding the close interconnections between scholarship
and nationalism,[10] he argues that Old Testament historiography has its roots in
Eurocentric nineteenth-century nationalism, has consequently shown a fascination with the emergence of a 'nation state' in ancient Israel, and has thus been the
ally, in effect, of modern nationalism, specifically Zionist nationalism. Archaeology has evinced similar commitments.[11] Biblical studies, in embracing an 'Israelite' reading of the Old Testament, and specifically in its refusal to use the term
'Palestinians' to refer to the population of the land in general, 'is, thereby, implicated in an act of dispossession which has its modern political counterpart in the
Zionist possession of the land and dispossession of its Palestinian inhabitants'.[12]
On such a view, the biblical texts are the creatures of the political interests of the
powerful not only at the point of their generation but also in the history of their
appropriation. They are in consequence unlikely to be available for constructive
theological or political thinking. Indeed, theological interpretation is apparently
foreclosed at the outset.[13]

There is, however, a contrary tendency in modern hermeneutics, in which
texts are precisely *not* bound by their original functions or intentions. In the search
for the location of meaning, attention has largely turned away from the world
'behind the text' to focus on the text itself, or the 'world of/within the text', and
the world 'in front of' it: meaning lies in an engagement between texts and those
who read them. There is no single form of this approach, with greater and lesser
freedom accorded to the reader, and greater and lesser constraints exerted by
the texts. Yet in common is the point that texts by their nature cannot control
the reading process. As Iser put it: 'The text represents a potential effect that is
realized in the reading process'.[14] In similar vein Umberto Eco spoke of 'open
texts',[15] and Paul Ricoeur of a 'surplus of meaning'.[16] The fundamental assump-

10. Whitelam, *Invention*, p. 20; Edward Said, *Culture and Imperialism* (London: Chatto and Windus, 1993), p. 51.

11. Whitelam, *Invention*, pp. 20–1. He cites Finkelstein's study of the 'Israelite settlement', as 'an interpretation of the archaeological data from the Late Bronze to the early Iron Ages which assumes the unity and identity of Israel, in effect an incipient nation state, in the Palestinian high-lands' (p. 21); I. Finkelstein, *The Archaeology of the Israelite Settlement* (Jerusalem: Israel Explo-ration Society, 1988).

12. Whitelam, *Invention*, p. 46.

13. E. T. Mullen, for example, refers to his study of the Pentateuch as a 'non-theological, secular analysis'; *Ethnic Myths and Pentateuchal Foundations: A New Approach to the Formation of the Pentateuch* (Atlanta: Scholars Press, 1997), p. 5.

14. Wolfgang Iser, *The Act of Reading: A Theory of Aesthetic Response* (Baltimore: The Johns Hopkins University Press, 1978), p. ix; cited A. C. Thiselton, ' "Behind" and "In Front of" the Text: Language, Reference and Indeterminacy', in Craig Bartholomew, Colin Greene and Karl Möller (eds.), *After Pentecost: Language and Biblical Interpretation* (SHS, 2; Carlisle: Paternoster Press/Grand Rapids: Zondervan, 2001), pp. 97–120 (100).

15. Umberto Eco in (for example) '*Intentio Lectoris*: the State of the Art', in Eco, *The Limits of Interpretation* (Bloomington and Indianapolis: Indiana University Press, 1990), pp. 44–63 (49–50).

16. Paul Ricoeur, *Interpretation Theory* (Fort Worth: T.C.U. Press, 1976), p. 45. The same concept appears as a 'principle of plenitude', that is, as Dan Stiver puts it, 'a text or event can mean

tion here is that texts are by their nature capable of becoming meaningful in new ways, independently of conditions that brought them to birth.

There is, furthermore, a specifically canonical dimension to this. Historically, the biblical texts have been predominantly read theologically, or canonically. That is, they have been heard to speak to faith communities in a multiplicity of settings, and they have been read in relation to each other. The potential of the canonical texts to become meaningful in fresh ways has been a basic postulate of biblical interpretation. George Aichele, describing the working assumptions of 'biblical theology' (though he does not share them) and alluding to Ricoeur, puts this well: 'The canonical text overflows with a surplus of meaning, an abundance of significance, that allows it to speak to all times and peoples'.[17]

In this discussion, as we have seen, a specific issue concerns whether the canon is the product of the narrow interests of a particular group, and thus tainted with oppressive ideology, or whether it is liberative and capable of speaking critically and prophetically. The importance of this dilemma in the political interpretation of the Bible may be seen from an exchange between Christopher Rowland and Itumeleng Mosala. Mosala thinks that black theology, to be effective, needs to understand both the history and culture that affects the reading of the Bible and the political agendas that lie behind the texts. He thus adopts what he calls a 'historical-materialist' method, 'to get to the bottom of real events, relationships, structures and so forth'.[18] Reading the Book of Micah accordingly, he addresses his enquiry not to the 'surface' of the biblical text, but to the disparate parts from which it has been composed. He does so on the grounds that these reveal the real oppression of the poor by the powerful strata of monarchical society. The canonical final form, in contrast, represents a re-appropriation of such by an élite that adduces themes from Davidic theology – namely 'stability, grace, creation, restoration, universal peace, compassion and salvation' – and now casts itself in the role of victim.[19] The affinities with Davies' reconstruction are clear. Rowland argues, in contrast, that it is the final form that preserves the variety of readings, readily conceding that liberative readings jostle with more accommodating ones (he refers especially to the Gospel of Luke), but arguing that this at least ensures the survival of the liberative voices, and that readers of

all that it can mean'; Stiver, 'Ricoeur, Speech-act Theory, and the Gospels as History', in Bartholomew *et al.* (eds.), *After Pentecost*, pp. 50–72 (58). Stiver refers there to Ricoeur, 'Metaphor and the Central Problem of Hermeneutics', in J. B. Thompson (ed.), *Hermeneutics and the Human Sciences: Essays on Language, Action, and Interpretation* (Cambridge: Cambridge University Press, 1981), pp. 165–81 (176).

17. George Aichele, *The Control of Biblical Meaning: Canon as Semiotic Mechanism* (Harrisburg: Trinity Press International, 2001).

18. Itumeleng Mosala, *Biblical Hermeneutics and Black Theology in South Africa* (Grand Rapids: Eerdmans, 1989), pp. 3–4.

19. Mosala, *Biblical Hermeneutics*, pp. 101–53; see pp. 102–3, 118–21. He goes on: 'Micah itself, as is true of most of the Bible, offers no certain starting point for a theology of liberation. There is simply too much de-ideologization to be made before it can be hermeneutically usable in the struggle for liberation'; p. 121.

Luke have had no difficulty in hearing them.[20] Rowland does not deny that Luke may have been produced by an élite, but he shows that the text could nevertheless not be reduced to an instrument of their ideology.[21]

In a different debate, Michael Wolter comes to a similar conclusion. Arguing that the formation of the (NT) canon was not the consequence of a consistent theological programme (but rather had a strong element of compromise), he claims that the plurality of the canon even has a positive significance, because it maintains that Christian identity can and must take different forms in different social contexts, without however becoming subsumed by any such context. [22] Here too, therefore, the forces that produced the canon cannot determine its interpretation in advance.

3. *The Text and its 'Worlds'*

The idea of 'worlds *behind, of/within*, and *in front of*' the text has already been introduced in the preceding pages. I propose to adopt it as a methodological basis in the study before us, because I believe it offers a conceptual possibility of doing justice to the complexity of interpreting a biblical text with an interest in its contemporary significance, as well as a measure of control.[23] Some further considerations are in place at this stage, however.

a. *'Behind the text'*

It may seem that the drift of the preceding argument suggests that any attempt to recover the 'world behind the text' cannot play an effective part in interpretation. But this would be unrealistic and unconvincing. I have argued only against allowing interpretation to be unduly influenced by over-confident theories of the text's origins, and by an excess of 'suspicion' about the motives for its production. In practice, texts can hardly be understood apart from some grasp of the world in which they were produced. Thiselton rightly counsels against detaching the text from 'the extra-textual world of reality'.[24] The problem with reading the Old Testament is that so much of what counts as knowledge about the specific origins

20. Christopher Rowland, 'In This Place: the Center and the Margins in Theology', in Fernando F. Segovia and Mary Ann Tolbert (eds.), *Reading from this Place: Social Location and Biblical Interpretation in Global Perspective* (Minneapolis: Augsburg Fortress, 1995), pp. 177–82.

21. Rowland, 'In This Place', p. 182.

22. Michael Wolter, 'Die Vielfalt der Schrift und die Einheit des Kanons', in John Barton and Wolter (eds.), *Die Einheit der Schrift und die Vielfalt des Kanons* (Berlin and New York: W. de Gruyter, 2003), pp. 45–68 (61–2).

23. Thiselton also claims that the three dimensions are inseparable from each other in the reading process; '"Behind" and "In Front of" the Text', pp. 102, 108. See also W. R. Tate, *Biblical Interpretation: an Integrated Approach* (Peabody, Mass.: Hendrickson, 1991), who adopts the concept throughout.

24. Thiselton, ' "Behind" and "In Front of" the Text', p. 100. See also his comments on p. 107, and reference to K. Vanhoozer, *Is There a Meaning in This Text? The Bible, the Reader, and the Morality of Literary Knowledge* (Grand Rapids: Zondervan, 1998), pp. 48–90, 229–59.

of texts is approximate and provisional. This difficulty is felt even by those who argue strongly for a particular setting. E. T. Mullen takes the view, like Davies, that the Pentateuch was formed in the Persian period by an élite in Judah under the auspices of the imperial authorities, arguing that its purpose was to establish an ethnic identity for the returned community and especially its leadership. Yet it proves impossible to locate the process of formation to that period, as Mullen sees:

> There can be little doubt that the process itself would have been much more complex than the factors mentioned above would suggest [viz. the need to form a tradition for the community in the context of Persian policy]. Since there is evidence that the Pentateuch was still open to modifications as late as the latter half of the third century BCE, then it is clear that caution must be taken in postulating a precise time at which the Pentateuch was completed.[25]

He finally concedes that the theory of the Pentateuch's composition in the Persian period by the returned exiles in Jerusalem 'has to be somewhat hypothetical, since there exists no direct empirical evidence for either the composition of the Pentateuchal traditions or the ways in which they were applied within the community'.[26] The Persian hypothesis finally suffers from the handicaps which Mullen claimed stood against the traditional theories about Pentateuchal formation, evidence for which 'is all internal to the argument itself and is supported only by its own presuppositions'.[27]

To this fundamental difficulty in historical research we may add a factor indicated by the Old Testament itself. Old Testament books do not point unequivocally to times of their composition. In the case of the Book of Isaiah, for example, the composition cuts across the two main periods to which its structure and content draw attention, the Assyrian and Babylonian. And this appears to be not merely a testimony to a long period of growth, but a strategy of the composition, which brings together the prophetic messages to Judah in the two periods (and probably beyond them) in a theological composition that is not determined by any one. B. S. Childs, drawing attention to this aspect of the book, thought that it was deliberately lifted out of specific historical contexts in order to apply more effectively to new contexts in which it might be read.[28] The same point holds for Deuteronomy, with the difference that specific settings (apart from the Mosaic) are not explicitly indicated. While it locates itself at a point prior to the entry of Israel to the land of Canaan, formal and theological indicators allow it to be read broadly against the background of ancient Near Eastern law and treaty, and particularly in relation to neo-Assyrian concepts; and it finally has a

25. Mullen, *Ethnic Myths*, pp. 73–4. For evidence for this late finalization of the Pentateuch he refers to G. Garbini, *History and Ideology in Ancient Israel* (New York: Crossroad, 1988), p. 146. He also points to Qumran as the earliest evidence for the Pentateuch and other OT literature as basically complete.

26. Mullen, *Ethnic Myths*, pp. 75–6.

27. Mullen, *Ethnic Myths*, p. 157.

28. B. S. Childs, *Introduction to the Old Testament as Scripture* (London: SCM Press, 1979), pp. 336–8.

post-exilic horizon.[29] Many books of the Old Testament are impossible to date with certainty.

However, the examples mentioned show that it is impossible to ignore the historical, social, religious and cultural matrix within which the texts were formed. While it is true that Deuteronomy cannot simply be identified with a vassal-treaty, whether Hittite or neo-Assyrian, a responsible reading of the book is bound to pay attention to the affinities it shares with these, as they are likely to be essential to a nuanced understanding of its character and purpose. The 'world behind the text', therefore, is indispensable. We simply have to enter the caveat that our knowledge of how the texts relate to that world is imprecise. The relationship between the text and the world 'behind' it always eludes complete description; it is rather a matter of ongoing comparison and modification, as part of the full range of the interpretative process. This modest approach to understanding texts historically is not only realistic, but also has the advantage of refraining from forcing texts into a mould cast by an overriding theory of origins.

b. *'Of/within the text'*
The idea of the world 'of' or 'within' the text recognizes that texts (whether historical or fictional) represent an imaginative construction of the world, which is then offered to the imagination of the reader. It is thus distinct from the world behind the text, since that is independent of the text. The world of the text is a construct entailed in its production, lying close to the idea of the text's 'horizon', which in Gadamer's hermeneutics has to be 'fused' with that of the reader if the text is to be understood.[30] A first concern in the study that follows is to identify a text within the Old Testament which offers the possibility to the reader to reflect on theology and politics. In choosing Genesis–Kings, I have decided to focus on the 'primary history' of the Old Testament.

It is increasingly recognized that Genesis–Kings forms a distinct entity. The designation 'primary history' for Genesis–Kings is owed to D. N. Freedman, who thought it was an exilic composition.[31] The concept, if not Freedman's specific hypothesis, has been followed by a number of writers. Davies adopts it in the context of his thesis that the scribal project in Yehud required a coherent account of the origins of Israel,[32] as does Mullen.[33] The basic justification for viewing it in this way is that it offers a complete account of the story of Israel from its origins to the exile.[34]

29. See below, Chapter 2, for more on the background of Deuteronomy.
30. See Stiver, 'Ricoeur', pp. 58–9, for this comparison. He refers to H. G. Gadamer, *Truth and Method*, (trans. J. Weinsheimer and D. G. Marshall; New York: Crossroad, rev. edn, 1991), p. 297. See also above, nn. 14–16.
31. D. N. Freedman, 'The Law and the Prophets', VTSup, 9 (1963), pp. 250–65; *idem*, 'Canon of the Old Testament', IDBSup (New York and Nashville: Abingdon Press, 1975), pp. 130–6.
32. Davies, *'Ancient Israel'*, pp. 124–5.
33. Mullen, *Ethnic Myths*, pp. 57–8.
34. It is the only such account, since Chronicles–Ezra–Nehemiah omits the formative events of exodus and Sinai.

This remains the case even though the canonical division between Torah or Pentateuch and Historical Books or Former Prophets cuts across certain narrative and theological interconnections between those blocks. These interconnections have long been recognized in critical scholarship, albeit in different ways. For example, the concept of a Hexateuch was based on the view that the Abrahamic land-promises of Genesis cannot be severed from the only story of their fulfilment, in Joshua.[35] Conversely, the Deuteronomistic theory thought the evident connections between Deuteronomy and some of the language and concepts of the historical books decisive, leaving a 'Tetrateuch' of Genesis to Numbers. Each view carried a certain weight, yet neither was a complete description. The Deuteronomistic analysis found it impossible to read Joshua without reference to material in the books preceding Deuteronomy (hence Noth's 'priestly' additions, including the participation of Eleazar the priest and the heads of the tribes in the distribution of land, Josh. 14.1–2; 19.51; 21.1–2, and the setting up of the Tent of Meeting at Shiloh; Josh. 18.1; 19.51).[36] And the clear echoes of the Exodus narrative throughout Joshua–Kings show that neither of the proposed boundary lines is definitive.[37] While there are real issues of composition here, it is finally inevitable to respect again the traditional linkages which present Genesis–Kings as a unified narrative.[38]

The considerations above are primarily literary, but the focus on Genesis–Kings is informed, second, by a certain 'canonical' interest. The reasons for invoking the idea of canon are first, that the literature has been shaped and preserved by a canonical process, so that its status as canon is bound to be acknowledged in its interpretation, and second, that it recognizes that the texts have a crucial theological dimension which should not be foreclosed at the outset.[39]

In adopting the notion of canon for the present enquiry, I do not mean the process of canonization, but rather what eventuates from the process, namely an invitation to read the books in terms of their shared canonical status (hence as an

35. The Hexateuch is associated particularly with G. von Rad in classical twentieth-century Old Testament interpretation: 'The Problem of the Hexateuch', in *The Problem of the Hexateuch and Other Essays* (trans. E. W. Trueman Dicken; London: Oliver and Boyd, 1966). In an important recent work, Konrad Schmid revives both the Hexateuchal idea and the unity of Genesis–Kings. The promises to the patriarchs and the exodus from Egypt constitute a double foundation for the origin of Israel. While promise and fulfilment of the latter are found within Exodus, the fulfilment of the patriarchal promises occurs in Joshua; *Erzväter und Exodus: Untersuchungen zur doppelten Begründung der Ursprünge Israels innerhalb der Geschichtsbücher des Alten Testaments* (WMANT, 81; Neukirchen–Vluyn: Neukirchener Verlag, 1999), pp. 196–7. See also his reflections on the relationship between Hexateuch and Pentateuch, pp. 290–3.

36. M. Noth, *Das Buch Josua* (HAT, I/7; Tübingen: Mohr-Siebeck, 1953), pp. 10–11.

37. K. Schmid, *Erzväter und Exodus*, p. 78; e.g. Josh. 2.8–11; 5.1; 9.9; 24.2–8; Judg. 2.1, 11; 6.8–9; 1 Sam. 4.8; 6.6; 2 Sam. 7.6; 1 Kgs 8.16; 8.51; 2 Kgs 17.7, 36; cf. C. Westermann, *Die Geschichtsbücher des Alten Testaments: Gab es ein deuteronomistisches Geschichtswerk?* (TBü, 87; Gütersloh: Kaiser, 1994), pp. 39–40.

38. For Schmid, Genesis–Kings is unified according to a structure of 'Heilsgeschichte' ('salvation-history') in Genesis–Joshua, followed by 'Unheilsgeschichte' ('judgement-history') in Judges–Kings; *Erzväter und Exodus*, pp. 290–1.

39. *Pace* Mullen; see above, n. 13.

aspect of the world *within* the text). In the case of Genesis–Kings, this canonical imperative operates initially in the obvious sense that Genesis–Kings is presented as a continuous narrative. (Here, therefore, canonical and literary considerations overlap.) The traditional intra-canonical divisions of Torah, Prophets and Writings do not tell against this point, since the canonical idea entails that ultimately all the writings in the canon should be read as constituting a unity. (In as far as the present study is a *canonical* exercise it is, by the same token, partial or preliminary.) Furthermore, the point at which 'Torah' gives way to 'Former Prophets', namely at Josh. 1.1, contains in its reference to the death of Moses just narrated at the end of Deuteronomy, a strong 'canonical' mark of continuity (canonical because it does more than establish a chronological linkage, but it implies a theological point about continuity between Moses and Joshua). However, the canonical imperative in the case of Genesis–Kings is not exhausted by the narrative logic that gives it its initial unity. Rather it implies a method of reading in which texts are understood in the light of each other. For example, the juxtaposition of texts about the creation of the world with texts about the formation of Israel, and the gathering of various law codes into the framework of the ministry of Moses between Sinai and Moab, invite theological reflection about the relationships thus composed. Such reflection will perceive not only surface-level continuities between events, but also discontinuities (for example between parts of the law codes), which give rise to perplexity on the reader's part. It is the canonical dimension, however, that poses the question to the reader how such elements might be read in the light of each other.[40]

The idea of the 'world of the text' impinges on our study in this connection. The 'imagined' world is laid out on a canvas that has both literary and canonical aspects, and the work of the reader is to engage with it in ways that pay attention to both.

c. *'In Front of the Text'*

The various 'worlds' are interconnected. The world within the text, as we saw, was an imagined construct that aimed at and required the participation of the reader. The reader's participation in the making of meaning corresponds to the text's 'openness', or 'surplus of meaning'. Iser's definition of the text as 'a potential effect that is realized in the reading process',[41] expresses the point succinctly. The idea of the world 'in front of the text' conveys the possibility inherent in the text for it to affect the worlds inhabited by its readers. The story of this potential, therefore, is told in the many ways in which texts have actually been read and used.

---

40. The idea of 'canon' is used in distinct but related ways. First it refers to the formal divisions of the Old Testament/Hebrew Bible, thus (in the style of the latter) between Torah, Former/Latter Prophets, Writings. But second, it is an approach to biblical interpretation in which the character of the Bible as a canon by definition proposes a hermeneutic in which the comparative analysis and evaluation of its parts is prominent; see Aichele, *Control of Biblical Meaning*, e.g. pp. 15–27, for a penetrating if not wholly sympathetic account.

41. See above, n. 14.

To say this is not to underestimate the great differences between ancient and modern societies and concepts, though the recognition of such differences often leads to pessimism about the usefulness of the biblical texts in contemporary ethical discourse of any sort. I accept the caution of Daniel Fleming in his enquiry into antecedents of 'democracy' at Mari (in second-millennium BCE Mesopotamia): 'I have tried to respect the world embodied in each ancient word, from "town" to "elder" to "king", recognizing that the reality behind every term is distant from anything in the modern world, so that we are too easily seduced into inappropriate interpretive frameworks'.[42] The concept of democracy itself illustrates the point well, as some scholars have claimed that the Old Testament contains democratic ideas, while others have found this to be hopelessly anachronistic.[43] The divergence of view on the point bespeaks fundamentally different appraisals of the capacity of ancient texts to engage with the urgent concerns of contemporary readers. But it is just here, I think, that attention to the reception and usage of texts enters necessarily into the process of their interpretation, since such usage discloses something of the actual potential of the text. Genesis–Kings has in fact a rich history of appropriation in theological political thinking, and we shall observe this at appropriate points and in conclusion.[44]

We shall therefore offer a reading of Genesis–Kings which a) learns from historical setting, b) reads the text in its integrity and interconnectedness, and c) aims to hear it in relation to modern issues. Our reading allows that it is bigger than any proposed original purpose. For example, in its concern for 'justice and righteousness', and its association of these with confession of the one God Yahweh, it engages with powerful concepts in such a way that the texts could not possibly be restricted in their meaning or effects to the agenda of any group.[45]

42. Daniel E. Fleming, *Democracy's Ancient Ancestors: Mari and Early Collective Governance* (Cambridge: Cambridge University Press, 2004), p. 20.

43. Frank Crüsemann writes concerning Deuteronomy: 'The sovereignty of the people underlying the law compels us to speak of something like a democracy', *The Torah: Theology and Social History of Old Testament Law* (Minneapolis: Fortress, 1996), pp. 246–7. For the contrary view, see D. A. Knight, 'Political Rights and Powers in Monarchic Israel', in Knight (ed.), *Ethics and Politics in the Hebrew Bible* (*Semeia* 66; Atlanta: Scholars Press, 1995), pp. 93–117. We shall revisit this at a later stage of the argument.

44. One account of the interpretation of Deuteronomy which offers a preliminary illustration of this point is S. Dean McBride, 'Deuteronomy', in John H. Hayes, (ed.), *Dictionary of Biblical Interpretation A-J* (Nashville: Abingdon Press, 1999), pp. 273–94.

45. See Thiselton on 1 Corinthians; ' "Behind" and "In Front of" the Text', pp. 108–9.

Chapter 2

THE OLD TESTAMENT AS CULTURAL CRITIQUE

1. *Monotheism under Attack*

In modern conflicts, the various allegiances of the warring parties to God often appear to be the main barrier to progress. This is nowhere clearer than in Israel-Palestine, with its long biblical resonances. Here the memory of Abraham, carefully tended to this day in his adoptive home at Hebron, might be a symbol of unity, as some have hoped.[1] Yet on the contrary, the 'tombs of the patriarchs' grace one of the most conflicted sites in that embattled land, the very divisiveness of Abraham fossilized in a shrine to complexity and hostility. The reality of the land of Israel-Palestine is an arena of competing populations, each informed at some level by their own version of Abrahamic monotheism. Marc Ellis, in his moving and searing appeal for an inclusive polity in modern Israel, finds the globalized expansionism of Christianity and Islam now to have borne fruit in a 'Constantinian Judaism':[2] '…monotheistic religions – Judaism, but also Christianity and Islam – are born in a cycle of violence of what becomes a particular religion, that violence continues within various understandings of these particular religions, with subsequent violence carried on between these religions.'[3]

The association of monotheism, violence and exclusiveness has been pursued programmatically by several writers. The Egyptologist Jan Assmann contrasts the Egyptian Moses of imagination with the Hebrew Moses of biblical tradition. The former was an object of Enlightenment fascination with the figure of Moses in an Egyptian cultural and religious context (with a debt to Acts 7.22: 'Moses was instructed in all the wisdom of the Egyptians'). The latter represented a transfer in ancient cultural memory of the monotheistic revolution of Akhenaten, which Assmann characterizes as exclusive and repressive, and found literary expression in the biblical narrative. Monotheism in its Mosaic form produces the 'Mosaic distinction' between true and false religion and the characterization of all that is not 'true' as pagan and idolatrous.[4] Assmann contrasts Mosaic exclu-

1. Karl-Josef Kuschel, *Abraham: a Symbol of Hope for Jews, Christians and Muslims* (trans. John Bowden; London: SCM Press, 1995).
2. Marc H. Ellis, *Israel and Palestine: Out of the Ashes; the Search for Jewish Identity in the Twenty-First Century* (London and Sterling VA: Pluto Press, 2002), pp. 69–86.
3. Ellis, *Israel and Palestine*, p. 75.
4. Jan Assmann, *Moses the Egyptian: the Memory of Egypt in Western Monotheism* (Cambridge, Mass.; Harvard University Press, 1997). With a debt to Freud, he finds the 'Mosaic distinction' to be not only intolerant in general, but (paradoxically) to be the root of anti-Semitism; pp. 5–6.

sive, violent monotheistic religion with ancient polytheism which, by its capacity for 'translation' (i.e. of the pantheons), was intrinsically hospitable to otherness: 'Whereas Moses the Hebrew is the personification of confrontation and antago- nism… Moses the Egyptian bridges this opposition…While the Biblical Moses personifies the Mosaic distinction, Moses the Egyptian embodies its mediation.'[5] In this perspective, modern pluralism finds ancient Egyptian polytheism conge- nial company, and biblical religion inimical.

Writing at the same time as Assmann, Regina Schwartz argues that the Bible's concern with identity has violence latent in it. She documents the uses of biblical monotheism for particularist, especially 'nationalistic', purposes. In the Old Tes- tament's portrayal of Israel as a nation taking its collective identity from its covenant with God lay the seeds of all nationalisms that claimed transcendent legitimation: 'Nations are the will of God. National borders are the will of God. National expansions and colonization are the will of God. National military confrontations are the will of God. Every nation is the one nation under God.'[6] Schwartz finds a few strands within the Bible that are in her terms open, gener- ous, plural. Citing other powerful re-readings of the Bible (Luther, Blake, Milton, Freud) she proposes her own 'alternative Bible', which 'subverts the dominant vision of violence and scarcity with an ideal of plenitude and its corollary ethical imperative of generosity. It would be a Bible embracing multiplicity instead of monotheism.'[7]

For Schwartz as for Assmann, pluralism or multiplicity is philosophically preferable to the all-inclusiveness of monotheism ('Not one, but many gods'), and monotheism is deeply opposed to it. This was experienced even by Israel, which having attached its identity to the one God Yahweh became vulnerable to that God when it turned away from him to other gods, and found that 'radical monotheism unleashes its fury against pluralism' (citing Hos. 13.4–8).[8] Even parts of the Old Testament which have often been felt to be the pinnacle of its religion are found guilty of oppressive singularity. Of Jeremiah's New Covenant, she writes: 'The religious life is one of complete possession and utter subjection.' And as for Hosea, his '"tenderness" (*ḥěsěd*), love, mercy, and com- passion of God…are in the service of an unrelenting ideology of possessive monotheism'.[9]

2. *Exclusivism and Deuteronomy*

Modern studies of Old Testament theology and religion often voice similar con- cerns, and here one notices a tendency to criticize Deuteronomy and the deuter- onomic strands of the Old Testament in particular. The reasons for this are clear.

  5. Assmann, *Moses the Egyptian*, p. 11.
  6. Regina M. Schwartz, *The Curse of Cain: the Violent Legacy of Monotheism* (Chicago and London: University of Chicago Press, 1997), p. 11, cf. pp. 58–62.
  7. Schwartz, *The Curse of Cain*, p. 176.
  8. Schwartz, *The Curse of Cain*, p. 46; cf. pp. 37–8.
  9. Schwartz, *The Curse of Cain*, pp. 73, 75.

Deuteronomy's policies seem to be intended rather one-sidedly for the benefit of the 'Israelite' to the exclusion of others. Deuteronomy enshrines the חרם (*cherem, ban of destruction*) as the basis on which Israel shall occupy the land that God has given (Deut. 2.34; 7.1–5). To the story of Moses' implementation of the ban in Transjordan against the Amorite kings Sihon and Og (2.26–3.7), it adds a command to do likewise to the peoples of the land west of the Jordan, showing no mercy (7.1–2). The religion and culture of these peoples was to be eradicated, and replaced root and branch with the symbols and practice of Yahwistic worship (12.2–7). The practices of Canaan were 'abhorrent' to Yahweh (12.29–13.1[12.32 EVV]). This thorough rejection of the Canaanite 'other' runs through the book, as the presupposition of its concept of Israel entering a land gifted to it by God, an empty land, whose goods were entirely at their disposal (8.7–10). The point is even laboured: the Israelites will occupy 'a land with fine, large cities that you did not build, houses filled with all sorts of goods that you did not fill, hewn cisterns that you did not hew, vineyards and olive groves that you did not plant...' (Deut. 6.10b–11). Furthermore, this is not a gift which may be taken or left. It comes with the force of divine command; God will be angry with Israel if they turn away from the project of claiming this land for Yahweh[10] by blending in with the religion of its non-Israelite occupants (6.14–15). The distinction between this particular land and other lands is pressed in the laws about warfare, in which mercy might be shown following victory in wars fought outside the land, but not in wars fought within it (Deut. 20.10–18).

The rigours of Deuteronomy have their counterpart in the narratives that follow. In Joshua, the deuteronomic land-occupation is effected by war and *cherem*, and Yahweh's ownership of it, and his covenanted gift of it to Israel, are proclaimed and celebrated in ceremonies at Mt. Ebal and Shechem (Josh. 8.30–35; 24). Rigour in the *cherem* is a matter of obedience, as is clear from the judicial execution of Achan and family following their breach of it in the sack of Jericho (Joshua 7), and also later in Samuel's execution of the Amalekite king Agag, negligently spared by King Saul (1 Samuel 15).

The 'ban' is widely regarded today as a figure for radical loyalty to Yahweh.[11] The uncompromising commands just observed stand alongside others which appear to represent a more realistic view (Deut. 7.3 after 7.2). Even here, however, Deuteronomy's social provisions sometimes deliberately distinguish between the Israelite 'brother' and the foreigner, from whom, for example, the Israelite may exact interest in business transactions, though not from a fellow-Israelite (Deut. 23.19–20).

---

10. This is the force of the command in 12.5 to 'place the name' of Yahweh at the place he will choose, as demonstrated recently by Sandra L. Richter, *The Deuteronomistic History and the Name Theology: l*ᵉšakkēn š*ᵉmô šām in the Bible and the Ancient Near East* (BZAW, 318; Berlin/New York: W. de Gruyter, 2002).

11. See R. W. L. Moberly; R. D. Nelson and G. Braulik, 'The Destruction of the Nations and the Promise of Return: Hermeneutical Observations on the Book of Deuteronomy', *Verbum et Ecclesia* 25.1 (2004), pp. 46–65.

Here, then, if anywhere in the Old Testament, the equation between 'monotheism' and nationalism is writ large. The charter to possess and dispossess, and to do so as a matter of obedience and right, lies on the surface of the book. The towering presence of Deuteronomy within the theology of the Old Testament does nothing to diminish the problem.

a. *Deuteronomic Nationalism in History*
The connection between deuteronomic 'nationalism' and historic nationalisms is brought out by a number of writers. Steven Grosby shows how Oliver Cromwell and the American Puritans applied deuteronomic election theology directly to their contemporary political agendas in England and New England.[12] F. Deist documented the 'dangers of Deuteronomy' in relation to apartheid South Africa.[13] Robert Jewett and John Shelton Laurence identify distinct currents within the adoption of biblical themes in American political consciousness, and find a dichotomy between what they call 'zealous nationalism' and 'prophetic realism'. They show a link between 'zealous nationalism' and the 'superhero' myth in popular American culture, from 'the Virginian' and the Lone Ranger, to Superman and Bruce Willis in the film *Armageddon*. And provocatively, they demonstrate parallels between the 'Captain America complex' and characteristics of Islamic jihad.[14] Grosby and A. D. Smith catalogue other times and places in which Old Testament sanction has been claimed for specific national programmes, particularly Christian nations, where the universality of Christianity has not diminished the particularistic drive.[15] For Jewett and Laurence, the strain in American consciousness that draws strength from Deuteronomy is also inimical to the democratic instinct.[16]

12.   Cotton Mather thought of the formation of a Puritan nation in America in terms that drew on the biblical account of the deliverance of Israel from Egypt, through the wilderness, and into a promised land: 'Unto the upright Children of Abraham, here [sci. 'in an American Desert'] hath arisen Light in Darkness... 'Tis very certain, that the greatest Entertainments must needs occur in the History of the People, whom the Son of God hath Redeemed and Purified unto himself as a Peculiar People...'. Again, he writes of John Winthrop, governor of Massachussetts: 'Accordingly when the Noble design of carrying a Colony of chosen people into an American Wilderness was by some Eminent persons undertaken, This Eminent Person was, by the Consent of all, Chosen for the Moses...'; Steven Grosby, *Biblical Ideas of Nationality Ancient and Modern* (Winona Lake, IN: Eisenbrauns, 2002), pp. 222–3. The quotations are taken from *Magnalia Christi Americana*, Hartford, 1855, pp. 27, 119. For Cromwell's understanding of the war on absolutism in terms of the biblical victories of Israel over Canaan, see Grosby, pp. 219–20, referring in turn to Wilbur Cortez Abbot, *The Writings and Speeches of Oliver Cromwell Vol. III* (Cambridge, Mass.; Harvard University Press, 1945), pp. 52–66, 434–43.
13.   F. Deist, 'The Dangers of Deuteronomy: a Page from the Reception History of the Book', in F. García Martínez *et al.* (eds.), *Studies in Deuteronomy in Honour of C. J. Labuschagne on the Occasion of His 65th Birthday* (VTSup, 53; Leiden: E. J. Brill, 1994), pp. 13–29.
14.   Robert Jewett and John Shelton Laurence, *Captain America and the Crusade Against Evil* (Grand Rapids: Eerdmans, 2003), pp. 24–5.
15.   Grosby, *Biblical Ideas of Nationality*, pp. 102, 204, 218; A. D. Smith, *Chosen Peoples* (Oxford and New York: Oxford University Press, 2003), pp. 66–94.
16.   Jewett and Laurence, *Captain America*, pp. 41–3.

b. *Deuteronomic Exclusivism in Old Testament Theology*
Writers of Old Testament Theologies are exercised by Deuteronomy's potential
for perpetuating exclusivistic ideologies. E. Gerstenberger traces Israel's belief in
one God to the sixth century (with its 'classic' formulation in Deut. 6.5–8), from
which time it became not only predominant in early Judaism but also foundational in western thought. The idea of one God, with its attendant exclusive
claim, passed into modern (western) consciousness as the axiomatic basis of all
religion. In our deeply pluralistic world, however, with its intolerance of all
absolutist claims, we must learn to think differently.[17] Pluralism is inevitable in
a modern ethic, and the deuteronomic tradition does not easily square with it.

W. Brueggemann depicts a God who wavers uncertainly between mercy and
severity. In Exod. 34.6–7 he finds what he calls a 'disjunctive rendering of God',
a stark juxtaposition of love and anger. These aspects are unreconciled, and capable of being taken up separately elsewhere in the OT (as in Nah. 1.2–3).[18]
Yahweh's sovereignty is 'endlessly unsettling and problematic'; there is 'something wild, unruly, dangerous' in his life,[19] so that Israel can never be quite sure
how he will act next. Brueggemann, like Gerstenberger, aims especially at
Deuteronomy: 'It is now a commonplace among Old Testament scholars that
Yahwism was quite variegated and that it was especially the Deuteronomic
tradition which imposed a certain exclusivistic view of faith…To be sure that
assertion of exclusivism was not completely successful, for traces of pluralism in
faith still remain in the text'.[20] Pluralism appears here too as a *bonum*, and while
the deuteronomic strand is against it, there are contrary signs of its emergence
in the Old Testament. For Brueggemann, it falls to Amos to 'de-absolutize' the
exclusive claims of the Old Testament's election tradition.[21] Together with the
Old Testament's violence, election theology illustrates what he calls its 'negativ-
ity', where the *positive* is all love and mercy. The concept of 'righteousness' is
only a 'proximate' resolution of the tension between the two poles of Yahweh's
character.[22] This tension is expressed vividly in such texts as Hos. 11.8–9; Jer.
31.20.[23] The overcoming of judgement by mercy, 'an emergence of pathos'
tending to incarnation, is a 'shaping of Yahweh' conducted in and through the
prophetic books: 'these texts permit us to watch while Yahweh redecides, in the
midst of a crisis, how to be Yahweh and who to be as Yahweh'.[24] (For Bruegge-

17. E. S. Gerstenberger, *Theologien im Alten Testament: Pluralität und Synkretismus alttestamentlichen Gottesglaubens* (Stuttgart: W. Kohlhammer, 2001), p. 166, cf. p. 176.
18. W. Brueggemann, *Theology of the Old Testament; Testimony, Dispute, Advocacy* (Minneapolis: Fortress, 1997), p. 270.
19. Brueggemann, *Theology*, p. 271. Brueggemann's language finds echoes in, for example,
Louis Stulman, *Order Amid Chaos: Jeremiah as Symbolic Tapestry* (Biblical Seminar, 57; Sheffield: Sheffield Academic Press, 1998).
20. Brueggemann, *Theology*, p. 264, n. 54.
21. Brueggemann, *Theology*, p. 178. Jewett and Laurence also cite Amos as an example of the
'prophetic realism' that they distinguish from 'zealous nationalism'.
22. Brueggemann, *Theology*, p. 283.
23. Brueggemann, *Theology*, p. 300.
24. Brueggemann, *Theology*, p. 302.

mann Israel's testimony is an 'uttering' of Yahweh.) But such resolutions are 'characteristically provisional and tenuous'; and 'the unsettling quality belongs definitionally to the character of Yahweh'. In spite of all, 'the sovereign self-regard of Yahweh' remains at odds with his 'covenantal relatedness'. Associated with the former (Yahweh's self-regard) are Yahweh's 'glory, holiness and jealousy', while his 'steadfast love and fidelity' belong with the latter.[25] The unpredictable in God is never settled once and for all in the Old Testament.[26]

For Gerstenberger and Brueggemann, therefore, the attempt to bring the Old Testament into fruitful engagement with the modern world seeks avenues to pluralism, and is critical of Deuteronomy in particular.

c. *Deuteronomic Exclusivism in Old Testament History*
Modern Old Testament history militates against the deuteronomic picture in a distinctive way. According to the prevalent opinion, the biblical narrative's portrayal of exodus from Egypt and conquest of land by a unified Israel is far removed from historical actuality. The Old Testament's account is widely regarded as possessing little historical value, and reconstructions of the history, religion and culture of the region depend much on archaeology and other sources. In its earliest stage, Israel was native to Canaan, and indistinguishable from the local population, in language, architecture and religion. In common with that population it was polytheistic, or 'pluralistic', as the recorded sayings of the prophets obliquely attest, when they find Israel habitually worshipping the god Baal in his various forms. Archaeological evidence in the form of inscriptions from Kuntillet-ʾAjrûd and Khirbet el-Qôm has led a number of scholars to think that Asherah was worshipped by some as Yahweh's consort.[27] Artefacts from the late Judean monarchy suggest a lively popular piety that employed goddess figurines, in stark contrast to the aniconic cult of Yahweh alone propounded by the canonical literature and especially by Deuteronomy. N. Lohfink thought that Josiah's reform was more likely directed against this renaissance of popular 'unofficial' religion than against the official religion of Assyria.[28] Gnuse adduces texts such as 1 Kgs 11.1–8; 2 Kgs 17.29–41, as evidence of polytheistic belief in Israel before the exile.[29] Because of such evidence, R. Gnuse thinks that '…the Israelites and Judahites were basically polytheistic throughout the pre-exilic

25. Brueggemann, *Theology*, pp. 302–3.
26. Brueggemann, *Theology*, pp. 312–13.
27. R. Gnuse, *No Other Gods: Emergent Monotheism in Israel* (JSOTSup, 241; Sheffield: Sheffield Academic Press, 1997), pp. 69–73. See also Mark S. Smith, *The Early History of God; Yahweh and the Other Deities in Ancient Israel* (San Francisco; Harper and Row, 1990), e.g. pp. 80–114. W. Arnold enters some cautionary notes: Bill T. Arnold, 'Religion in Ancient Israel', in David W. Baker and Bill T. Arnold (eds.), *The Face of Old Testament Studies* (Grand Rapids: Baker/Leicester: Apollos, 1999), pp. 391–420, e.g. pp. 411–13.
28. N. Lohfink, 'The Cult-Reform of Josiah of Judah: II Kings 22–23 as a Source for the History of Israelite Religion', in P. D. Hanson (ed.), *Ancient Israelite Religion: Essays in Honor of Frank Moore Cross* (Philadelphia: Fortress, 1987), pp. 459–75.
29. Gnuse, *No Other Gods*, pp. 179–81.

period, and Yahwism was a complex religion with indigenous polytheistic cultic activities'.[30]

We have already seen how this sort of historical analysis has a powerful hermeneutical dimension.[31] Deuteronomy's mono-Yahwism represents a late, minority development in Israel, and it is the achievement of the deuteronomic movement to have re-written history so as to present Israel as a pristine unity, committed to aniconic Yahwism from its earliest existence, having originated outside the land, and thus independently of the Canaanite religion and culture which it found there. Deuteronomy is the ideological centre of a canonizing programme that is nothing other than 'history written by the winners'. It is a dominant religious programme which has silenced other voices, and repudiated diversity. On this 'minimalist' view, aniconic mono-Yahwism, far from being a dangerous idea that changed the world, has become the dead hand of orthodoxy shoring up the ruling powers in the imperial province of Yehud. The typology of 'exodus' serves the purposes of the returnees at the expense of others. The 'exclusive' nature of mono-Yahwism is asserted once again. And Whitelam, as we saw, found connections between the Persian-period Yahwists and the oppression of modern Palestinians.

The revisionist historians, therefore, bring us back full circle to the critique of Marc Ellis, with which this chapter began. In the echoes which he finds between ancient Israel in Canaan and modern Israel in Palestine, he too portrays Old Testament mono-Yahwism as nationalistic and repressive.

Responses might be made in a number of ways to the above analyses. The pessimistic view of the relationship between the Old Testament and the writing of pre-exilic history is strongly challenged from other quarters within Old Testament scholarship.[32] Equally, the picture of early Israel as typically polytheistic and only gradually evolving a mono-Yahwistic religion is open to question. Richard Bauckham has argued against Gnuse that the Old Testament's monotheism (a term which he accepts with careful qualification) is not an evolutionary culmination, but rather a matter of perpetual dispute with Canaanite polytheism. This picture fits very well with Kings' concept of a clash of cultures, religion and politics stretching from Solomon to Josiah, and manifested in the polemics of the prophets.[33]

It is not our immediate concern, however, to reconstruct Israelite history, but rather to consider the nature and effect of the Old Testament's political ideas. The account of the legacy of the Old Testament, and of Deuteronomy's mono-Yahwism in particular, briefly reviewed above, focuses on its concept of one people in one land worshipping one God, and finds this to be precisely the

30. Gnuse, *No Other Gods*, p. 179; cf. pp. 58–61.

31. See above, Chapter 1.

32. See for example John Day (ed.), *In Search of Pre-Exilic Israel: Proceedings of the Oxford Old Testament Seminar* (JSOTSup, 406; London: T&T Clark, 2004).

33. R. J. Bauckham, 'Biblical Theology and the Problems of Monotheism', in C. Bartholomew *et al.* (eds.), *Out of Egypt: Biblical Theology and Biblical Interpretation* (SHS, 5; Grand Rapids: Zondervan, 2004, pp. 187–232).

problem in its confrontation with the modern world. In a pluralistic world, as Gerstenberger saw, it is not surprising that this book and its theological traditions have encountered special resistance. Here surely is unpromising material for a political theology.

There is, however, another way of looking at the texts, which may encourage us to continue.

3. *Yahwism as Critique of Oppression*

The picture of the baneful effects of biblical religion sketched above pays too little attention, in my view, to the contexts in which the texts emerged. It is admittedly the case that certain nationalistic and even oppressive types of society have appealed expressly to the biblical account of Israel in order to justify themselves. However, the larger claim that 'monotheism' has the germs of violence in it requires scrutiny. First, the idea of 'monotheism' is a coinage of the Enlightenment,[34] and Old Testament scholars have long doubted its usefulness in discourse about Old Testament religion. Aside from the question whether texts that insist on the worship of Yahweh alone actually imply that only one God exists,[35] there is the further factor that the concept is somewhat levelling and reductionist. It is a catch-all term that aims to embrace types of belief that are quite different, and may therefore apply badly to all of them.

The difficulty of applying the term to the Old Testament is felt even by some of those who want to criticize biblical monotheism. Schwartz admits: '...there is strictly speaking no such thing as monotheism in (the Hebrew Bible)'.[36] Indeed, the Old Testament narrative of Israel in practice undermines some of the simple unities that it appears at first glance to promote. The text '...founds itself on the notion of a covenanted community and then takes pains to demonstrate how fragile, how easily broken that is.'[37] Because of this self-critical, even contradictory character of the Old Testament, Schwartz occasionally agrees that it is not the Bible itself that propounds a radically exclusive view of group identity,

34. It has been attributed to David Hume, who believed that all religions that insisted on the oneness of God were intolerant, e.g. by N. Lohfink, 'Gewalt und Monotheismus: Beispiel Altes Testament', *ThPQ* 153.2 (2005), pp. 149–62 (149).

35. It has become customary to think of 'monolatry' or 'henotheism' instead of monotheism, that is, the worship of one God without the denial in principle that others may exist. For a recent development of this idea in relation to Deuteronomy see Nathan MacDonald, *Deuteronomy and the Meaning of "Monotheism"* (FAT 2/1; Tübingen: Mohr-Siebeck, 2003). It seems to me that certain Old Testament texts carry the confession of faith in Yahweh alone to a point where the existence of other gods is put in doubt, e.g. 1 Kgs 8.60. However, even here we do not have the language of ontological speculation.

36. Schwartz, *The Curse of Cain*, p. 17.

37. Schwartz, *The Curse of Cain*, p. 20. In her own note on this statement she cites, in support of the Hebrew Bible's self-critical tendency, Robert Alter, *The Art of Biblical Narrative* (New York: Basic Books, 1981); Mieke Bal, *Death and Dissymmetry: the Politics of Coherence in the Book of Judges* (Chicago: University of Chicago Press, 1988).

but rather those who have read it for 'racist' and other exclusive ends.[38] That the Bible has been used by dominant groups for their own advantage is indisputable. But this recognition that the connection between it and such applications is not straightforward is significant. The biblical story must be read carefully as what it is, and not made to conform to some pre-conceived critique.

Having noted the tendentiousness of the term monotheism, it is also in place to query the claim that religion that insists on the worship of one God necessarily leads to violence. The necessity of this connection is insisted on by Assmann: 'If one wishes to rescue the monotheistic idea, it must first be stripped of its inherent violence' (author's translation).[39] Such an assertion leaves monotheism no right of reply.[40] Yet, the connection so confidently posited is probably beyond demonstration. (Are non-monotheistic ideologies free from the tarnish of violence? What sort of mix does it take to produce a holocaust?) The evidence of ancient polytheism counsels caution: the Old Testament has no rival to the Canaanite depiction of the goddess Anat wading in the blood of her enemies.[41] And we come in a moment to the polytheistic religion that drove the Assyrian lust for conquest.

a. *Yahwism as Counter-Culture*

Critiques of monotheism have not always adequately considered the picture of Yahwism that actually emerges from the Old Testament. Here is no interest in a philosophical singularity. Nor does the idea of a dominant ideology ring true. Rather, biblical Yahwism is found, through the pages of the Old Testament, in critical dialogue with the powers and ideologies of the region, and in life-or-death conflict with them. Israel's confession of the 'oneness' of Yahweh (Deut. 6.4) is embedded in a work that is itself a redrawing of the religious and ideological map of the ancient world. The belief in Yahweh as one is a response to the monopolistic imperialisms that perennially threaten to absorb and obliterate Israel. Such was indeed the fate of the northern kingdom, when its people were deported and assimilated into the Assyrian conglomerate (2 Kings 17). Here was a kind of diversity that resulted in displacement and the annihilation of identity in the service of monolithic power (2 Kgs 17.29–34). In this context, the oneness of Yahweh is more than an assertion of the rights of this god over against that god, more even than the means whereby a vulnerable people preserved its identity, but part of an alternative view of power and order in the world.

In order to substantiate this, we begin with the 'Shema' itself, the great confession of faith in Yahweh alone (Deut. 6.4). The Hebrew of v. 4b[42] (literally,

---

38. Schwartz, *The Curse of Cain*, p. 103.

39. J. Assmann, 'Monotheismus und Ikonoklasmus als politische Theologie', in E. Otto (ed.), *Mose: Ägypten und das Alte Testament* (Stuttgarter Bibelstudien, 189; Stuttgart: Katholisches Bibelwerk, 2000), pp. 121–39 (139).

40. N. Lohfink's response is to the point: 'I find this sentence in itself to be an act of violence' (author's translation), 'Gewalt und Monotheismus', p. 149.

41. 'The Ba'lu Myth', in W. W. Hallo and K. Lawson Younger (eds.), *The Context of Scripture I: Canonical Compositions from the Biblical World* (Leiden: Brill, 1997), pp. 241–74 (250–1).

42. ‏יהוה אלהינו יהוה אחד‏.

'Yahweh our God, Yahweh one') is open to several translations,[43] the most persuasive in my view being 'Yahweh our God, Yahweh is one'. The question that concerns us, however, is whether the force of the word *'echad* ('one') is that Yahweh *alone* is God, or that Yahweh's 'oneness' refers somehow to the manner of Yahweh's being. The former sense certainly coheres with the thrust of Deuteronomy, since plainly it requires covenant loyalty to Yahweh alone. The covenantal home of the language of 'love' was established long ago by W. L. Moran, and more recently R. W. L. Moberly has found that the 'Shema' declares that Yahweh alone is worthy of covenant love.[44] However, the implication of oneness may also be that Yahweh is one and indivisible.[45] The corollary of this would be that he is capable of undertaking entirely for Israel's life, giving land and other blessings, and delivering from danger. Conversely, he is entitled to Israel's undivided devotion. The oneness of God thus corresponds to the unity of reality itself as perceived in Deuteronomy, where the enjoyment of good in the natural order is a counterpart of doing good in the religious and moral order (e.g. Deut. 6.24–25). Deuteronomy faces a world in which religion, politics and the natural order are closely connected. Its confession of the oneness of Yahweh takes its significance in critical interaction with that world. How precisely this is so will be seen as we look further at how Israel's confession of one God bears upon competing claims about the nature of reality, and also (in ensuing chapters) how the political vision of Deuteronomy is developed in the Old Testament narrative and in the book itself.

The Old Testament's engagement with Assyria now requires closer examination. Assyrian kings took the title 'king of the four regions', meaning king of all the world (as in the case of Esarhaddon).[46] This was in effect an imperative laid on Assyrian kings to embark on campaigns of conquest. As is shown by prophecies to Esarhaddon and the Assyrians following a successful campaign across the Tigris, conquests were ratified by prophetic oracles of 'peace' (*šulmu*), and ceremonial acts of 'covenant' (*adê*).[47] A covenant between the king and the god Ashur is followed by one between the king and his subjects and vassals, now sponsored by the goddess Ishtar, and celebrated with a meal. Parties to the covenant are solemnly exhorted not to 'forget' it, but to 'remember' Ishtar (cf. Deut. 8.18–19). The demand for loyalty on the part of vassals was impressed

43. See J. G. McConville, *Deuteronomy* (AOTC, 5; Leicester; Apollos, 2002), pp. 140–1.

44. W. L. Moran, 'The Ancient Near Eastern Background of the Love of God in Deuteronomy', *CBQ* 25 (1963), pp. 77–87; R. W. L. Moberly, 'Toward an Interpretation of the Shema', in C. Seitz and K. Greene-McCreight (eds.), *Theological Exegesis in Honor of Brevard S. Childs* (Grand Rapids; Eerdmans, 1999), pp. 124–44. See also MacDonald, *Deuteronomy*, pp. 62–70.

45. In contrast perhaps to the multiple manifestations of Baal (1 Sam. 7.4). In this text Yahweh is worshipped לבדו, 'alone', so the Yahweh-alone point emerges more clearly here than in the Shema. Even so, there seems to be a contrast with the plurality of the Baals and Ashtaroth in themselves.

46. SAA 9 3.2 line ii 3; see M. Nissinen, C. L. Seow and Robert K. Ritner, *Prophets and Prophecy in the Ancient Near East* (Writings from the Ancient World, 12; Atlanta; SBL, 2003), p. 119.

47. SAA 9 3.3, lines ii 26–27; Nissinen, Seow and Ritner, *Prophets*, p. 120.

upon them also by the well-known blessing and curse conventions in the vassal treaties, supported by appeal to a multitude of deities as witnesses.[48]

This powerful religious and ideological imperative to dominate lies behind the experience of Israel and Judah recorded in the Old Testament. At stake was the legitimacy of dominion in any given region, and appeal was made to divine sanction in order to establish it. The Assyrian divine imperative appears in words attributed to the conqueror, as in Isa. 10.8–11, where his confident progress is driven by belief in the superiority of his gods, and where the 'idols' and 'images' of Samaria and Jerusalem are considered lightweight opposition.

For a depiction of war as a realization of beliefs about the ultimate nature of order, the confrontation between Sennacherib's commander, the Rabshakeh, and the besieged populace of Jerusalem (701 BCE) can hardly be bettered. The account illustrates the Assyrian practice of negotiating terms of surrender while the siege was already under way, a practice also displayed in a palace-relief of Sargon II. This practice is expressly opposed in Deut. 20.10–11, which requires the offer of terms of peace prior to siege, and thus not under the immediate pressure of it.[49] The biblical author's critical portrayal of the threat is evident also in his staging of the negotiations, namely in the Rabshakeh's replication of the Old Testament's 'deuteronomic' language, conceived to express Israel's debt to Yahweh for all its life and well-being (2 Kgs 18.31–35; Isa. 36.16–20; cf. Deut. 7.13; 8.7–10; 30.19). The power-play for the popular mind is perfectly caught in the Jerusalem leadership's vain plea that the Rabshakeh use the diplomatic language of Aramaic so that the ordinary people might not understand (2 Kgs 18.26). He on the contrary persists with the vernacular for his own purposes, determined that his naked threat shall be very clear to all within the walls. The deep connection between rhetorical language, appeal to the religious imagination, and power politics is perfectly illustrated. The biblical record of this episode sheds light on the nature of the impact of Deuteronomy, which echoes so much of the language and conceptuality of the Assyrian political world. The use of 'deuteronomic' language in the mouth of the Rabshakeh highlights with sharp irony the direct confrontation between the two worldviews. In its similarities to Assyrian concepts of power, yet with profound differences, Deuteronomy is designed to make an impact on the *Realpolitik* of its day.[50]

The ideological clash with Assyria has affected much of the Old Testament literature, especially Kings, Isaiah, Hosea and Amos. But the impact of ANE claims upon allegiance is more thoroughgoing. The great imperial contenders of a millennium or more walk the pages of the biblical texts. Israel is born into freedom in a separation from Egypt, the substance of a foundational narrative and pervasive memory (Exodus 1–24; Deut. 26.5–11). In its covenant documents, especially Deuteronomy, it borrows forms which have Hittite as well as Assyrian

---

48. Again, the Vassal Treaties of Esarhaddon (VTE) exemplify the form; see *ANET*, pp. 534–41.

49. See E. Otto, *Krieg und Frieden in der Hebräischen Bibel und im Alten Orient* (Stuttgart: W. Kohlhammer, 1999), p. 101.

50. The political ideology of Deuteronomy is developed below, in Chapter 5.

resonances. It records its campaign for its land in warfare against the peoples of Canaan. Following the Assyrian depredations of the northern kingdom, its southern rump (mainly Judah) suffers exile in Babylon, and a continued reduced existence under Persia. The Book of Daniel is stalked by the figure of the Seleucid king Antiochus Epiphanes IV.

Furthermore, the record is such that the distinctions between one level and another have become blurred in the canonical texts. This appears to be a deliberate effect in certain books. Isaiah is structured around a progression from Assyria to Babylon, with the impact of the two empires portrayed in relation to each other. (The miraculous deliverance of Jerusalem from Assyria, Isaiah 36–38, becomes an earnest of the later deliverance of the exiles from the power of Babylon.) Again in Isaiah, the imagery of the exodus from Egypt is re-applied to the return to the promised land from Babylon (Isa. 43.2–3, 16–17). In some places the names of the empires are used metaphorically for a rhetorical purpose. In Ezra 6.22 the Persian king Cyrus, whose policy had allowed the exiles to return to their land, is referred to as 'the king of Assyria'. This has the effect that the whole nexus of events from the devastation of Israel by the actual Assyrians to the reconstitution of a Jewish people in the ancient land is placed in a unified perspective, all subject to the purpose of Yahweh. Similarly, Egypt sometimes stands for any place of exile, as in the deuteronomic curse (Deut. 28.68). In Jer. 2.18, Egypt and Assyria are in effect melded into one. Finally, the book of Daniel depicts the rise and fall of empires, characterized equally as unnatural, 'beastly' forms of power rising from the sea of Chaos, their common destiny being displacement finally by the kingdom of God (Daniel 7).

The counter-cultural nature of the biblical texts runs deep. The early chapters of Genesis, for example, display a critical orientation towards Babylonian religion in particular, most pronounced in the story of the Tower of Babel (Gen. 11.1–9), which lampoons Babylonian temple-towers. The first creation narrative (Gen. 1.1–2.3/2.4a), and the flood-narrative (Gen. 6.5–8.22) are also widely regarded as asserting a Yahwistic view of God, the world and humanity in opposition to Mesopotamian concepts.[51] However, the Babylonian orientation of these texts is by no means exclusive. In some respects creation accounts echo both Egypt and Canaan. John Day argues that Genesis 1 is to an extent dependent on Psalm 104 which in turn shows parallels to Akhenaten's fourteenth-century BCE Hymn to the Sun. On the other hand, the word םוהת (*tehom*, 'the deep'), is in his view closer to a Canaanite form than to the name of the Babylonian sea-monster Tiamat, with which it is frequently compared.[52] The creation poetry of

---

51. See for example G. J. Wenham, *Genesis 1–15* (WBC, 1; Waco, TX: Word Books, 1987), pp. 159–66, who demonstrates convincingly the close connections between Genesis and the Mesopotamian flood-myths, and the critical stance of the former.

52. John Day, *Yahweh and the Gods and Goddesses of Canaan* (JSOTSup, 265; Sheffield: Sheffield Academic Press, 2000), p. 101. See in contrast, however, D. Tsumura, *The Earth and the Waters in Genesis 1 and 2: A Linguistic Investigation* (JSOTSup, 83; Sheffield: Sheffield Academic Press, 1989), pp. 51–2, 65. Tsumura thinks *tehom* cannot be shown to depend directly on either the Canaanite or the Babylonian forms.

the Old Testament, notably in those texts in which Yahweh is depicted as slaying the primaeval chaos monster or dragon, bearing names such as Leviathan and Rahab, echoes myths known from the environment (e.g. Pss. 74.13–16[12–15]; 89.10–11[9–10]; 93.1–4; Isa. 27.1).[53] Closest perhaps is the Canaanite story of Baal's overcoming of the sea-god Yam. Yet when the motifs of the dragon-myth are incorporated into the cult of Yahweh this is, again, not simply an argument with Canaan, but can be applied to the controversy with Babylon. This is apparently the case in Ps. 74.12–17, an exilic Psalm, in which the kingship of Elohim/ Yahweh is asserted in the face of Babylonian creation-political claims.

The attempt to disentangle the elements of the cultural and religious background to the Old Testament is extremely complex. This is in part because of continuities between the cultures of Canaan and Mesopotamia, where deities in one region have close affinities with deities in others (for example Canaanite Astarte was equated with Greek Aphrodite. And the abode of Canaanite El was apparently at the source of the two great rivers of Mesopotamia.[54]). In part it is because the mythological fragments in the Old Testament seem to take distinctive forms, so that it is not possible to align them simply with known myths.[55] Their employment in the service of political polemic, however, is clear. The myth of the 'Day Star, son of Dawn' (Isa. 14.12–21) is a case in point, being assimilated to an oracle of judgement against the king of Babylon.

b. *Counter-Culture and Yahweh's Oneness*
The Old Testament's assertion of Yahweh's supremacy is more than the tribal claim that Israel's god was better than others. Rather, it involves an understanding of how the world was ordered, in the natural, religious and political realms. The creation narratives of Genesis are famously two distinct accounts (1.1–2.3/4a and 2.4/4b–3.24). Elohim creates the heavens and the earth in six days, resting on the seventh; then Yahweh Elohim, in a garden, makes the woman for the man, and they in turn test the limits of the environment Yahweh has made. Yet the 'twoness' of the accounts is one in Genesis. There is no distinction here between a god of heaven and a god of earth (as in Babylon, between Ea and Anu, both in turn subject to En-Lil). This is effected in several ways: by the linking passage in Gen. 2.4a, which echoes 1.1 and also takes a form which is elsewhere always introductory in Genesis (5.1; 6.9; 10.1 etc.);[56] by the name Yahweh Elohim, which affirms that these two are one; and by numerous commonalities running through Genesis 1–3, such as the ironic echo of 1.26 in 3.5, 22. It is the one God Yahweh, also called Elohim, who authors this world-order that is marked out from the type of world-order imagined in the religious environment.

---

53. Cf. F. M. Cross, *Canaanite Myth and Hebrew Epic* (Cambridge, Mass.: Harvard University Press, 1973), pp. 135–6.

54. Day, *Yahweh and the Gods and Goddesses*, pp. 171–2, and pp. 30–1.

55. See, for example, the myth of the 'Day Star, son of Dawn', Isa. 14.12–21, and Day, *Yahweh and the Gods and Goddesses*, pp. 171–84.

56. Wenham, *Genesis 1–15*, p. 49.

Yahweh's oneness is also an important feature of the flood-narrative. Whereas in Mesopotamia, the activities of flood-bringing and salvation from flood are attributed to different gods (En-Lil and Ea) whose purposes are at odds,[57] in Genesis the two activities are concentrated in Yahweh. (The 'twoness' of Yahweh and Elohim, if it once implied disparateness, is overwritten in the account as we have it, the fusion itself testifying to the meaning of the text.) The antinomy of Yahweh as both destroyer and saviour is felt keenly in Gen. 6.8, which logically contradicts vv. 5-7. The oneness of Yahweh is proclaimed without apology, in all cognizance of the theological issues that ensue, especially that of the origin of evil. At stake is the unity of the created order. This is not unity for its own sake, however; rather, it is marked by the characteristic immediately predicated of Noah: 'Noah was a righteous man (צַדִּיק, *tsaddiq*), blameless in his generation' (Gen. 6.9). This צְדָקָה, *tsedaqah* (justice-righteousness) is imprinted on Yahweh's universe, as we shall see more fully in the next chapter.

The polemical aspect of the assertion of Yahweh's oneness is seen in the Old Testament's aniconism itself. A non-imaged Yahweh is at once incapable of being rendered multiply in images, specifically not both male and female, and yet also susceptible of metaphorical imagining in both male and female modes. A non-imaged Yahweh cannot be humiliated like a Dagon (1 Sam. 5.1–5), or like the many idols that were ritually transported into exile in the ebb and flow of imperial domination; rather, the non-imaged Yahweh may be imagined enthroned over Babylon, as in Ezekiel 1. Yahweh as one and non-imaged is also, and by the same token, creator of all the world.

Closely linked with aniconism is demythologization. The oneness of Yahweh Elohim corresponds to the non-deity of sun, moon, stars, earth, sea and other living beings. Herein lies one of the major contentions of Gen. 1.1–2.3, with its portrayal of the heavenly bodies as suspended lights (1.14–19), and its resolute distinctions between God, earth and living creatures.[58] And in the Song of the Sea (Exodus 15), it is Yam/Nahar merely as a body of water that stands opposed to Yahweh, the more serious opposition being the human power, in its totalizing form, of Pharaoh and his hosts.[59]

In all these cases the affirmation of the oneness of Yahweh does not rest with belief about the supreme deity in itself but is carried into the realms of nature and politics. A natural world that is not animated cannot be the source of terror. As for the domain of human power, the analogies between the power systems of heavenly and earthly realms have been well demonstrated.[60] How extensive the implications of Yahweh's oneness for political order are must be carefully

---

57. See Atrahasis, in Stephanie Dalley, *Myths from Mesopotamia* (Oxford: Oxford University Press, 1991), pp. 1–38.

58. See Wenham, *Genesis 1–15*, pp. 36–40.

59. Cross, *Canaanite Myth*, pp. 131–2.

60. For example by Lowell K. Handy, *Among the Host of Heaven: the Syro-Palestinian Pantheon as Bureaucracy* (Winona Lake, IN: Eisenbrauns, 1994); Dale Launderville, *Piety and Politics: The Dynamics of Royal Authority in Homeric Greece, Biblical Israel, and Old Babylonian Mesopotamia* (Grand Rapids: Ecrdmans, 2003).

unfolded. But we have hints already from this preamble. The creation of humanity as 'the image of God' (Gen. 1.26) makes two distinct but related polemical points: the 'image' (צֶלֶם, *tselem*) of God is to be found not in manufactured idols but in humanity, since Hebrew *tselem* is a standard word for such idols; moreover, it is humanity as such and not kings that enjoys 'royal' status (since the Akkadian counterpart of Hebrew *tselem, ṣalmu*, 'representative', is used for the king in Assyria).[61] And in the account of the one Yahweh's confrontation with Pharaoh in Exodus 1–15, culminating in the Song of the Sea, the oneness of Yahweh is linked not only with his appearances in the past to Abraham, Isaac and Jacob (Exod. 3.13; 6.3), but to the creation itself (note the echoes of Genesis 1 in the overcoming of 'the deep', *tehom*, Exod. 15.5, 8[62]). That is, Yahweh's defeat of Pharaoh's Egypt is an extension of his primaeval triumph over the forces of Chaos, now in the political sphere. And the whole nexus is woven into a narrative whose central theme is the deliverance of a people of Yahweh from slavery under a totalitarian tyranny into freedom.

As with the Song of the Sea, so with the account of the conquest of the land in Joshua. The 'holy war' texts noticed above are no doubt the most difficult of all. These too, however, are a kind of demythologization. To maintain this depends on taking them as theoretical constructs, with an ideological purpose. That is, in accordance with modern reconstructions of Israel's early history, as well as stylized features of the narrative itself (notably in the story of the conquest of Jericho), they are not factual accounts, but symbolic of loyalty to Yahweh. As such, they adopt ancient Near Eastern conventions pertaining to conquest accounts.[63] Narratorially, they are linked with the account of the exodus, the crossing of the Jordan (Joshua 3–4) plainly echoing the crossing of the Reed Sea. And following from the Song of the Sea, they continue to historicize the mythological primaeval conflict between a god of order and the forces of Chaos. Their polemic also has a political edge, however, aimed at the ideology of perpetual war exhibited especially by Assyria, and rooted in its religio-politics (we shall see more on this in a moment). In Joshua, the holy war is located in the past and confined to the borders of the land of Israel (as in Deut. 20.16–18, which gives the narrative a rationale in commandment). The most severe 'holy war' texts are often seen as distinct from and inferior to the deuteronomic theol-

61. E. Otto, referring to Deut. 17.14–20, makes the point that the Judean king could not ground his authority in creation, since according to Ps. 8 and Gen. 1, *all* human beings were 'kings'. Genesis' use of *tselem* specifically polemicizes in this way; Otto, *Krieg und Frieden*, pp. 89–91. See also Wenham, *Genesis 1–15*, pp. 28–32; Westermann, *Genesis 1–11* (trans. John J. Scullion; Minneapolis; Augsburg/London: SPCK, 1984), pp. 145–58; Andreas Schüle, 'Made in the "Image of God": The Concepts of Divine Images in Gen 1–3', *ZAW* 117 (2005), pp. 1–20. The Egyptian 'Instruction to King Merikare', however, has the idea of humanity created as God's 'images'; see Miriam Lichtheim, *Ancient Egyptian Literature I: the Old and Middle Kingdoms* (Berkeley: University of California Press, 1975), p. 106.

62. On the cosmic significance of the victory over the 'sea', see further T. E. Fretheim, *Exodus* (Interpretation; Louisville, KY: John Knox Press, 1991), pp. 165–70.

63. This is documented by K. Lawson Younger, *Ancient Conquest Accounts: A Study in Ancient Near Eastern and Biblical Historiography* (JSOTSup, 98; Sheffield: JSOT Press, 1990).

ogy of nationhood.[64] But viewed in the way described they too are part of the Old Testament's profound contention with the mythological ideologies of its world.

The politics of Yahweh's oneness goes well beyond Genesis and Exodus. E. Otto sees in Hosea, set in the period shortly before the fall of the northern kingdom to the rampant expansion of Assyria set in motion by Tiglath-Pileser III, a key text for the opposition of Yahwism to the religio-politics of that power. In Hosea 11–12, the prophet censures Israel, under King Hoshea, for its duplicity in making alliances with Assyria and Egypt at the same time. It has in fact been treacherous from its youth, as illustrated by Hosea's allusions to the Jacob tradition (Hos. 12.2–3).

Hosea 11 exhibits something of the stark contradictions that we saw in the flood-narrative. At the beginning of the chapter, God expresses his intention to give Israel over to slavery again as in its origins, because of its persistent unfaithfulness (Hos. 11.5). Yet this purpose is precisely that which is now revoked by the remarkable enunciation of the conflict within Yahweh himself, between the impulse to act in wrath and the stronger urge to have mercy (Hos. 11.8–9).[65] This text exhibits God's self-mastery, which becomes a model for Israel to repent of its false dependence on other powers.[66] Moreover, there is in this self-mastery a critical echo of Baal dying and rising. In the Baal-Mot myth, as in Hosea, there is an overcoming of the theme of warfare and death by means of a suffering god. However, in that myth Baal is passive, and while he lies defeated by Mot, it is the goddess Anat who continues the struggle and succeeds in freeing him from the underworld.[67] In Hosea this struggle takes place within the person of the one God, who overcomes his own wrath and so liberates Israel from its consequences. Otto sees this conflict as a victory over violence itself. Furthermore, it is a projection of the primaeval creation conflict onto the political plane, challenging the concept of war as a 'continuous creation'. With a model of divine self-restraint the inevitability of war is refuted, and political theology is totally transformed.[68] Here Israel's mono-Yahwism is portrayed as a potent means of engaging critically with contemporary ideology. And significantly, the ultimate overcoming of conflict in the world is located in the nature of the one God.

The contention between Israel's Yahwism and the surrounding cultures reaches a climax in the book of Isaiah. In Isaiah 40–66, the Old Testament's critique of the worship of other gods is at its most astringent (Isa. 40.18–20; 44.9–20). This section of Isaiah opens with an extended argument about the incomparability of Yahweh (Isaiah 40). But the argument claims more than mere incomparability. Rather, it is part of the contention of the Book of Isaiah (as of Kings) that Yahweh alone is the mover in all the affairs of Israel and the nations. Yahweh spurs kings to action, not the gods of Assyria or Babylon. He has brought

---

64. E.g. Otto, *Krieg und Frieden*, pp. 105–7.
65. Otto, *Krieg und Frieden*, pp. 77–9.
66. Otto, *Krieg und Frieden*, pp. 81–3.
67. Otto, *Krieg und Frieden*, pp. 84–5.
68. Otto, *Krieg und Frieden*, pp. 85–6.

exile on Judah and now he brings deliverance. This is why the theme of Yahweh as creator is so dominant here. It is the God who created all things who now 'creates' the new thing that is the deliverance of the exiles, the restoration of Zion, the ultimate establishment of 'new heavens and a new earth' (65.17). No other divine agent can frustrate his designs.

Finally, it is only with such a view of God that there can be grounds for the vision in Isaiah of an ultimate inclusive peace beyond the warfare in which nations are embroiled (Isa. 42.4; 49.6; cf. 2.2–4). The outcome of the Old Testament's underlying narrative in such a vision is its strongest answer to the concept that belief in one God engenders violence. On the contrary, it is a portrayal of history under the hand of the one God Yahweh that leads in the Old Testament story to a hope of eschatological peace that transcends conflicts both primaeval and political.[69]

4. *The Setting of the Old Testament's Oppositional Stance*

The above survey sets the Old Testament in contention with the ideologies of its world. But can a setting be determined for this stance? The question can hardly be answered conclusively, and in general, settings for Old Testament books can be only broadly determined. Nevertheless, it is fruitful to consider large parts of the Old Testament in relation to Assyria, and especially the crisis in the eighth and seventh centuries BCE. For Otto, deuteronomic political theology, emanating from priestly and wisdom circles and represented in Deuteronomy 13; 28, directly opposed Assyrian monopolistic claims. Nor is this anti-Assyrian orientation limited to a deuteronomic strand narrowly defined. The life of Moses, as told in Exodus, is subversive of Assyrian claims. The similarities between the story of Moses' rescue from the river as a baby (Exod. 2.1–10) and that of Sargon I of Akkad, around 2300 BCE, are well known, and the biblical version may be read so as to see Moses as antitype to the Assyrian 'great king'.[70] The idea of covenant with Yahweh implied a rejection of Assyrian state-prophets' understanding of a covenant between Esarhaddon and Aššur (SAA 9 3) in order to legitimate Esarhaddon's wars of conquest. Prophetic intellectuals in Israel and Judah went beyond a 'theological deconstruction' of neo-Assyrian hegemonic claims to a fundamental critique of their own society, to explain why it was exposed in such weakness to the great powers. The Assyrian conquests as victory of Aššur are turned round, to be a work of Yahweh.[71]

The Assyrian setting for the deuteronomic level of political theology in particular is advocated by many scholars.[72] In terms of the 'social location' of the

69. This is Lohfink's response to the charge that monotheism is a recipe for violence, 'Gewalt und Monotheismus'.
70. Otto, *Krieg und Frieden*, p. 76.
71. Otto, *Krieg und Frieden*, pp. 76–7.
72. Among recent influential scholars may be named M. Weinfeld, *Deuteronomy and the Deuteronomic School* (Oxford: Clarendon Press, 1972); *idem, Deuteronomy 1–11* (AB; New York, Doubleday, 1991); B. M. Levinson, *Deuteronomy and the Hermeneutics of Legal Innovation* (New

deuteronomists it is espoused among others by P. Dutcher-Walls, who memorably imagines the position of Judah in relation to Assyria as 'sleeping with the elephant'.[73] In current debate about this, a much later setting is favoured by, among others, R. Person, who thinks that deuteronomistic polemical theology has its principal context in the Persian period.[74]

It is intrinsically difficult to resolve such a debate. In the nature of the case, what holds for Assyria may hold also for Babylon, Persia and so on. Indeed, the biblical literature itself exploits the possibilities for typology inherent in the language and imagery it employs, as we saw above. Nor is it essential to our study to establish the setting or settings of the literature. Whether the Old Testament emerges in dialogue with Assyria or another power, it is clear that Israel's Yahwism never takes the form of the domination of the weak by the strong. On the contrary, it is advocated in political weakness, and in the face of such power. Nor is it generally triumphalistic in its visions of the future, as its inclusive tendencies attest. The Old Testament's mono-Yahwism, therefore, has a particular colour, distinct from a stereotype of violent monotheism. Its concept of the one God Yahweh, furthermore, is not incidental to its peaceable tendency, but essential to it.

In pursuit of this perspective on the Old Testament's political theology, we shall next explore further the setting of its central texts in Deuteronomy in the narrative from Genesis to Kings.

York: Oxford University Press, 1997). On Deut. 13 see P. Dion, 'The Suppression of Alien Religious Propaganda in Israel during the Late Monarchical Era', in B. Halpern and D. Hobson (eds.), *Law and Ideology in Monarchic Israel* (JSOTSup, 124; Sheffield: Sheffield Academic Press), pp. 147–216; and on Deut. 28, U. Steymans, *Deuteronomium 28 und die adê zur Thronfolgeregelung Asarhaddons: Segen und Fluch im Alten Orient und in Israel* (OBO, 145; Göttingen: Vandenhoeck & Ruprecht, 1995).

73. In a paper at SBL in San Antonio, 2004. Question: 'What happens when a mouse lies in bed with an elephant?' Answer: 'The mouse doesn't get much sleep.' See also her, 'The Social Location of the Deuteronomists: a Sociological Study of Factional Politics in Late Pre-Exilic Judah', *JSOT* 52 (1991), pp. 77–94.

74. Raymond F. Person, *The Deuteronomic School: History, Social Setting, and Literature* (Studies in Biblical Literature, 2; Leiden: E. J. Brill, 2002).

Chapter 3

THE JUDGE OF ALL THE EARTH: GENESIS

1. *Towards an Old Testament Political Theology*

a. *What Kind of Politics?*

We have seen that the Old Testament's political theology can be viewed as a critical dialogue with the dominant powers in ancient Israel's world. But what kind of political ideas does it articulate? With this question we immediately encounter the enormous diversity of the Old Testament, together with the fact that it does not offer treatises or tracts. The political picture changes with the exigencies that faced Israel at various times: as tribal society became centralized state, as a united and independent monarchy divided and fell into vassaldom, as the last symbols of nationhood were lost in the Babylonian ravages, and as a new kind of society re-formed under Persian tutelage. Furthermore, the picture displays the struggle of ideas. Should Israel have a king 'like other nations' (1 Sam. 8.5), or rather maintain a de-centralized form as remembered in the Book of Judges? Should it be exclusive (Ezra) or assimilationist (Ruth)? Should it accept imperial rule or try to shake it off and restore a kind of Davidic monarchy (a debate that may be reflected in Chronicles–Ezra–Nehemiah)? The Old Testament story does not present any of the forms taken by Israel as ideal, for each is portrayed in its vulnerability, not only to external forces but also to inner corruption.

We shall look to the story itself as the source of the Old Testament's political ideas. I have explained above the reasons why this study focuses on the primary history of Genesis–Kings, in its literary and canonical aspects.[1] In any case, Old Testament political theology can hardly be understood apart from Genesis and Exodus in particular. The former establishes a relationship between Israel and creation, and between Israel and other nations. The latter tells the archetypal story of the exodus from Egypt, places Israel in covenant with Yahweh, and in the same connection proclaims the first laws. A rounded understanding of the Old Testament's political theology cannot overlook these early stages of its narrative, nor can an attempt to respond to the challenges noticed in the preceding chapter. For those who think Deuteronomy has theological pre-eminence, this is not compromised by the proposed approach. On the contrary, Deuteronomy retains a certain centrality in the story, as we shall see.

---

1. In Chapter 1.

The thesis in what follows is that the 'primary history' places Israel in relation to the other nations. Israel is at once with, separate from, and for the other nations. It is *with* them in that it shares with them its place in God's created order, and also the fundamental institution of law. It is *separate from* them in the sense that it is separated from both Egypt and Canaan, at the beginning and end of its journey into land. This separation has religious, moral and political aspects. And it is *for* them, in the sense that it is called to display to them what a nation might be like under the one God Yahweh.

b. *Creation Order and Political Order*
I have said above that Old Testament political history cannot be understood apart from Genesis and Exodus. The prominence of the Book of Exodus in an account of Israel's political theology hardly needs demonstration, but the place of Genesis needs elucidation. This is because Old Testament interpreters formerly saw a sharp distinction between the religion of creation or 'nature', and the religion of history and salvation. Creation-theology was suspect both because of the fertility religion of Canaan and the creation ideologies of Mesopotamia. The religion of Baal, as portrayed in the Old Testament, postulated causal connections between well-being in the regularities of life and appropriate fertility rituals, in which the world might be manipulated by technical know-how. In Babylon, primaeval conflict between the gods led to the sustaining of order in the world through the victory of Marduk who reigned from Babylon. In this way creation ideology served to underwrite a political system. For reasons such as this, Old Testament scholars insisted that the religion of Israel was about salvation or redemption, not about creation. The belief is generally associated with the early work of G. von Rad, though he was later more hospitable to creation categories. In recent times the work of Claus Westermann, H. H. Schmid, and R. Knierim has led the way to a recovery, and Walter Brueggemann has documented and welcomed its reinstatement.[2] The loss of it had entailed a disjunction between the faith of the Old Testament and the ordinary processes of life. And its recovery brings with it fresh possibilities for engagement with modern debates about ecology and the bearing on each other of religion and science.[3] Brueggemann remains wary of political applications, rightly warning that creation ideology remains open to ideological abuse, for example 'when the

---

2. An account of the reinstatement of creation in Old Testament theology is given by Brueggemann, *Theology*, pp. 159–64; cf. *idem*, 'The Loss and Recovery of "Creation" in Old Testament theology', *TTod* 53 (1996), pp. 177–90. Von Rad's seminal essay was 'The Theological Problem of the Old Testament Doctrine of Creation', in *The Problem of the Hexateuch*, pp. 131–43 (originally 1936). As Brueggemann points out, von Rad's writing on wisdom marked a shift towards a more receptive attitude to creation theology: von Rad, *Old Testament Theology I*, pp. 418–59; *Wisdom in Israel* (trans. James D. Martin; London: SCM Press, 1972); Brueggemann, *Theology*, pp. 160–1. Westermann's conviction about the centrality of 'blessing' in Old Testament religion arose from his study of Genesis: *Genesis 1–11*; see also *idem*, *Blessing in the Bible and the Life of the Church* (trans. Keith Crim; OBT, 3; Philadelphia: Fortress, 1978). On Schmid and Knierim, see further below.

3. Brueggemann, *Theology*, pp. 160, 162–3.

order of creation is equated with a preferred social order, such as by appeal to "natural law".[4]

However, the recovery of creation theology brings in its wake the question of its relevance to the political order. Important pointers have been given in this respect by H. H. Schmid and R. Knierim. Schmid argued that there was an order in the world that embraced nature, law, ethics and politics. The key Old Testament concept which expresses this unity is *tsedeq/tsedaqah*,[5] terms often translated by 'justice' or 'righteousness', but which cannot be rendered satisfactorily by any single term in English. Schmid saw in *tsedeq* 'the right, Yahweh-willed, salvific order of the world' and correspondingly in *tsedaqah* 'right, salvific behaviour – also in the judicial process'.[6] Schmid developed his thesis in his landmark essay, in which he proposed a comprehensive order of creation embracing law, nature and politics, and therefore that creation constituted the 'broad horizon' of Old Testament theology.[7] Here too *tsedaqah* is fundamental, understood as wholeness ('Heil') in all these spheres.[8] Kingship guarantees this cosmic order (as in Ps. 72),[9] and prophets proclaim it.[10] Creation is not in one category while history, politics and salvation are in another. Rather, salvation is restoration to how things ought to be. This is why the language of salvation in II-Isaiah freely intertwines creational and historical themes (e.g. Ps. 74.13–15; Isa. 51.9–11).[11]

R. Knierim also rejected the primacy accorded to history in Old Testament studies, but took the enquiry in a more radical direction. Following Schmid, he accepted the significance of *tsedeq* as representing 'an all-encompassing world order', but not content with affirming the close relationship between cosmos and historical-political sphere, he asserted the primacy of the former. Knierim welcomed certain moves in the direction of re-establishing an emphasis on the created order, the universals in human experience, and even cyclic time, in the work of Westermann and others.[12] But for him, in a reversal of the older view, history is actually subservient to cosmos. That is, it points, or should point, to the realities

    4. Brueggemann, *Theology*, p. 163.
    5. See above, Chapter 2, on Noah.
    6. H. H. Schmid, *Gerechtigkeit als Weltordnung: Hintergrund und Geschichte des alttestamentlichen Gerechtigkeitsbegriffes* (BHT, 40; Tübingen: Mohr-Siebeck, 1968), pp. 178–80: '[*tsedeq*] bezeichnet die richtige, jahwegewollte, heilvolle Ordnung der Welt, [*tsedaqah*] das ihr gemässe, richtige, heilvolle Verhalten – auch im Vollzug des Gerichts'.
    7. H. H. Schmid, 'Creation, Righteousness and Salvation: "Creation Theology" as the Broad Horizon of Biblical Theology', in B. W. Anderson (ed.), *Creation in the Old Testament* (Philadelphia: Fortress, 1984), pp. 102–17 (105). He says in the same context: 'the repulsion and destruction of the enemy, and thereby the maintenance of political order, always constitute one of the major dimensions of the battle against chaos', p. 104.
    8. Schmid, 'Creation, Righteousness and Salvation', p. 107.
    9. Schmid, 'Creation, Righteousness and Salvation', p. 115 n. 9.
    10. Schmid, 'Creation, Righteousness and Salvation', p. 107. He cites *tsedaqah*-texts in Isaiah: Isa. 45.8, 23–24; 46.12–13; 51.6, 8; 54.14, 17.
    11. Schmid, 'Creation, Righteousness and Salvation', p. 108.
    12. Rolf Knierim, *The Task of Old Testament Theology: Substance, Method and Cases* (Grand Rapids: Eerdmans, 1995), pp. 183–4. He cites Westermann, *Genesis 1–11*, p. 347.

that exist independently in the created order. Yahweh himself is closely related to and manifest in the creation: '…*world order* explicated what it meant for Israel to say "Yahweh" '.[13] And this is reflected in the portrayal of key concepts, such as justice, righteousness (*tsedeq*/*tsedaqah* and מﬦﬡﬦ, *mishpat*), truth, steadfast love, faithfulness and peace as '(present) in this order', in such a way that Yahweh himself is seen to be present in it.[14] As evidence for this contention, Knierim points to texts in Psalms and Isaiah in which the qualities in question are predicated of the natural order. For example:

> Steadfast love and faithfulness will meet;
> righteousness (*tsedeq*) and peace will kiss each other.
> Faithfulness will spring up from the ground,
> and righteousness will look down from the sky.
> The LORD will give what is good,
> and our land will yield its increase.
> Righteousness will go before him,
> and will make a path for his steps (Ps. 85.11–14[EVV 10–13]).[15]

The use of such texts for his argument requires acknowledgement that the language is highly metaphorical, and some attention to the way in which it operates here. An account of the level of correspondence between vehicle and tenor would make the case more convincing. Yet arguably the correspondence is in this case rather high, since there are also texts, such as Psalms 104, 148 and Genesis 1, in which the orderliness of creation and its relationship to God are in the forefront. Psalm 104 emphasizes the inner harmony of the world; Psalm 148 portrays the many parts of creation even giving him praise, animate and inanimate alike.[16] And Genesis 1 places God, humanity and the world in a harmonious tripartite relationship. The analogy between God and creation might be further strengthened by observing the attribution of the epithet *tsaddiq*, related to *tsedeq*, directly to God in two texts (Deut. 32.4; Ps. 119.137).

Knierim wants to go further, however, and establish the God-revealing character of the creation independently of history. In doing so, he runs the risk, in my view, of re-establishing a divide between creation and history, albeit in favour of the former.[17] His leading concern, however, is to redress the balance between

13. Knierim, *Task of Old Testament Theology*, p. 199.
14. Knierim, *Task of Old Testament Theology*, p. 200.
15. Knierim, *Task of Old Testament Theology*, p. 200.
16. Knierim, *Task of Old Testament Theology*, p. 201.
17. Knierim thinks the Old Testament portrays the first human sin as affecting the created order as well as the moral condition of the human beings (Gen. 3.14–19). Indeed, the disharmony resulting from human sin evidently crosses the boundaries of the earthly and heavenly spheres (Gen. 6.1–4). Knierim also encounters difficulty when he tries to relate his analysis to the New Testament, because its theology of the cross and resurrection of Christ has implications for cosmic renewal (e.g. Rom. 8.19–23). And he poses as a rhetorical question whether the New Testament assumes '…a cosmic realm in which God's creation has always been intact, over against a realm that is not intact' (citing also Matt. 6.10; *Task of Old Testament Theology*, p. 223). His final hesitation over whether the initial creation is intrinsically bound together with human history or separate from it is illustrated by the series of open questions posed in this context (pp. 223–34).

creation and history which had formerly tipped too far towards history, and he rightly challenges the older suspicion of creation-based religion as being necessarily in thrall to natural or political necessities. The insistence in both Schmid and Knierim on God's *tsedaqah* as a governing principle of the universe, and its priority over human history, stands in direct opposition to such theories of necessity. Rather than preclude creation, therefore, from an account of the Old Testament's view of politics, it is better to ask whether and in what way the Old Testament's creation traditions are accommodated to its political theology. When history is taken to serve the purpose of creation, it has the important corollary that Israel's political institutions are by definition not final. If the locus of *tsedaqah* is in God and the created cosmos itself, then it may or may not be realized in the history and institutions of Israel.[18] Only the history itself will tell. And it is this history that unfolds in Genesis–Kings. Our study of Genesis–Kings, therefore, is part of an answer to the question of how the Old Testament responds to the religio-political claims of the ancient world.

2. *The Politics of Genesis*

a. *The Primaeval History*
We saw in Chapter 1 that elements in the primaeval history, the notion of humanity as being 'in the image of God', and the flood as the work of the one God Yahweh, were consonant with the Old Testament's advocacy of God as One and thus its oppositional stance. We now enquire further about the political orientation of the Genesis story.

Genesis unfolds on the broad canvas of Israel's geographical and political environment from Mesopotamia to Egypt. Abraham comes from Ur and his journey takes him to the house of Pharaoh (Gen. 11.27–12.20). His first arrival in the land that Yahweh showed him (12.1) was fleeting, his life in it immediately jeopardized by famine. And he and his descendants barely achieve a settled existence there. Rather, the story displays a restless motion, between the land and Egypt, the land and Aramaean Haran. In this way the lives of the ancestors echo the uncertain existence of Israel itself in the land, with its fragile geography, at best precariously held between the thrusting civilizations to the east and south. The narrative intimates the political realities of Israel's life at several points. The Tower of Babel story (Gen. 11.1–9) aims critically at Babylonian religion. The campaign against the cities of the plain (Genesis 14) conveys the perpetual danger of war in the region. The potential enmity between Israel and its immediate neighbours, such as Ammon, Moab and Edom, is expressed in the tormented ancestral origins of these (Gen. 19.30–38), especially in the near-fratricidal relationship between Jacob and Esau (Gen. 27.41), and in the estranged kinship between Jacob and Aramaean Laban, marked by linguistic and religious difference (Gen. 31.19, 47). Yet the very possibility of belonging in the land itself is made problematical by the need for Abraham's people to intermarry with these

18. Knierim, *Task of Old Testament Theology*, p. 212.

alien kin rather than with their closest neighbours (Gen. 24.2–4; 27.46–28.1). Genesis closes with the story of Jacob and his sons (Genesis 37–50), expressing fascination and awe at the mighty Egypt, in which the sharp differences with Palestine are marked again by language, as also by custom self-consciously maintained (Gen. 42.23; 43.32). Genesis brings and leaves the descendants of Abraham here, having been 'shown' a land but now sojourners in another, exposed to the will of an empire whose actions will be driven by its own inner logic, rather than by any sense of the privilege or destiny of Israel. Israel is even partly estranged from itself by the Egyptianization of Joseph, faceless and unrecognized for much of the narrative (Gen. 42.8), his two sons Ephraim and Manasseh, whose descendants would form the backbone of Israel in the land, borne by the daughter of an Egyptian priest (Gen. 41.50–52).

Genesis thus foreshadows in its portrayal of the ancestors the life-cycle and condition of the nation of Israel, told in the primary history (Genesis–Kings). As Abraham came from Babylonia and his family took refuge in Egypt, so the people of Israel would follow the same trajectory in reverse, coming out of Egypt, dwelling precariously in the land (so the book of Judges), and finishing in exile in Babylon.

It is to this story that an appraisal of the politics of Genesis must be orientated. Its depiction of Israel in the wide world is prefaced by creation narratives which place humanity as such in universal or unspecified settings. As we have already observed,[19] the first creation account (Gen. 1.1–2.3)[20] may in effect demythologize both Canaanite and Babylonian cosmologies. In fact it would be better to say that it takes its place in a world of creation myths whose full extent and interrelationships are unknown to us. Yet its conscious orientation to that mythological world is unmistakable in, for example, the pointed designation of the sun and the moon as 'the two great lights' (Gen. 1.16). The universal view found in Gen. 1.1–2.3 has often been attributed to its origin in the Pentateuchal P source, and thus to the experience of Babylonian exile. Whether or not this is so, that universalism is striking, both because of its literate awareness of other cosmologies, and because it is with this broad view of the world that the story of Israel begins.

The second creation narrative (Gen. 2.4–3.24) was classically assigned to J, dated to the early monarchy, and thought to express the nationalistic confidence of that time.[21] Yet here too there is critical engagement with the myths[22] and an

---

19. In Chapter 2, at n. 52.

20. The ending of the first creation account is frequently put at Gen. 2.4a. Whether 2.4a is a colophon to 1.1–2.3 or an introduction to the ensuing account, according to the usual function of the תולדת formula in Genesis (as in Gen. 10.1), is a moot point. I take it both to enclose the first account with an echo of 'the heavens and the earth', and also to herald what follows.

21. So, for example, S. R. Driver, *The Book of Genesis* (London: Methuen, 1904), pp. xvi, xxi–xxii.

22. In Genesis the forming of the first human from clay (Gen. 2.7) may be compared with Atrahasis, where he is formed from a mixture of clay and the blood of a sacrificed god (Dalley. *Myths*, pp. 15–16); similarly, the serpent sheds some of his magical connotations, and becomes merely one of the creatures (Gen. 3.1).

orientation that is rather universal. This is clear not least from the ways in which themes from Genesis 2–3 are still engaged today as significant for the fundamental understanding of the place of humanity in the world.

So it is that the biblical story of Israel begins simply with humanity (אדם, *'adam*) placed on the earth to work the ground (אדמה, *'adamah*). The context is first as broad as possible ('the heavens and the earth'), then a garden, unspecific, where hints of ordinary Mesopotamian geography are mixed with the mythic (Gen. 2.10–14). Humanity as such, in the 'image' of God (1.26),[23] shoulders the 'royal' responsibility of God's vicegerent on earth, and has dominion over the creation (1.28). Elemental human issues are played out here: the hard toil required to live, pain, sexual relationship, childbirth, the human moral and religious condition, death. The first fratricide and its consequence in displacement (Genesis 4) is a still-powerful paradigm of inter-human violence and alienation.[24] It is humanity (*'adam*) as such who calls on the name of Yahweh (4.26b). In Noah's survival of the flood it is in reality humanity who receives afresh its primacy in the created order, the 'image' reaffirmed, with its corollary in a fundamental law demanding respect for all human life (9.1–6). A 'covenant' is made with 'all flesh', that no such cosmic disaster should occur again (9.16–17). The universalizing picture is disturbed by Noah's curse on Canaan for the enigmatic sin of his father Ham (9.25–27), to which we return shortly. But the creation mandate to 'fill the earth' is realized in the 'table of nations', depicting a world of diverse nations and languages as a fulfilling of the blessing-command to 'fill the earth' (Genesis 10), before that diversity should be cast as a 'scattering' in consequence of the pretensions of Babel (11.1–9).[25]

The primaeval history depicts a whole world. The first signs of distinctions among peoples are indeed here, and must be seen in the light of the unfolding story. But the story is essentially that of humanity as such. And in Noah, the post-diluvian ancestor of all humanity, the goal of God for creation is adumbrated, namely in his 'righteousness' (Gen. 6.9, נח איש צדיק, 'Noah was a righteous [*tsaddiq*] man'). This theme will develop as the story proceeds.

b. *The Chosen Line: an Exclusive or a Universal View?*
If the primaeval history supports the idea of a divine purpose for the whole world, the ancestral history (Genesis 12–50) puts that purpose in a different perspective. Here, with an echo of the tripartite division of humanity in Gen. 9.25–27, one Shemite family line is distinguished from all others. The land that is shown to Abraham will in due course belong to his descendants. And there is

---

23. See Chapter 2 for the 'image' as making the political point that it is humans as such, and not kings only, who represent God on earth.

24. This is well illustrated by David Gunn and Danna Nolan Fewell in their review of interpretations of Genesis 4, culminating in applications of it to recent South African history by Alan Boesak and Itumeleng Mosala: Gunn and Fewell, *Narrative in the Hebrew Bible* (Oxford: Oxford University Press, 1993), pp. 12–33.

25. This take on the relationship between Genesis 10 and 11.1–9 was suggested by D. J. A. Clines, *The Theme of the Pentateuch* (JSOTSup, 10; Sheffield; JSOT Press, 1978), pp. 68–9.

room, it seems, for only one branch. The plotline, indeed, might be described as a separation in each generation of those who would possess from those who would not. And those who would not are compelled to head 'east', out of the land, rather like Cain, who 'went away from the presence of the LORD, and settled in the land of Nod, east of Eden' (Gen. 4.16).

The pattern begins with Lot, ancestor of Moab and Ammon, who takes the way of the Jordan valley, 'because the land could not support both of them [Abraham and Lot] living together' (Gen. 13.6, 10–11). If Lot thought the boun-tiful Jordan promising, still his parting from Abraham is occasioned by strife over land, and the point is reinforced by the narrator's remark: 'At that time the Canaanites and the Perizzites lived in the land', with its ominous foreshadowing of future conflicts (cf. Deut. 7.1–2). Lot's choice, moreover, does not fulfil its immediate promise, for his settlement in Sodom is short-lived, and his story becomes one of continued displacement and homelessness (Gen. 19.30). Lot's journey east leads in the fullness of time to the settling of the peoples of Ammon and Moab in Transjordan. Displacement ends in placement. But the origins of Ammon and Moab in Lot's drunken relations with his daughters in a cave (Gen. 19.30–38) puts this peopling of the world under a shadow of shame.

The branching of the line continues in Genesis, with Isaac preferred to Ish-mael, and Jacob to Esau. In each of these cases there are territorial entailments, with Ishmael populating desert areas to the south of Judah (Gen. 25.12–18), and Esau accepting craggy Edom (Gen. 33.16–17; 36.6–8). The echo in this last text (36.6) of Lot's parting from Abraham (13.7) shows how much the Genesis story is concerned with the capacity of land to support population, and the territorial entitlements of peoples.

But what view is taken of this settling of the world around Israel? Is it mere apologia for rightful Israelite possession of the land shown to Abraham? There is indeed a 'line of blessing' running from Seth to Jacob. Substantial parts of the narrative are expended on insisting that the promise to Abraham continues through Isaac, not Ishmael (Genesis 15–21), and on Jacob's expropriation not only of Esau's birthright but of his blessing too (Gen. 25.29–34; 27). However, this pattern of separation does not fully account for the texture of the narrative. On the contrary, the double view that was already apparent in the primaeval history, where the progress of humanity was portrayed under the signs of both blessing and curse, continues in the story of the ancestors. Abraham is indeed to become 'a great nation' (12.2), but his countless descendants (15.5) are to include 'nations' and 'kings' (17.6, 16). And the proliferation of these is part of the fulfilment of God's promise to Abraham. Ishmael is to be blessed with numerous offspring (like Abraham), and become the father of 'twelve princes' (like Jacob) (Gen. 17.20, cf. 25.12–16), and 'a great nation' (21.18).

The inclusion of Ishmael in the divine plan is also borne out by the story of Hagar. On one level the birth of Ishmael is a misstep on the part of Abraham and Sarah. Yet (like other human missteps in the biblical story) it is brought within the divine purpose. Hagar becomes more than the convenient surrogate, but rather a personality with whom God deals directly, in an encounter which has no parallel in Sarah's story (Gen. 16.7–14). She receives a promise of many off-spring in her own right (v. 10, cf. Gen. 15.5). And her son is to be called 'Ishmael', ('God hears'), because 'the LORD has given heed to your affliction' (v. 11). There are echoes here not only of the name given to Samuel, another child born to a woman in great distress (1 Sam. 1.20),[26] but also of the grounds for God's salvation of Israel in Exodus, namely their distress under the Egyptian yoke (Exod. 2.23–25). In all these cases the common element is 'God hearing'. It is Ishmael who bears this name in Genesis (while Isaac's name more ambigu-ously connotes 'laughter', Gen. 17.17; 21.6). The 'blessing' of Ishmael conveyed to Hagar (Gen. 16.12) looks less unequivocal than that in Gen. 17.20, yet it is on a par with several of the blessings given to Jacob's sons (Genesis 49). And his part-Egyptian parentage has a close parallel in that of Ephraim and Manasseh, as we have noticed already (Gen. 41.50–52). Abraham's fatherly instincts with regard to his firstborn, therefore (Gen. 17.18; 21.11), are questioned by the nar-rative, but by no means negated by it.

The Genesis narrative accounts for the existence of the nations in the region of the world known to Israel, and traces their presence to the creation of all things by the one God Yahweh. Its purpose, therefore, is an explanation of the way things are, with all its potential for good and ill. The 'table of nations' in Genesis 10 prepared us to see the spread of distinct peoples in the world as, from one point of view, a fulfilment of the creation mandate, and the story of the ancestors begins to add colour to that sketch. Even the basic postulate of the narrative, from Lot to Esau, that the land could not support the ever-increasing progeny of Abraham (Gen. 13.6; 36.7) cannot be viewed only as a function of conflict. On the contrary, the premise that Yahweh would make Abraham's offspring too numerous to count, and that they would comprise many nations, requires pre-cisely such divergence in order to be realized. The vast multiplication of off-spring is regarded as a good in itself, from Gen. 1.28 through the terms of the repeated promises to the ancestors.

The potential for conflict is also part of the story, however, and that theme too is rooted in Genesis 1–11. Human interrelationship has the capacity to be benign or internecine. The dual possibilities appear strongly in the character of Esau, who begins with an echo of Cain, in his desire to kill his brother (Gen. 27.41), but who ends with a paradigm of reconciling generosity which expressly refuses to try to turn the clock back, and accepts the integrity of his brother-neighbour in spite of the crooked means by which the brother-neighbour acquired his entitle-ment (Genesis 33). Esau's renunciation of Jacob's offered gift (33.9), with its strong connotations of the blessing once stolen (especially in the use of the word ברכה [*berakah*], 'blessing', for the gift, v. 11), shows what it takes to realize brotherhood in a world in which fratricide always threatens. Esau's generosity does not prove to be determinative for the biblical story of Israel and Edom. Yet it is the more important for that, as charting one possible path for human relations.

---

26. The name Samuel conveys the idea of 'God hearing', even if Hannah's explanation of it is based on the verb 'ask', which is more suitable to the name 'Saul'.

The dual possibilities for human interrelating are also illustrated by the role of Egypt. Egypt is predominantly benign in Genesis, thanks to its generous life-giving role in the lengthy story of Jacob's sons (Genesis 37–50). A darker possibility is hinted at earlier in Genesis, with the pharaoh's assimilation of the matriarch of Israel into his harem (Gen. 12.15), leaving questions about her integrity which are only obliquely answered in Gen. 20.4. The dark side of this great power emerges more strongly when the benevolence of Joseph's Egypt abruptly gives way to the xenophobic harshness of the pharaoh 'who did not know Joseph' in Exodus (Exod. 1.8).

c. Resolving the Ambiguity of the Non-Elect Nations
The above account has attempted to resolve the ambiguities in the stories of the ancestors by showing that they affirm at once the distinctive position of Israel and a positive view of the other nations. An alternative appraisal of the ambiguities should be noticed at this point, however. R. C. Heard understands the Genesis narrative in the context of Persian Yehud, and argues that the systematic separation of the Abrahamic line through Jacob from other Abrahamic lines is designed to secure the exclusive rights of the dominant group of Yahwists at that time to occupy the ancestral land.[27] The Genesis narrative, he thinks, is part of that group's programme to establish its identity by reference to the Abrahamic tradition. His reading, which is indebted to both literary and sociological studies, finds that the narrative portrayal of key characters such as Lot, Ishmael and Esau has ambiguities which are left to the reader to resolve, yet that the ultimate outcome is unambiguous, namely the exclusion of the 'diselect' from inheritance rights in the land. Thus, the 'blessing' of Ishmael (Gen. 16.12) may be given a positive or negative spin, and Esau may be read either sympathetically or unsympathetically, but the conclusion of their stories is unavoidable, that by the decision of Yahweh those who are regarded as their descendants have no land-entitlement in Yehud.[28]

The case of Ishmael bears additionally upon the specific issue of intermarriage, and so shares a concern with Ezra-Nehemiah. The insistence in Genesis that Isaac and Jacob take wives from the ancestral family in Mesopotamia, rather than from the peoples of the land, corresponds to the concept that the 'holy seed'

27. R. C. Heard, *The Dynamics of Diselection: Ambiguity in Genesis 12–26 and Ethnic Boundaries in Post-Exilic Judah* (SBLSS, 39; Atlanta: SBL, 2001), pp. 8–16, 171–84. Heard takes a cue from a number of studies which call for Ezra and Nehemiah to be read with a view to the interests of the authors or group that produced them. The group in question identified itself with the returning Babylonian exiles and demarcated itself from those who had not been in exile. Heard cites among others P. R. Davies, *'Ancient Israel'*; *idem*, 'Scenes from the Early History of Judaism', in Diana Vikander Edelman (ed.), *The Triumph of Elohim: from Yahwisms to Judaisms* (Grand Rapids: Eerdmans, 1995), pp. 145–82; Lester L. Grabbe, 'Reconstructing History from the Book of Ezra', in P. R. Davies (ed.), *Second Temple Studies, 1: Persian Period* (JSOTSup, 117; Sheffield: JSOT Press, 1991), pp. 98–106; Mullen, *Ethnic Myths*; R. P. Carroll, 'Textual Strategies and Ideology in the Second Temple Period', in Davies (ed.), *Second Temple Studies I*, pp. 108–24. See also above, Chapter 1.

28. Heard, *Dynamics*, pp. 175, 177–8.

should not be mixed with 'the peoples of the lands' (Ezra 9.2). Abraham's readiness to turn out Hagar and Ishmael, however reluctant, becomes a warrant for husbands in Yehud to do likewise, leaving their wives and children to the mercy of God.[29] Intermarriage with women from Mesopotamia, however, is put in a more favourable light than intermarriage with Moabites, Edomites, 'Arabs' and Egyptians, this being a function of the community's positive attitude to the Persian authorities, extending perhaps to intermarriage of the élite in Yehud with 'leading Mesopotamian families' as a measure to secure political advantage.[30] The narrative, therefore, is finally in thrall to a strong political commitment: '...*the will of the Achaemenid rulers is an expression of the will of Yahweh*' (emphasis original).[31]

Heard's account differs from the one offered above in its conception that the text serves the interests of the Yahwistic community of Yehud, and especially its élite. His method of dealing with the ambiguities in the narrative is governed by this conception. He argues that the possibility of a favourable reading of the characters of Lot, Ishmael and Esau tells nothing in itself about the orientation of the narrative: whatever the reader may think of these (and their descendants) a supervening voice asserts unambiguously that they have no place in the land. Heard does find a kind of universalism in the stories. Laban appears to acknowledge the oneness of Abraham's God (Gen. 31.49, 50, 53); the ratification of his covenant with Jacob in both Hebrew and Aramaic (Gen. 31.47) shows that Mesopotamians and the ' "descendants of Abraham" can use different words for the same external referent' (and so they might talk of the same god in different language);[32] and these features, together with Abraham's use of the divine names 'God Most High, Maker of Heaven and Earth' (Gen. 14.19, 22) and 'the God of Heaven [and Earth]' (Gen. 24.3, 7) agree with 'the notion of "inclusive monotheism" in the Achaemenid period'.[33] This universalism, however, is such as to nurture an advantageous relationship with Persia, and protect the interests of the powerful in Yehud.

Heard's view of Genesis 12–36 through the lens of Achaemenid Yehud is in my view too narrowly focused. Genesis gives less support than he thinks to his thesis that it opposes marriages to Edomites, Ammonites and Egyptians while permitting Mesopotamian marriages. Abraham is not finally a suitable model for a programme like Ezra's, since he not only has a child by the Egyptian Hagar, but also marries Keturah, who becomes the mother of other non-Israelite peoples (including Midian; Gen. 25.1–4). Genesis offers no comment on the ethnic origin

29. Heard, *Dynamics*, p. 176.

30. Heard, *Dynamics*, pp. 179–80. Heard is indebted for this thesis to Daniel L. Smith-Christopher, 'The Mixed Marriage Crisis in Ezra 9–10 and Nehemiah 13: a Study of the Sociology of the Post-Exilic Judaean Community', in Tamara C. Eskenazi and Kent H. Richards (eds.), *Second Temple Studies, 2: Temple Community in the Persian Period* (JSOTSup, 175; Sheffield: JSOT Press, 1994), pp. 243–65.

31. Heard, *Dynamics*, p. 184.

32. Heard, *Dynamics*, p. 182.

33. Heard, *Dynamics*, pp. 181–2.

of Keturah, nor criticism of Abraham's fathering these peoples. On the contrary, the reader is entitled to infer that his productive match with Keturah is one fulfilment of the promise to him in Gen. 17.6. The expulsion of Hagar and Ishmael may justify Abraham from the perspective of Ezra, but no such interpretation is possible with Keturah.

Finally, Heard's limitation of his study to chs 12–36 means that the place of the non-Israelite nations in Genesis as a whole is not fully considered. In general, the book's breadth of interest in the peoples of the world, as in the Table of Nations (Genesis 10), is underestimated. A pro-Mesopotamian stance is difficult to maintain in respect of the creation, flood and Babel narratives. And on the other hand, he does not consider Joseph's Egyptian marriage (Gen. 41.50–52), and thus the Egyptian origins of Ephraim and Manasseh.[34] There is indeed a universalism in Genesis, but I do not believe it is accounted for by appeal to the narrow interests of Persian Yehud.

3. *Universalism in Genesis*

a. *Yahweh*

In Genesis, the possibilities of human life in relation to God are placed prior to and outside the life of Israel. Following the elemental beginnings – the heavens and the earth, humanity male and female, the first struggle with human identity before God, fratricide – comes the enigmatic: 'At that time people began to call on the name of the LORD' (Gen. 4.26b). The occurrence of the name Yahweh in Genesis, in bold anticipation of Exod. 6.2–3, is well known, and was once thought a classic case of the proposed theological divide between J and P.[35] Recent scholarship has explained the presence of the name in Genesis, alongside other divine names, as a more complex theological engagement between Mosaic Yahwism and pre-Mosaic religious concepts.[36] Of all the occurrences of the name, however, this one is the most striking. Here people are said to have begun to call on the name of Yahweh at that time (that is, at the birth of Enosh). This seems odd at first glance, since the name Yahweh has been used throughout Gen. 2.4–4.26. However, it is likely that it functions to affirm that worship was

34. The possibility that this might reflect a critical attitude towards Ephraim and Manasseh in Yehud would seem to be ruled out by the generally favourable portrayal of Joseph in Genesis. The old idea that the books of Chronicles took a critical stance towards the former northern territory has been effectively refuted by H. G. M. Williamson, *Israel in the Books of Chronicles* (Cambridge: Cambridge University Press, 1977) and Sara Japhet, *Ideology of the Books of Chronicles and Its Place in Biblical Thought* (trans. Anna Barber; BEATAJ, 9; Frankfurt/M: Lang, 1989); *idem, I and II Chronicles* (OTL; Louisville, KY: WJK, 1993). Ephraim is mentioned in Ezra-Nehemiah only in the name of the Ephraim Gate (Neh. 8.16; 12.39).

35. C. Westermann finds that Gen. 4.26b coheres with Exod. 3 within the perspective of J, and thus is in line with the traditional critical view that J assumed the name Yahweh was known prior to the Mosaic period; *Genesis 1–11* p. 339.

36. This view was propounded influentially by R. W. L. Moberly, *The Old Testament of the Old Testament: Patriarchal Narratives and Mosaic Yahwism* (OBT; 2; Minneapolis: Fortress Press, 1992; repr. Eugene, Oregon: Wipf and Stock, 2001), especially pp. 79–104.

'a fundamental constituent of human life and the beginnings of civilization'.[37] This is indicated, indeed, by the naming of Seth's son Enosh, a word meaning 'human being',[38] and also by the grammatically impersonal formulation (hophal, literally, 'it was begun to call on the name of Yahweh'), which points to the generality of human experience.

But this does not explain why the name Yahweh should be used to make a point about universal worship. To account for this adequately, it is not quite enough to say that the writers were merely following the convention of their time, well aware that the name of Yahweh was not actually used before the time of Moses. The point is not only that early human beings worshipped, but that they worshipped the God known to Israel as Yahweh. This is one of those places in Genesis where the particular history of Israel is deliberately placed within a universal context. When first Abraham then the people of Israel later meet Yahweh, they are meeting the God of all humanity. The unexpected allusion to Yahweh-worship in antediluvian times is a careful splicing of the universal and particular. It is part of the developing picture of a story of Israel that is also a story of the world.

b. *Tsedaqah*

We turn now to the concept of *tsedaqah* in Genesis. It occurs relatively infrequently, but at significant moments. It is first introduced when Noah is said to be *tsaddiq* (Gen. 6.8–9). In the world before the flood, human relating to God is made possible by 'righteousness'. It is with the 'righteous' Noah that God makes a 'covenant' (6.18), a concept which will in turn become important in the story. Yet Noah's righteousness has priority here, and is not overtly made subject to a theology of divine grace. The point about Noah's righteousness is to contrast it with the wickedness of the world which has brought about its condemnation. This is the quality that must characterize humanity if the world is to survive. What is entailed in *tsedaqah* remains to be further disclosed by the narrative. The end of the flood-narrative imposes one fundamental obligation on the survivors, namely human beings' respect for each other's lives as being in the 'image of God' (9.1–6). The flood-narrative is therefore framed by the postulate of *tsedaqah* and the prohibition of murder by appeal to humanity's god-likeness. In this Old Testament version of the well-established ANE topic of flood-survival by an individual, a foundation is laid for human interrelationships, rooted in the essential nature of humanity.

The concept of *tsedaqah* next appears in the famous ascription of faith to Abraham: 'And he believed the LORD, and he [the LORD] reckoned it to him as righteousness (*tsedaqah*)' (Gen. 15.6). In the unfolding Genesis narrative this

---

37. Moberly, *Old Testament*, p. 68, who cites also Westermann, *Genesis 1–11*, pp. 339–41. See G. J. Wenham, *Genesis 1–15*, pp. 115–16, for a similar view.

38. John Van Seters draws attention to this generic meaning of Enosh as the founder of religion, and finds a parallel in a story of Philo about Genos and Genea, the first human pair, who invented worship; John Van Seters, *Prologue to History: the Yahwist as Historian in Genesis* (Louisville, KY: WJK, 1992), p. 142.

premise of Abraham's *tsedaqah* follows unmistakably on the characterization of Noah as *tsaddiq*, and the parallel is strengthened by Yahweh's making a covenant with Abraham in the immediate context (15.18). The portrayal of Abraham as possessing *tsedaqah* in this important dialogue between him and Yahweh heightens the profile of the concept in Genesis.

It is striking that Abraham's possession of *tsedaqah* is presented in different terms from Noah: while Noah was simply said to have been *tsaddiq*, Abraham is said to have had *tsedaqah* reckoned to him because of his faith in Yahweh's word. Does this mean that Abraham's possession of *tsedaqah* is different from Noah's? What exactly is involved in the 'reckoning' of righteousness to Abraham is difficult to establish clearly from analogous texts. Some think that righteousness is imputed to Abraham by analogy with texts in the realm of holiness and sacrifice, where a person might be declared to be clean or accepted on the grounds of a proper ritual performance (e.g. Lev. 7.18; 13; 17.4; 25.31; Num. 18.27, 30). In these cases the thing that is 'reckoned' is not intrinsically the case, and the relationship between what is done or offered and what is 'reckoned' is therefore a kind of exchange. But the analogies proposed are not close enough.[39] The closest parallel to Abraham in this respect is Phinehas in Ps. 106.31, the only other place where the verb חשׁב (*chashab*, 'reckon') occurs together with *tsedaqah*. In that case an act of loyalty to Yahweh is considered as righteousness, and the performance is not so much a substitute for *tsedaqah* as a demonstration of it. A text in the deuteronomic law (Deut. 24.13), though it lacks the verb *chashab*, also lies close, with its promise that the act of returning at night a garment held in pledge against a loan would be seen as *tsedaqah*. If these analogies hold, Abraham's faith might best be seen as an instance or demonstration of *tsedaqah*, rather than something accepted in place of it.

In support of this view we may consider other texts in which Abraham is said to be obedient to Yahweh or morally upright (Gen. 18.19; 22.16, 18; 26.5). In 18.19 Abraham is said to have been chosen by Yahweh 'to keep the way of the LORD by doing righteousness and justice' (*tsedaqah umishpat*), and this is a means whereby the promises to him might be fulfilled. In 26.5 his obedience is couched in terms reminiscent of Deuteronomy: he 'obeyed my voice and kept my charge, my commandments, my statutes and my laws' (cf. Deut. 4.30; 5.31). In addition, his willingness to sacrifice Isaac is portrayed in a similar way ('you have obeyed my voice', 22.18). There is therefore a connection in Genesis between Abraham's *torah*-obedience and his possessing *tsedaqah*, also as in Deuteronomy (Deut. 6.24–25). For reasons such as these, Abraham is often thought to be portrayed finally in Genesis precisely as one who is faithful to Mosaic law.[40]

---

39. The idea that the present text is best explained by reference to cultic actions was proposed by G. von Rad, 'Faith Reckoned as Righteousness', in von Rad, *Problem of the Hexateuch*, pp. 125–30. Westermann rightly points to a broader background for the idea, citing Deut. 24.13; *Genesis 12–36* (trans. John J. Scullion; Minneapolis: Augsburg, 1985), p. 223.

40. For example by Moberly, who thinks that thus Abraham, whose religion is largely distinct from the Mosaic, is adopted by Yahwistic editors to show that he was in fact the true ancestor of

At this stage our interest in the 'righteousness' of Abraham must be pursued within Genesis. In Gen. 15.6 it is established that the quality of *tsedaqah* is postulated, even presupposed, as the quality that must be exhibited by the bearer of the divine commission for the world. The topic is returned to in Abraham's dialogue with God over the fate of Sodom (Gen. 18.16–33). This is the place in Genesis where the nature of God's rule in the world is aired most penetratingly. At the heart of Abraham's prayer for Sodom lies his appeal to Yahweh, 'Shall not the judge of all the earth do what is just?' (18.25b). Yahweh is שׁפֵט (*shophet*, 'judge'), who rules the world with *mishpat*, 'justice'.[41] These concepts combine here with *tsedaqah*, 'righteousness', in a passage that addresses squarely one of the Old Testament's pervading issues, the justice of the divine government of the world. The repetition of the 'righteous-wicked' opposition in Abraham's prayer makes the centrality of the theme evident. In the Sodom episode it is affirmed that God differentiates between righteous and wicked, and that he will not compromise in his pursuit of justice.

Equally significant is the responsibility that falls consequently on Abraham. Abraham's righteousness now appears (along with *mishpat*, 'justice') as an obligation laid upon him, his children, and his 'house', in consequence of his chosenness (Gen. 18.19).[42] The debate that is about to follow therefore takes place within the framework of the role in the world assigned to Abraham in 12.1–3, that in his descendants 'the nations of the earth' might be blessed.[43] In the purpose of Yahweh, it is an implication of Abraham's mission that he should comprehend what is involved in the divine judgement concerning righteousness (vv. 17–18). The judgement of Sodom and Gomorrah, therefore, is a paradigm of the criteria by which nations, set to be blessed through Abraham, will be judged.

The judgement of Sodom is a judgement in the strict sense.[44] Following an established pattern in the Genesis judgement-history, Yahweh declares that he will 'go down and see' (cf. 6.5; 11.5) whether what he has heard is true.[45] Here is

their faith; *Old Testament*, pp. 142–6, cf. pp. 97–8. Similarly G. J. Wenham describes Abraham as 'the archetypal Israelite', *Genesis 1–15*, p. 335. Once again the question is raised whether the patriarchal stories are told in the interests of elect Israel, or whether they have a truly universal orientation. The answer will depend on the outcome of our study more broadly.

41. *Shophet* means not only 'judge' but 'ruler'; *mishpat* is variously 'justice', 'righteousness', 'right'. On these and related terms see further below, Chapter 7.

42. On Abraham's responsibility for 'justice and righteousness', cf. James K. Bruckner, *Implied Law in the Abraham Narrative: a Literary and Theological Analysis* (JSOTSup, 335; Sheffield: Sheffield Academic Press, 2001), pp. 133–4, 142, 146. The verb translated 'chosen' (NRSV) in v. 19 is strictly 'known' (יָדַע), (cf. Amos 3.2), which adds to the choosing a connotation of intimacy. Yet 'chosen' is the natural translation.

43. Here the phrase is 'nations of the earth' (גּוֹיֵי הָאָרֶץ), while in 12.3 it is 'families of the earth' (מִשְׁפְּחֹת הָאֲדָמָה). The phrases are presumably synonymous, though the form met here lends itself more naturally to the idea of nationhood. Whether the niphal of בָּרַךְ, 'bless', should be read as a passive or reflexive in these two texts need not be resolved here.

44. Cf. Bruckner, *Implied Law*, pp. 124–70. Bruckner shows that the consideration of the case of Sodom by Yahweh and Abraham is couched throughout in the terms of a legal enquiry.

45. Cf. G. J. Wenham, *Genesis 16–50* (WBC, 2; Dallas: Word Books, 1994), p. 50.

the investigating judge, to whom specific complaints have come, presumably from those who have suffered at the hands of the wicked cities.[46] The 'outcry against Sodom and Gomorrah' (v. 20, cf. 19.13) that has come to Yahweh echoes the cry that went up to God from the oppressed Hebrews under the pharaoh of Exodus (Exod. 2.23; cf. also Prov. 21.13). The crucial assumption of the narrative is that there might in principle be 'righteous' people in Sodom, even if in fact there are not, as Gen. 19.4 may imply.[47] As Lyons puts it, this premise 'is accepted by both Abraham and YHWH and indicates that it is possible for those outside the covenant between Abraham and YHWH to be considered "righteous" by the investigating deity'.[48]

The dialogue and judgement that follow show that Yahweh-God continues to act as judge over the whole world, just as in Genesis 1–11. Indeed, extensive parallels between the Sodom and flood narratives have been observed.[49] The essence of both is that God distinguishes between the righteous and the wicked. The flood-narrative portrayed a general judgement in which a single righteous man and his family were spared, and the outcome of the Sodom narrative is similar. (Lot is not expressly said to be righteous, but the logic of the story makes it necessary to assume it.) But Abraham's intercession in the Sodom narrative raises a new issue, namely whether God would judge a whole city if there were a number of righteous people in it, and then how many righteous it would take for him to spare it. It may be presumed that Abraham has an underlying concern for Lot, but the story is not determined by that. Rather it takes on a theoretical character. Indeed, the number game that Abraham plays with God has a certain artificiality: Abraham does not continue to question God beyond the number ten, and God does not answer Abraham's question with a fixed figure. But the relationship between righteousness and judgement is put in a new framework here. Noah and Lot are spared as righteous individuals. But now we are asked to consider how righteousness at an individual level relates to the idea of a righteous city or people. It is the *cities* of Sodom and Gomorrah that have offended against the standard of righteousness in their dealings with others. The nature of their 'sin' (18.20) is unspecified, but the concept now appears for the first time since Cain (Gen. 4.7), and is applied to corporate entities. The outcry that God has heard is against the cities as such, rather than particular individuals.

It is possible that different issues are interwoven in Abraham's intercession, indeed the particular concern of Abraham has been found to be elusive.[50] However, the story takes forward the account of righteousness and judgement in God's world. There are two important outcomes of it. First, this display of God's moral framework is made with a people that is not related to the chosen line, and therefore is declared (again) to be a universal criterion; and *tsedaqah*, as God's

46. So also William John Lyons, *Canon and Exegesis: Canonical Praxis and the Sodom Narrative* (JSOTSup, 352; Sheffield: Sheffield Academic Press, 2002), p. 183.

47. Bruckner, *Implied Law*, p. 126.

48. Lyons, *Canon*, p. 183.

49. See Wenham, *Genesis 16–50*, pp. 42–3; Bruckner, *Implied Law*, p.168.

50. Lyons, *Canon*, pp. 186–93.

basic ethical requirement, is predicated of peoples as such in their dealings with each other. Second, as Bruckner has shown, the relationship between the moral ordering of the world and the cosmological or physical ordering is a feature of the story. The judgement on Sodom results in a convulsion in the creation itself, leaving the 'Plain' uninhabitable. The transforming of Lot's wife into a 'pillar of salt' symbolizes this rendering of the earth inhospitable to life.[51]

The possibility of non-Abrahamic peoples exhibiting *tsedaqah* recurs almost immediately in the account of Abraham's encounter with King Abimelech of Gerar (Genesis 20).[52] Here as in Gen. 12.10–20, Abraham declares to a foreign king that Sarah is his sister, with the result that she is taken into the king's harem (20.2). There are a number of interests in this narrative (including the concern to protect the reputation of the matriarch, v. 4a, one which may be read back into 12.10–20). But an important dimension is the righteousness of Abimelech and Gerar, asserted by Abimelech in response to the threat posed by Abraham's deceit (v. 4). The narrative has in common with the Sodom narrative that God is in the role of judge, and his justice is questioned by a human character.

Abimelech's assertion of his people's 'righteousness' is made in the context of his fear that they might be unfairly judged. It is taken for granted in the story, by the narrator, the characters and God, that Abimelech would have been guilty if he had approached Sarah sexually, since she was the wife of another man. This is why Abimelech is so angry with Abraham for having endangered him and his people by his deceit (20.9–10). Abraham's new plea in mitigation that Sarah actually is his sister (v. 12) takes nothing away from the treachery of the initial act. The accent is therefore thrown back on to the righteousness or innocence of Abimelech and Gerar. Would God be so unjust as to punish a people that was righteous on the grounds of an unwitting sin?

Again it is significant that this issue is aired by means of a non-Abrahamic people. Assumed here are the responsibility of a non-Abrahamic people to be righteous, the possibility of this actually being the case, and the direct communication between Abimelech and God. Abimelech uses the name אֲדֹנָי (*'adonay*, lord), and the narrator אֱלֹהִים (*'elohim*, God). But the God of Abimelech and the God of Abraham are clearly one and the same. The answer to Abimelech's question is that God would not indeed punish an innocent/righteous nation, and this is demonstrated by his intervention to warn Abimelech not to touch Sarah and thus overcome the danger posed by Abraham's deceit (v. 3). Indeed the issue is settled before Abimelech even asks the question, since it is only after he has been warned that he becomes alert to the danger.

Before concluding on the story of Abimelech, two points need to be settled. First, is Abimelech's concern really about his people or more narrowly about himself? When he asks whether God will destroy a 'righteous [*tsaddiq*] people' (הֲגוֹי גַּם צַדִּיק תַּהֲרֹג, v. 4), there is some tension between this idea and the focus of God's interest in the narrative on Abimelech himself. This is compounded by a doubt about whether the noun גּוֹי (*goy*, 'people') is authentic to the text. Yet

---

51. Bruckner, *Implied Law*, pp. 158–69.
52. See again Bruckner, *Implied Law*, pp. 171–98.

the textual objection is not decisive,[53] and there are other reasons to think that
Abimelech's case involves his nation also. Not only does the challenge to God's
justice regarding a judgement on a people echo unmistakably the issue in the
immediately preceding Sodom narrative, but also Abimelech knows that his own
guilt will have consequences for his kingdom (v. 9).

Second, is the translation of *goy tsaddiq* as 'a righteous nation' an overinter-
pretation, or might the phrase be better rendered by the somewhat weaker 'an
innocent people' (NRSV)? This understanding of it has some plausibility, since
tsaddiq is rightly rendered 'innocent' in the context of legal verdicts (Deut. 25.1).
In favour of the stronger view however is, again, the fact that the possible righteousness of a people has been the issue in the preceding narrative. Furthermore,
Abimelech's declaration of his own innocence in the matter of Sarah uses language from the vocabulary of the moral life in Israel's own spirituality ('the
integrity of my heart and innocence of my hands', v. 5[54]), and his declaration is
accepted and reaffirmed by God (v. 6). The expression is used a number of times,
notably in the Psalms and often of kings, to refer to integrity of character.[55] The
term תמים, related to תם (*tam*), 'integrity', was also used of Noah in parallel with
צדיק (*tsaddiq*).

In Abraham's encounter with Abimelech, therefore, the moral credit goes to
the latter. It is Abimelech who stands within Old Testament patterns of righteousness, who teaches Abraham what 'ought not to be done' (v. 9), and who
provides Sarah with public vindication of her honour, which Abraham had put at
risk (v. 16). He also acts generously by allowing Abraham to settle in his land.
The passage is remarkable for the favourable portrayal of Abimelech and his
people, showing once again that the basic obligations that lie upon God's created
humanity can in principle be met in any people. It is remarkable too because the
righteousness of Abimelech is played out in contrast with the dishonourable
behaviour of Abraham, the one declared righteous, and who just previously has
interceded for Sodom, holding God to account for acting justly in the world.
Abraham's commission is therefore not consistently matched by his performance. Indeed the irony of the situation is driven home when Abraham's plea in
self-defence – 'I thought, there is no fear of God at all in this place' (v. 11) –
reveals his lack of true perception. There is also an uncomfortable incongruity
between his moral ineptitude and his role as 'a prophet' who must intercede for

53. The word נוֹי is often regarded as a dittography on the following גוֹי (Westermann, *Genesis
12–36*, p. 318; BHS). However, LXX, while it varies from MT, has ἔθνος, representing נוֹי. Wenham
thinks emendation unnecessary, 'despite the unparalleled interpolation of גוֹי between a noun and its
qualifier'; *Genesis 16–50*, p. 67.

54. בתם־לבבי ובנקין כפי.

55. The expression 'integrity of one's heart' is predicated of David in Ps. 78.72, and again of a
royal figure in Ps. 101.2 (David in the superscription). It is suggestive to cast Abimelech in the role
of the king in this Psalm and Abraham as the deceiver! The phrase also appears in Pss. 7.9 [EVV 8];
26.1, 11; 41.13 [EVV 12]; Job 4.6; 21.23; Prov. 2.7; 10.9 etc. In 1 Kgs 9.4 it is a duty laid on Solomon in parallel with the keeping of the Mosaic commandments. There are further echoes of Abimelech's declaration in the Psalmic entrance liturgies: Ps. 15.2 (ופעל צדק ודבר אמת בלבבו);
Ps. 24.4 (נקי כפים הולך תמים).

Abimelech in order to remove any effects of Sarah having been introduced into the royal harem (vv. 7, 17–18). This role of Abraham in Gerar echoes his intercessory role at Sodom in a rather hollow way.

The story of *tsedaqah* in Genesis, therefore, does not correspond tidily with the story of the line of Abraham. The same point appears in the case of Judah and Tamar, the wife he took for his son Er (Genesis 38). Tamar is presumably 'Canaanite', like the mother of Er and Judah's other sons Onan and Shelah (vv.1–7). The unfolding story turns on the relationship between Judah and Tamar, in which Judah behaves treacherously and murderously towards her, but, his deceitfulness and double standards finally exposed, has to admit: 'She is more righteous than I'[56] (v. 26). To the catalogue of the chosen line's moral failures we might add Jacob's egregious claim that his *tsedaqah* will answer for him in his false dealings with Laban over his herd of goats (Gen. 30.33). His appeal to *tsedaqah* in the act of deception seems even to pour contempt on it as an obligation or ideal.

It is a paradox of Genesis that the line of Abraham, the one 'known' by God 'to keep the way of the LORD by doing righteousness and justice' (18.19), so carefully distinguished as a line of blessing that inherits Abraham's promise and commission, conforms rather little to the fundamental standard for right behaviour set at the flood with the attribution of 'righteousness' to Noah (6.9). In Lyons' view, the story of Sodom is intended to show that 'if Sodom can be pronounced righteous, then Sodom's exemplar status requires that Abraham and Israel can also be pronounced *unrighteous*' [emphasis original].[57] This is true, though the role of Sodom should not be narrowly conceived to act as an 'exemplar' for Israel only. Rather, Genesis lays out the possibilities for righteous behaviour among the nations. In this context, the role of Abraham and thus Israel is portrayed as problematical. The moral failures of Abraham and his line make it clear that 'rightness' will not inhere in the chosen line; rather, its vocation will be subject to God's higher aim of seeing righteousness established in the world.

This account, unlike Heard's, supposes that the stories are told, not in the service of the theology of Israel's election, but in that of God's purpose for the whole of creation. As we saw, Heard had to postulate an incongruity between the openness or ambiguity of the stories of the patriarchs and the dominant factor of the election of Israel which overrode the ambiguities. On our account, the portrayal of the chosen line as morally unreliable belongs essentially to the message. The struggle of nascent Israel to fulfil its calling does not simply pose the narrow question whether Israel can be righteous, but what a righteous nation might be like. As we have seen, other nations share in the demonstration of this.

4. *Conclusion*

In Genesis the created order is at the same time political, and contains a mandate, grounded in the divine character, for humanity to exhibit righteousness in its

56. צדקה ממני.
57. Lyons, *Canon*, p. 184.

corporate life. Yahweh is 'the judge of all the earth', committed to ruling in justice and righteousness. Abraham and one line of his descendants bear special responsibility to embody and witness to this righteousness as the proper condition of human relationships. Yet the story of Genesis makes it clear that Yahweh's ultimate interest is in his entire creation, and that the standard of righteousness is demanded equally of all. Moreover, Abraham and his line are sometimes exceeded in righteousness by others. The choice of the patriarch, therefore, and so the nation of Israel, is not pure privilege, but a vocation that extends beyond itself.

The story of Israel's forebears in Genesis is a necessary prelude to the Mosaic beginnings of Israel the nation. The obligations assumed to lie upon humanity in general are logically and canonically prior to the laws later given to Israel through Moses at Sinai.[58] Patriarchal religion should therefore not be contrasted with Mosaic in the sense that it is thought to have no moral framework or theology of judgement.[59] The fundamental standard for all the world is set here. Nor should the concept that the Old Testament knows two quite separate narratives of origins (the patriarchal and the Egyptian)[60] distract from the strong narrative logic that leads from Genesis to Exodus and beyond. Rather, the stories of Abraham and Israel should be read both sequentially and in mutual illumination. The faltering beginning of Abraham shows that Israel's success in its mission may not be taken for granted, and already opens the possibility that it too may falter. In the immediate sequel, however, the nature of its vocation will first be more fully elaborated.

---

58. Cf. also Bruckner, *Implied Law*, p. 170.
59. So Moberly, *Old Testament*, pp. 97–8, citing 15.6; 18 as exceptions.
60. As in K. Schmid. *Erzväter und Exodus*.

Chapter 4

FROM TYRANNY TO FREEDOM: EXODUS TO NUMBERS

1. *The Politics of Exodus*

We turn now to the part played by Exodus–Numbers in the narrative of Genesis–Kings as it relates to politics. Exodus has a reputation as one of the Bible's most politically potent books. At its heart is the act of liberation from oppression which becomes Israel's most characteristic confession, and most influential theological concept, in the Old Testament.[1] In the modern world too, the exodus has had a major role in shaping liberation theology.[2] I aim to show that the story of God's purpose for the world, begun in Genesis, is continued in these narratives of the formation of the nation Israel. Here as in Genesis this will require a consideration of how the idea of one nation chosen from among others can serve a purpose larger than the interests of that nation alone.

The particularity of Israel stands out, if anything, more sharply in Exodus than in Genesis. Here Israel is separated from Egypt, lately its host and the means of its survival, by a series of afflictions brought upon Egypt, culminating in the terrible sentence of death passed on all its firstborn (Exodus 5–14). The liberation of Israel has this act of the divine anger as its counterpart, and it becomes the centre of the most characteristic feast of Israel, the Passover, the narrative of the event being at the same time the institution of the feast (Exodus 12–13). Following the exodus is the Sinai covenant (Exodus 19–24), in which Israel is constituted Yahweh's 'special possession' (Exod. 19.5), and promised that he will take them to a land from which he will drive out the present inhabitants for their benefit (Exod. 23.23–33). The final major section of the book (Exodus 25–40) provides for the place of worship, the tabernacle, which in due course will serve as the focus for the military advance of Israel upon its promised land (Num. 10.11–36).

The particular focus on Israel has often dominated its interpretation. Moberly finds a sharp contrast between Genesis 12–50 and Exodus because of the effect of the latter's theology of 'holiness': as against Genesis' 'open, unstructured, and nonlocated unagressive nature...', Exodus, from 3.5 onward, manifests an 'exclusive, demanding, regulated, mediated, sanctuary-centred relationship between YHWH and Israel'.[3] There is, furthermore, a habit in Old Testament studies,

1. See for example Ps. 78; Isa. 43.1–3.
2. See, e.g., George V. Pixley, *On Exodus: a Liberation Perspective* (Maryknoll, NY: Orbis Books, 1987).
3. Moberly, *Old Testament*, p. 104.

since Wellhausen, to see the tabernacle as in effect a cipher for the Jerusalem temple, thus limiting its capacity to speak about worship as such, but rather concentrating attention on the nation of Israel. A modern version of this approach is the sociological analysis which sees Exodus–Numbers as part of an attempt to establish the identity of the post-exilic returnees as the true Israel, organized around the rebuilt temple.[4]

Approaches such as these tend to minimize the narrative and theological links between Genesis and Exodus. Mullen finds few links back to the patriarchal promises (only at 13.5, 11; 32.13; 33.1), and other reminiscences of Genesis are marginalized as 'editorial'.[5] He opposes reading Exodus as if it were part of a coherent literary unit following from Genesis, arguing that this is 'modern, or at least post-biblical'. Rather, the Pentateuch consists of units, used 'as wholes or in part' according to the need of the moment in respect of establishing ethnicity, their locus being the cult.[6] The stories of Exodus were read in the post-exilic period according to the typology of exile-restoration, and further, this is *the only way* to understand them: 'each of these sets of traditions can be understood only against the background of the ideologies constructed by the Persian restoration community in Jerusalem'.[7] Exodus is a 'legitimizing myth of restoration', utilizing temple traditions while conforming to the Persian policy of 'temple economy'.[8] In this analysis, the sociological reading, which finds the texts to support the interests of a particular group at a particular time, is married to one which plays down the 'canonical' dynamic that invites reading across the biblical books.[9] In the approach followed here in contrast, the latter sort of reading is taken to be theologically decisive, for reasons already offered.

The continuities from Genesis to Exodus are both narrative and theological. (In classical criticism they were attributed to the dominant sources, especially J and P.) As the Genesis narrative ended with the descent of Jacob's family into the Egypt of Joseph, so Exodus opens with the people dwelling there, consisting of the families of the twelve sons of Jacob (1.2–5). The growth of Israel to a numerous people signals that the promise to Abraham of countless descendants (Gen. 15.5) is beginning to find fulfilment. It is this factor that provides the first spring of the action in Exodus, since it is the increasing population of Israel that leads to the change of official attitude to them under a Pharaoh who 'did not know Joseph' (1.8), and so the oppression from which Yahweh will in due course deliver them. The narrative, furthermore, is at pains to stress that the God of the exodus is the same God who made himself known to Abraham, Isaac and Jacob (Exod. 3.15–16; 6.3), and this at key moments in Moses' encounters with God.

---

4. So Mullen, *Ethnic Myths*, pp. 163–281.
5. Mullen, *Ethnic Myths*, p. 163. In this he is close to K. Schmid, *Erzväter und Exodus* (see above, Chapter 3).
6. Mullen, *Ethnic Myths*, p. 165.
7. Mullen, *Ethnic Myths*, p. 166.
8. Mullen, *Ethnic Myths*, p. 167.
9. In one sense Mullen and others, such as P. R. Davies, do offer a view of canon, as we observed above, Chapter 1.

An indication that Genesis and Exodus together are part of a larger story is gained from such texts as Gen. 15.12–21, which anticipates the long Egyptian enslavement and ultimate entry to land, and is thus connected with Exod. 23.23–33. These links are often explained, not surprisingly, as 'deuteronomic', since it is in Deuteronomy that the theme of land-possession receives its fullest exposition. However, this should not pre-empt discussion of how they affect the way in which the text might be read. The motif of circumcision makes another connection between Abraham and Moses (Gen. 17.10; Exod. 4.24–26).

These narrative links already point to the theological ones. The story, with its aspects of promise and covenant, is about the formation of a nation among others. The family of Jacob is introduced at the outset (by the new Pharaoh) as 'the *people* of the sons of Israel' (עַם בְּנֵי יִשְׂרָאֵל, 1.9), and from Yahweh's perspective 'my people' (עַמִּי, 3.7). The story of the covenant will now take the form of a bond between Yahweh and this nation. The foundation-narratives of the people of Israel are in this way spliced into the patriarchal narratives and presented as a development of the themes of Genesis.

a. *Pharaoh, Israel and Yahweh: A Creation Conflict*
In Exodus themes of creation, politics and worship are intertwined. The strong creational theology of Exodus has been demonstrated by Fretheim, who portrays the new Pharaoh's tyranny as specifically a challenge to God's created order, showing that the exodus-liberation has cosmic implications and dimensions.[10] The subjection of God's people to slavery is a negation of the created purpose of humanity, in which *'adam* as such is in God's 'image', with its royal connotations, and exercises dominion over the created order (Gen. 1.26–28). This perversion of the creational purpose is evident from Pharaoh's opening deliberation (Exod. 1.8–14). Here rule is in the hands of an all-powerful figure, whose concern for order, however, is characterized by fear and the readiness for domination by force. In Pharaoh's mind, the world threatens his order with war and sedition, and this leads inexorably to a policy of repression and cruelty.

Pharaoh's plan to constrain the growth of Israel runs counter to the creation theme of 'filling the earth', as well as to God's purpose for Abraham's descendants that they should be numerous. His 'lest they multiply' (v. 10)[11] directly contradicts God's blessing-command spoken to the first human pair (Gen. 1.28), in which their multiplying was precisely a concomitant of their 'ruling the earth'. Indeed, Pharaoh stands in the place of God and opposed to him. While God's purpose for humanity is generous, that they should possess the earth together in freedom and abundance, Pharaoh's plan is that *he* should possess the earth, and in defending it for himself deny to those outside his sphere their inheritance as children of *'adam*. For him, the 'land' (הָאָרֶץ, *ha'arets*) that is his domain equates

---

10. T. E. Fretheim, *Exodus*, pp. 12–14.

11. פֶּן־יִרְבֶּה. The pronouns and suffixes referring to Israel in vv. 10–12 are singular in MT, presumably following עַם (*'am*, people) in v. 9. The major ancient versions have plurals. The singular can be retained, and may have the effect of emphasizing the 'peoplehood' of Israel.

in effect with the 'earth'. In his hostility to Israel he does not seek their expulsion; his fear on the contrary is that they should escape from the boundaries of his rule. When he declares his determination that they should not leave (literally, 'go up from the land/earth',[12] v. 10d), he resists God's intention for Israel, that he should in due course 'bring them up' from '*this* land to the land that he swore to Abraham, to Isaac and to Jacob' (Gen. 50.24)[13]. The same phrase will in due course be applied to the memory of the deliverance itself (e.g. Exod. 17.3; 32.1–33.15 [9×]).[14]

Pharaoh's impulse to exercise sole and absolute rule has echoes of the Babel narrative (Gen. 11.1–9). Both passages portray attempts to unify humanity and so to concentrate its power and resources. Each in its own way resists the spreading of humanity, the Babelites construing this as a 'scattering' and disintegration, while Pharaoh sees the growth of Israel as a threat to his hegemony. The motif of city-building is also shared, with some echoes in the Exodus passage of the extensive wordplay in Gen. 11.1–9 based on 'Babel' and 'building' (בנה). The city in both places symbolizes in bricks and mortar the desperate search for security. Pharaoh, prefacing his call to action with 'Come' (הבה, v. 10a), stands both in the place of the Babelites and of God, each of whom uses the same word in their declarations of intent (Gen. 11.3–4, 7). The contest for control played out there is thus in the background here, with Pharaoh not only renewing the defiance of the Babelites, but placing himself in direct opposition to God.

The hostility to the creational purpose also bears fruit in the corruption of productive work into slave labour. The creation narratives, in both Genesis 1 and Genesis 2, give the human beings responsibility for the world in which they are placed, but portray work as benign, a proper function of humanity. In the first narrative they are in the position of stewards over the creation (1.28), and in the second they are to 'work' the land (2.5). The benign face of human work is already corrupted in Gen. 3, when as a result of the human rebellion there it becomes hard toil (Genesis 3.17–18). Exodus develops this corruption of work in its own way, now portraying it as the enslavement of the weak by the powerful; while the product goes to the overlords, the prospect for the workers is only death. The echo of the second creation narrative in the enslavement of the Israelites is heard clearly in the use of the root עבד (*'abad*; 'serve', 'work') in 1.13–14;[15] cf. Gen. 2.5. 'Labour' as work dedicated by force to Pharaoh becomes in Exodus the antithesis of human freedom and the ground of Israel's appeal to Yahweh for deliverance (Exod. 2.23; 5.11; 6.6 etc.).

At stake in the labour-activity of Israel is not only the nature of labour, but also its object. In certain contexts the term has to be translated as 'service', with its further connotations of 'worship' (Exod. 7.26[EVV 8.1]). Within Exodus, the pervasive issue concerns the directedness of Israel's labour-worship, whether to Yahweh or to Pharaoh. Yahweh demands that Israel be released from its labour-

---

12. ועלה מן־הארץ.
13. והעלה אתכם מן־הארץ.
14. Curiously, these all occur in contexts in which Israel itself resists God's redemptive purpose.
15. עבד hi., v. 13; עבד qal, v. 14; עבדה, v. 14, 3x.

service to Pharaoh in order to give its labour-service to Yahweh (7.26[8.1]). The Passover, the act of worship which corresponds to this demand of Yahweh, is twice described by the same term (12.25; 13.5). In the Decalogue, Yahweh prefaces his commands with a reminder that he has delivered Israel from Egypt, 'the house of slaves' (עבדים, 20.2), and then prohibits them from 'worshipping other gods' (עבד, 20.5). He also institutes the Sabbath (20.8–11), rooted in the charter for humanity in Gen. 1.1–2.3, and tempering work (עבד) with the rest that is a sacrament of humanity's true nature. By the end of Exodus a full circle has been turned, because the completion of the tabernacle is pointedly described as עבדה (*'abodah*), a work of obedience done at Yahweh's command (Exod. 39.32, 40, 42). The term refers both to the work of constructing the tabernacle and to the activity of worship for which it was made. The latter is to the fore in v. 40, while the sense of 'work' prevails in vv. 32, 42. Labour and worship are thus conceptually close. And the force of Exod. 39.32–43 is to portray the duty of Israel towards Yahweh symbolized in its worship at the tabernacle as a precise antithesis to the allegiance extracted from it forcibly by Pharaoh. In its synthesis of constructive work, worship and rest, Exodus offers a revolutionary antithesis to Pharaoh's degradation and enslavement of humanity.[16]

b. *Exodus: Political and Religious Geography*
Israel's deliverance from the tyranny of Egypt, therefore, is not separable from its duty of worship to Yahweh. The book of Exodus is pervaded by a head-to-head contest between Pharaoh and Yahweh. Israel is Yahweh's 'son', not Pharaoh's slave, and Yahweh will demand his son from Pharaoh if necessary at the cost of Pharaoh's own firstborn son (4.22). In doing so he will exert his true claim as opposed to Pharaoh's false claim, for the earth is Yahweh's, not Pharaoh's (19.5, contrast 1.10d).

The book of Exodus, indeed, is structured by this fundamental conflict over Israel's true identity, nature, loyalty and place. This last (place) is highly significant, because the narrative of Exodus is about an exchange of places, where place is both geographically real and religiously and politically symbolic. The movement from Egypt to Sinai to tabernacle is carefully marked. The first change of place takes Israel from Egypt into the wilderness by way of the Reed Sea. As we observed earlier, the Sea is not only a physical boundary and a place of Yahweh's victory over the full strength of Pharaoh, but also symbolic of primaeval conflict.[17] The victory of Yahweh over the Egyptian hosts is at the same time a demonstration of his power over the waters. The mythological element is suggested already in 14.9, where the Egyptian army camps by the sea (*yam*), before Baal-Zephon. The verse brings together the names of the gods Baal and Yam known from Canaanite myth, and the struggle in which Yam, symbolizing the

16. Cf. N. Lohfink, *Theology of the Pentateuch: Themes of the Priestly Narrative and Deuteronomy* (trans. Linda M. Maloney; Edinburgh: T & T Clark, 1994), p. 132.
17. See above, Chapter 2 and n. 61. See also F. M. Cross, *Canaanite Myth and Hebrew Epic* (Cambridge, Mass.: Harvard University Press, 1973), pp. 121–44.

Chaotic waters, is overcome by Baal. The mythological connotations are even stronger in Exodus 15, the 'Song of the Sea'. Here we find a number of names for the waters, suggesting that the power of the waters themselves is in focus (15.4–5, 8, 10). Among them is תהמת (vv. 5, 8), a plural form of *tehom*, 'the deep', that covered the earth at the beginning of God's creative work (Gen. 1.2). The story of the warrior Yahweh's victory over Pharaoh echoes a more fundamental conflict, his triumph over Chaos itself. The adoption of motifs from Ancient Near Eastern mythology is typical of the Old Testament's assertion of the unrivalled power of Yahweh in the cosmos.[18]

But here as elsewhere the creative act is also a political-historical one.[19] Yahweh's overcoming of Chaos now takes the form of his defeat of Pharaoh. The deliverance of Israel, with its correlative in the gift of the land of Canaan, is an assertion of his cosmic rule, and a step towards the redemption of the political sphere. In the rival claims of Pharaoh and Yahweh upon the life and allegiance of Israel both are portrayed as 'king'. At stake, then, is the true nature of ultimate royal authority and how it relates to the condition of people. The arena of the contest between Yahweh and Pharaoh is the creation itself. Its outcome, in the deliverance of Israel through Sea, is that 'Yahweh will reign (יהוה ימלך) for ever and ever' (Exod. 15.18).

The narrative now takes Israel to Mt. Sinai, where in the metaphor of covenant, the implications of Yahweh's kingship in Israel will begin to unfold. In this transition, the double geography of Exodus continues to operate. In the physical geography Sinai is a wilderness space between Egypt and the promised land, a hard, dry place between well-watered Egypt and well-watered Canaan, which by its nature creates desire for rest and plenty. And so wilderness as physical space shades into wilderness as metaphor. It corresponds readily to a narrative space between the time of bondage which is past and the time of possession, still in the future. This narrative space is no mere limbo, but highly conflictual, an arena of battle for Israel's soul. After Pharaoh's attempt to resist Yahweh's purpose to bring Israel into his own sphere comes the resistance of Israel itself, with its nostalgic backward look (Exod. 16.2–3; 17.2–3). Other more serious hesitations will come as the story progresses (Exodus 32; Numbers 25).

In this context Sinai itself is not only a mountain but a metaphor of the divine presence. Like the ground on which Moses stood when he witnessed the bush that burned without being consumed (Exod. 3.2–6), it is 'holy'. The description of the mountain and Israel's encounter with Yahweh there corresponds to the concept of holiness and divine presence exemplified in the tabernacle. That is, there are gradations of holiness whose lines must not be infringed (Exod. 19.12–13, 21–23), actions of consecration of the people for the encounter with God (19.10–15), and certain persons who are authorized to approach more closely to

18. Ps. 93.3–4 offers a parallel to Exod. 15.4–8, with its proclamation of the kingship of Yahweh and its accumulation of 'water'-vocabulary echoing Canaanite myth (here ים and נהר, occur, names for the god Yam in the Baal conflict). Cf. also Ps. 74.13–14; Job 3.8; Isa. 27.1.

19. Cf. Isa. 43.15; Psalm 74.

the centre than the ordinary people (19.23–24, cf. 24.1–2).[20] The summit of the
mountain, where Moses and Aaron meet Yahweh, and where even the ordinary
priests may not go, anticipates the tabernacle's 'most holy place', which only
the high priest may enter, and then only once a year on the Day of Atonement
(Leviticus 16). This religious symbolism of presence has a strong political
dimension in the logic of Exodus, for the space represented by Sinai is absolutely distinct from the space of Pharaoh's Egypt. Israel has now entered a
different political sphere, with Yahweh at the centre. The holiness-geography of
Exodus is in direct opposition to that of Egypt, with the people in a different
presence, under a different authority, and in a different spatial organization.
Yahweh is lord of 'the whole earth'; and Israel in its entirety has the dignity of
'a priestly kingdom' (Exod. 19.6).

The final spatial shift in Exodus is from Sinai to the tabernacle. The connection between these two locations is firmly established by the narrative. As the
presence of God on the mountain is signified by a cloud and fire (19.16, 18;
24.15–18, so a cloud and fire also indicate his presence at the tabernacle (40.34–
38); in each case the cloud is closely associated with his 'kabod-glory' (כבוד)
(24.15; 40.34, and cf. the עַנָן כָּבֵד,[21] in 19.16). As God spoke to Israel from the
mountain, so he will speak to them from the most holy place (25.22, cf. 26.31–
35). As only a specially chosen personnel might approach the divine presence
on the mountain, so now Aaron and his sons are consecrated to serve in close
proximity to the divine presence in the tabernacle (chs 28–29). As the encounter
on the mountain was prepared for by actions of consecration, so now actions of
consecration prepare both priests and the tabernacle for the regular meetings
between Israel and God there (29.35–30.10). The unique meeting on the mountain gives way to the regular meetings at the tabernacle. Indeed, not only does
Yahweh undertake to 'meet' Israel at the tabernacle but he will 'dwell' among
them. The concomitance of meeting and dwelling is intimated in the architecture
of the most holy place, since the configuration of atonement-cover (כפרת) and
cherubim, above which Yahweh will speak to his people, resembles that of a
throne.[22] This dynamic of presence, embodying both encounter and permanence,
is forged especially by the commands concerning the daily burnt-offerings in
Exod. 29.38–46, with its repetition of the vocabulary of both meeting (vv. 42–44)
and dwelling (vv. 45–46) vocabulary. The undertakings to 'meet' and 'dwell'
point forward into a future of regular mutual presence of God to Israel and Israel
to God.

However, the vehicle that most clearly secures the transfer of the divine
presence from Sinai to tabernacle is Exod. 34.29–35. In this passage Moses
descends from Mt. Sinai, his face shining because of his recent encounter with

20. For the essential aspects of the geography of holiness see P. Jenson, *Graded Holiness*
(JSOTSup, 106; Sheffield: JSOT Press, 1992).

21. Translated as 'thick cloud', NRSV; but the adjective is also 'heavy', and related in form to
kabod, 'glory'.

22. Cf. 2 Kgs 19.15, where Hezekiah's 'sitting [upon] the cherubim' (ישב הכרבים) seems to
be an image of enthronement.

God (vv. 29–30). The transition from unique meeting at Sinai to regular meeting at the tabernacle is signalled by a change of tense. Up to v. 33 Moses' actions are described in the usual tense for sequential narrative in the past (the imperfect with waw-consecutive). But at v. 34 a different sequence of temporal clauses begins, using the perfect tense (mostly with simple waw) to indicate repeated actions in the past. The beginning of this series is best translated 'Whenever…', and the following verbs with the English form 'he would take the veil off' etc. (as NRSV).[23] The tabernacle is not mentioned explicitly in the text, but the context makes it clear that it is in view. The passage is thus a direct counterpart to 40.34–38, when a single initial filling of the completed tabernacle with God's glory gives way to a portrayal of the cloud repeatedly coming to the tabernacle during Israel's journeyings.[24] The narrative from ch. 24, therefore, carefully constructs the transition from the unique encounter at Sinai to the regular worship life of Israel around the tabernacle.[25] At the end of the book, Israel is in a position to move on with Yahweh, since the lines of its spatial relationship to him have been fully laid down.

The representation of God's presence in the tabernacle must also be viewed in the context of the larger picture of the narrative of Genesis–Kings. It is in this context that one must consider the location of the institution of the tabernacle worship in the wilderness. Is this merely a contingency of the narrative, providing a foundational story from antiquity, or is the wilderness location of the essence of the text's meaning? As we have noticed, some still take the view that the tabernacle is a cipher for the temple, in the context of the temple administration of Persian Yehud. For Mullen, the tabernacle is simply an anachronism, designed to give the Persian-period cult a 'religio-mythological charter'.[26] The worship prescribed for it is part of the drawing of boundaries around Israel intended to secure its identity as a nation. 'Israel' is recreated and maintained by cultic means of reintegration.[27] But the real force of the narrative was to sustain the ascendancy of the Jerusalem priesthood, to which the idea of the 'kingdom of priests' (Exod. 19.6) applied in reality.[28]

---

23. 34.34 opens with a temporal clause using the preposition ‏ב‎ and the infinitive construct of ‏בוא‎, 'come'. The construction does not indicate regular action in itself; rather this is indicated by the verbs that follow.

24. The sequence of tenses in 40.34–38 is different from that in 34.29–35. Here we have an initial waw-consecutive with imperfect (‏ויכס‎), followed by a series of perfects which in this case seem to refer to the single instance of the glory's appearance upon the tabernacle's completion. When the change comes at v. 36, with a temporal structure analogous to that in 34.34 (‏ב‎ + infinitive construct), the subsequent repeated actions are conveyed by the simple imperfect tense.

25. On the transition from unique event to regular worship, see also B. Janowski, *Sühne als Heilsgeschehen: Studien zur Sühnetheologie der Priesterschrift und zur Wurzel KPR im Alten Orient und im Alten Testament* (WMANT, 55; Neukirchen–Vluyn, 1982), pp. 306–8.

26. Mullen, *Ethnic Myths*, pp. 220–1; cf. pp. 252–3.

27. Mullen, *Ethnic Myths*, p. 232.

28. 'Despite the ideal that the whole community was to become a "kingdom of priests," not just any Israelite held the status necessary to approach the sacred precincts of the Tabernacle…', Mullen, *Ethnic Myths*, p. 258.

However, the equation of temple and tabernacle has been contested, in my view justifiably. In contrast to the temple, the tabernacle is neither a permanent structure nor is it situated necessarily in a particular place. R. E. Clements argued that the concept of it conveyed the impermanence of God's presence at any time.[29] J. D. Levenson emphasized the contrast between the impermanence of the wilderness tabernacle and the permanence of the city-cult of Zion.[30] The debate has sometimes focused on the use of vocabulary. It has been claimed, for example, that the verb שׁכן connotes permanent dwelling in the Jerusalem theology, and therefore that it conveys the same thing in the portrayal of the tabernacle. But Janowski has rightly contested this by arguing that the meaning of the language of divine presence in the priestly parts of the Pentateuch must be shown from within the literature of which it forms a part.[31]

In the interpretation of the tabernacle in Exodus, the key issue is its relationship to the accounts of creation in Genesis. That there is a connection between the first creation account (Gen. 1.1–2.3/4a) and the portrayal of the tabernacle in Exodus is widely recognized.[32] The progression that we have already noticed, from Sinai to tabernacle, is therefore only a part of a larger movement beginning in Genesis. The connection arises from a view of reality, shared widely with the ancient world, in which the place of worship corresponds to the cosmos as a space in which God and humanity meet.[33] In the Old Testament the creation and the worship space are linked by means of echoes and developments within the narrative of Genesis–Exodus. The most striking analogy between the two sections involves the pattern of six plus one days in the creation week and in Moses' encounter with God on Sinai (Exod. 24.15–16; 25.2) in which six days of cloud-covered silence are followed by a seventh on which God imparts the instructions for the tabernacle. The close affinity between God's creative work and the mak-

29. R. E. Clements, *God and Temple* (Oxford: Blackwell, 1965), p. 117. Clements thinks of the tabernacle as a theological image for the temple, intended to assert the primacy of Yahweh's dwelling in heaven, which alone could explain the absence of a temple at Jerusalem during the exilic years.

30. 'YHWH's self-disclosure takes place in remote parts rather than within the established and settled cult of the city. Even his mode of manifestation reflects the uncontrollable and unpredictable character of the wilderness rather than the decorum one associates with a long-established urban religion, rooted in familiar traditions'; Jon D. Levenson, *Sinai and Zion: An Entry into the Jewish Bible* (Minneapolis: Winston, 1985), pp. 21–2; cf. pp. 89–92.

31. Janowski, *Sühne*, pp. 297–9. He argues against R. Schmitt, *Zelt und Lade als Thema alttestamentlicher Wissenschaft: eine kritische forschungsgeschichtliche Darstellung* (Gütersloh: Mohn, 1972). Janowski means the priestly narrative beginning at Genesis 1. I propose to look at the narratives of Genesis–Exodus more generally, as will appear below.

32. See for example M. Weinfeld, 'Sabbath, Temple and the Enthronement of the Lord; the Problem of the *Sitz im Leben* of Genesis 1:1–2:3', in A. Caquot and M. Décor (eds.), *Mélanges bibliques et orientaux en l'honneur de M. Henri Cazelles* (AOAT, 212; Kevelaer/Neukirchen–Vluyn, 1981), pp. 501–12, esp. 502–3; J. D. Levenson, 'The Temple and the World' *JR* 64 (1984), pp. 275–98; *idem, Sinai and Zion*, pp. 142–5; *idem, Creation and the Persistence of Evil: The Jewish Drama of Divine Omnipotence* (San Francisco, 1988), pp. 78–99, esp. 84–6.

33. Janowski, *Gottes Gegenwart* (BTAT, 1; Neukirchen–Vluyn: Neukirchener Verlag, 1993), pp. 216–23; cf. Clements, *God and Temple*, pp. 6–9.

ing of the tabernacle is confirmed at the other end of the Exodus section when Moses is said to have 'finished the work' of erecting the sanctuary (ויכל משה את־המלאכה, Exod. 40.33c), exactly echoing God's 'finishing the work' of creation in Gen. 2.2 (ויכל אלהים...מלאכתו). [34]

In the Exodus narrative, therefore, God's creation rest is reflected in earthly experience in two ways, first in the pattern of weekly sabbatical rest from work (Exod. 20.8–11), and second in the place of worship. As the weekly pattern of productive work followed by Sabbath mirrors God's activity in the regularities of human life, so the tabernacle expresses the creation rest in terms of the presence of God and humanity to each other in worship. When the glory fills the completed tabernacle (Exod. 40.34) a fruition of the creative purpose of God is signalled. Fellowship between God and humanity, intended at creation, is established. The mutuality of God and humanity in the sanctuary evokes the idea of humanity as 'image of God' (Gen. 1.26–27), humanity becoming truly itself in worship. [35] The narrative of Exodus closes by pointing into a future in which such fellowship will continue based on the sanctuary. A further ratification occurs at Lev. 9.22-24, after the first sacrifices celebrated by the newly ordained priesthood at the place of worship.

But does the establishment of this connection between the creation and the inauguration of the worship of Israel mean that the divine purpose at creation has now been fulfilled? On one reading, which pursues the story into Israel's possession of the land of Canaan, this is precisely the case. N. Lohfink points to the echo of the creation command to 'subdue the earth' (Gen. 1.28) in Josh. 18.1, where Israel sets up the tabernacle in the land at Shiloh, and we read: 'The land lay subdued before them' (in each case the verb כבש is used, together with the noun הארץ, translated respectively 'earth' and 'land'). [36] For Lohfink, 'That the creation has here reached its successful outcome and that Israel has achieved its salvation are one and the same thing'. [37] He attributes this picture of a completion of creation to the Priestly narrative. P, like the Atrahasis epic, portrays a world that has arrived at a condition of stability after critical disruptions that had resulted from 'the human and animal *deviation from the God-given order of things*' (emphasis original). [38] P depicts an order that has been brought out of chaos, that consists in nations peacefully dwelling in their lands, and that should

---

34. Janowski, *Sühne*, p. 309; *idem, Gottes Gegenwart*, e.g. p. 238–9 and n. 102, where he cites others for the same view. See also Lohfink, *Theology of the Pentateuch*, pp. 130–1; *idem*, 'Macht Euch die Erde untertan', in Lohfink, *Studien zum Pentateuch* (SBAB, 4; Stuttgart, Verlag Katholisches Bibelwerk, 1988), pp. 11–28, esp. 26–8.

35. Lohfink makes this connection, at the same time noting a contrast with the place of humanity in the Babylonian myth of Atrahasis, in which humans, as 'images of god', were made to carry out onerous tasks which the gods refused to undertake; *Theology of the Pentateuch*, pp. 131, 133.

36. Lohfink, *Theology of the Pentateuch*, pp. 127–8. Joseph Blenkinsopp also observed a connection between the episodes of creation, construction of the tabernacle and its establishment in the land of Israel; 'The Structure of P', *CBQ* 38 (1976), pp. 275–92 (275–8), and cf. Levenson, *Creation*, pp. 84–5.

37. Lohfink, *Theology of the Pentateuch*, p. 128.

38. Lohfink, *Theology of the Pentateuch*, p. 123.

continue just as it is.[39] In his understanding, P provides a theology for the sustaining of the world as God's creation in opposition to other views that make it available for exploitation.[40]

However, the stability envisaged by the Pentateuchal narrative may be overstated. The erection of the tabernacle does not complete a hitherto imperfect creation;[41] rather the inception of tabernacle worship occurs within an ongoing story in which the relationship with God is broken and compromised. The story is characterized by repeated ruptures and new beginnings, the most notable ruptures being the first rebellion in Eden, the sin of humanity that brings the flood, the sin and destruction of Sodom, and the 'Chaos' of enslavement in Egypt.[42] The pattern continues into the second half of Exodus, with the Golden Calf narrative set into the tabernacle sequence. In each case there is a new beginning, often with a strong emphasis on God's grace (Gen. 3.20–21; 8.21–22; Exod. 34.6–9), together with the sense that the sin of humanity continues to have an effect (the expulsion from the Garden, the acts of judgement in the flood, at Sodom and at Sinai, Exod. 32.25–29). Parallels between these various interruptions have been well recognized. We have noticed already the echo of the salvation of Noah in Lot's escape from Sodom;[43] similarly, the renewal after the Golden Calf idolatry echoes the renewal after the flood.[44] The final setting up of the tabernacle enters into this pattern, because the date of it corresponds to the date of the end of the flood (in each case the first day of the first month of the second year; Exod. 40.17, cf. Gen. 8.13). In this way the gift of the tabernacle to Israel, and thus the possibility of God's presence, is likened to the renewed gift of life to humanity after the flood.[45]

The pattern of rupture and renewal is sometimes attributed to the P-narrative. Lohfink based his concept of stability forged out of disruption on a reading of P.[46] But when P is read in isolation, the recurrent effect of sin and violence is diminished. As Lohfink notes when referring to the sin of Israel in the P-account of Numbers 13–14, P rarely addresses the subject of sin. War too is expurgated, since the P-account of the taking of the land does not involve war, and P is even described as 'pacifistic'.[47]

Yet the reconstructed priestly account cannot entirely dim the voices that threaten the created order, and these voices are heard more clearly if one takes the Pentateuchal narrative as a whole, so bringing in the Eden story, Lot, and the Golden Calf. The Eden narrative (Gen. 2.4–3.24) has its own links with the

---

39. Lohfink, *Theology of the Pentateuch*, p. 125.
40. Lohfink, *Theology of the Pentateuch*, p. 133–4.
41. So rightly Janowski, *Gottes Gegenwart*, pp. 239–40.
42. The aggression of Pharaoh comes into the category of 'das Schöpfungswidrige' (hostile to creation), according to Janowski, *Gottes Gegenwart*, p. 243; cf. Fretheim, *Exodus*, p. 13.
43. See G. Wenham, *Genesis 16–50*, pp. 42–3.
44. See R. W. L. Moberly, *At the Mountain of God: Story and Theology in Exodus 32–34* (JSOTSup, 22; Sheffield: JSOT Press, 1983), p. 91, for the parallel between Gen. 8.21 and Exod. 34.9.
45. Cf. Janowski, *Gottes Gegenwart*, pp. 231–2; and see his further bibliography on pp. 238–41.
46. Lohfink, *Theology of the Pentateuch*, p. 123.
47. Lohfink, *Theology of the Pentateuch*, pp. 126–7.

tabernacle aside from those made by the first creation account. The typological relationship between the tabernacle and the Garden of Eden has been demonstrated by G. J. Wenham.[48] For example, the cherubim placed at the eastern entrance to the garden preventing immediate access to the presence of God (Gen. 3.24) correspond to the cherubim attending his near presence in the most holy place (Exod. 25.17–22); and in each case the direction of approach is from the east (Exod. 27.13; 38.13). The effect of these echoes in Exodus 25–40 of the primaeval story of human rebellion and loss of the immediate presence of God is to emphasize the restricted access to God's presence represented by the symbolism of graded holiness and regulated approach in the geography of the tent, and the imperfect nature of the relationship between God and humanity. It also emphasizes the perpetual possibility of dis-order and return to Chaos because of the frailty of humanity.

The completion of the tabernacle, therefore, is not an end in the sense of a perfecting. Rather it represents the possibility of a continuing relationship between God and humanity notwithstanding the ongoing story of human sinfulness, the very issue that is aired in the Golden Calf episode (Exodus 32–34),[49] in the midst of the tabernacle sequence. The fine balance between the presence of God with Israel and his potential absence is nowhere better expressed than in the Day of Atonement rituals. The double symbolism of the tabernacle, signifying both presence and inaccessibility, is expressed by the phrase '[the tent of meeting] which remains with them (הַשֹּׁכֵן אִתָּם) in the midst of their uncleannesses' (Lev. 16.16). In the Levitical theology of holiness both the physical location of God's presence among people and the people themselves must be atoned for in order for the people to be 'clean before the LORD' (Lev. 16.30), and so continue in relationship with him. In Aaron's approach once a year to the near presence of God in the holy place is the closest echo of the paradisal intimacy between God and human beings. Yet his approach is fraught with the danger inherent in the contact between holy and unholy, and Aaron must handle it properly on pain of death (Lev. 16.2). His exclusive and restricted access to the most holy place once a year to make atonement for Israel recalls by a *via negativa* the far freer communion between God and humans in the lost paradise. The prohibition of all human presence in the tabernacle precincts during Aaron's atoning ritual ('No human being [*'adam*] shall be in the tent of meeting…') symbolically negates the created presence of God and human to each other pending completion of the atoning ritual. The use of *'adam* in this text has connotations of humanity as such,[50] and may even recall the moment when there was a creation but not yet *'adam* (Gen. 2.5c).

48. G. J. Wenham, 'Sanctuary Symbolism in the Garden of Eden Story', in *Proceedings of the Ninth Congress of Jewish Studies* (Jerusalem: World Union of Jewish Studies, 1986), pp. 19–25; see also Gregory K. Beale, *The Temple and the Church's Mission: A Biblical Theology of the Dwelling-Place of God* (Leicester: Apollos/Downers Grove; IVP, 2004), pp. 66–80.

49. See, for example, Exod. 33.1–3; and Moberly, *At the Mountain of God*, pp. 49–50, 56–63.

50. Cf. John E. Hartley, *Leviticus* (WBC, 4; Dallas: Word Books, 1992), pp. 9–11, on Lev. 1.2, and thus on the use of *'adam* generally in Leviticus.

This last point brings us to the crucial question of how the picture of renewal relates to the role of Israel in Exodus. Lohfink, observing that this is the most difficult question in the interpretation of P, and also its neglect by Old Testament scholars, writes: 'This is the question whether, for the priestly writing, Israel is really a special chosen people of God, or whether it is only a nation whose history is narrated as an example, even though, strictly speaking, a similar history would have to be traced for every nation on earth.'[51]

At one level the tabernacle account signifies a renewal or re-creation of Israel itself. The dwelling of God with Israel in the sanctuary after covenant-breach and renewal enacts within Israel what had happened to all humanity at the flood. The story has at least an intermediate goal in this recovery of the presence of God in Israel. But the extensive affinities between tabernacle account and the story of humanity since creation mean that the accommodation between God and this people occurs in the face of a still open question about the destiny of humanity. The pattern of rupture and renewal, and the occurrence within Israel of the flaws of humanity in general, creates a certain kind of expectation, a tension consisting of hope and doubt that has an eschatological aspect. But what is the nature of this eschatological message? Is it a message of reassurance to post-exilic Israel, declaring that in its reconstituted worship it already experiences that which has not yet become a reality for the world in general?[52]

In my view the relationship between Israel and humanity in the portrayal of the tabernacle should be expressed differently. Because the story of Israel in Genesis–Exodus is also that of humanity, the experience of Israel reveals the possibilities for humanity with God. The logic of the narrative is such that the assertion of God's presence can be predicated of both Israel and humanity. Janowski conveys this with 'both-and' expressions. For example, at Sinai, we see what God's purpose in creation was, namely 'to have *fellowship with humanity/Israel*' (emphasis original).[53] The creation-redemption pattern means that Israel cannot be imagined without this interface with human destiny. The tabernacle (das Heiligtum) is constitutive for history 'as the place of encounter *between God and humanity or/and between Yahweh and Israel*' (emphasis added).[54]

In the presencing of God in the worship life of Israel the narrative expresses the possibility of reconciliation between God and humanity. Israel's role is in

51. Lohfink, *Theology of the Pentateuch*, p. 129. He admits that he does not see a clear answer to this question, but considers it possible that 'the cultic presence of God as salvation' applies somehow to the whole world. He clearly sees the theological significance of P from this perspective.

52. This is how Janowski frames it: P portrays 'a dynamic history, always surpassing itself and pointing towards an unforeseen eschaton' (author's translation); yet this history has its goal in the dwelling of the creator God with Israel. The tabernacle-cult represents Israel's hope for after the exile: they already know as reality what for the world has not yet come to pass; *Gottes Gegenwart*, pp. 243–4.

53. '*Gemeinschaft mit dem Menschen/Israel* zu haben', *Gottes Gegenwart*, p. 238. He also cites Genesis Rabbah 3.9, on the tabernacle as the completion of the creation, realizing God's fellowship with *humanity/Israel* (p. 245, emphasis added).

54. 'als Ort der Begegnung *zwischen Gott und Mensch bzw. zwischen JHWH und Israel*', *Gottes Gegenwart*, p. 246; cf. *idem*, *Sühne*, pp. 311–12.

part representative or exemplary, yet it is itself part of the story, a story that awaits an outcome. That outcome, as we shall see, is not achieved by the establishment of the nation in its land with permanent institutions. In this sense it is significant that this people of God is not yet in a land that bears its name, it is gathered around a tent not a temple, and it continues towards its land convicted of apostasy and only by grace. Moreover, the story, at least in the 'primary history', is one in which land and temple are lost; it is a story that has as yet no certain outcome. The tabernacle narrative affirms the possibility of human continuing with the creator God, but looks into an open future.

2. *Israel's Law and God's Creative Purpose*

The covenant between God and Israel at Sinai involves not only arrangements for worship but also for the regulation of life according to law. The first of the Pentateuchal law codes, the Book of the Covenant (BC), is given to Moses while Israel is gathered around the mountain (Exod. 20.22–23.22). The giving and accepting of law, therefore, is an essential part of the formation of Israel as Yahweh's people. From the perspective of Yahweh, Israel's obligation to obey his commands and laws is a consequence of his deliverance of Israel from slavery (Exod. 20.2), in a logic reflecting that of ANE treaties and law codes. The loyalty to him which is the fundamental requirement laid upon the people stands over the commands of the Decalogue (Exod. 20.3–17), and also dominates the laws of BC, which themselves open on the topic of worship (20.22–26). From Israel's perspective, their submission to the laws of Yahweh is a matter of voluntary acceptance, expressed both at the beginning and the end of the sequence of theophany and lawgiving, as an essential part of the covenant-making (Exod. 19.3; 24.3, 7). Here in Israel's experience is what might be called its 'initial moment of political faith'.[55] By submitting voluntarily to the law of Yahweh, with the implication of responsibility for its implementation (e.g. 23.6–8), Israel accepts a vocation to nationhood.

The covenantal law, like the arrangements for worship, both marks the uniqueness of Israel and exhibits its exemplary role within the story of creation and humanity. As the provisions for worship created a space for ultimate loyalty aside from loyalty to Pharaoh, so the laws given to Israel are a part of the demonstration of Yahweh's rule in its life in contrast to Pharaoh's. The giving of the laws is prepared for by the disengagement of Israel from Egypt, from the sphere of Pharaoh into the sphere of Yahweh. Both in terms of the broad sweep of Exodus and of the logic of the lawgiving itself, the laws assert the authority of Yahweh alone in Israel's life. This is expressed first in the Decalogue (Exod. 20.2–17), declared from heaven in the hearing of the whole people (v. 22b) with the result that they are terrified (vv. 18–19). In these commands, which lay

---

55. The phrase is O'Donovan's, *Desire of the Nations*, p. 33. He, however, assigns the moment differently, to the point at which Israel asserts Yahweh's kingship in the doxological *Yahweh malak*, as in Pss. 93, 96–99.

out with laconic solemnity the allegiance that Israel owes to Yahweh in all of
life, his unmediated authority is most starkly expressed. After the direct address
of the Decalogue, the people demand that Moses henceforth mediate the speech
of God to them (v. 19), and this is then the format for the laws of BC. But the
point about Yahweh's direct rule has been irreversibly made; Moses will merely
be a mouthpiece.

Yahweh's sovereignty over all aspects of life continues to be expressed in the
mix of laws found in BC, incorporating religious as well as social, economic,
juridical and criminal matters. This belongs entirely within the view of reality
proposed by the Pentateuchal narrative, a view that is sometimes regarded as
'deuteronomic', because it is in Deuteronomy that its implications are most fully
elaborated. However, it is established in principle already in BC and its exodus-
Sinai context.[56] The close connection between law and the rule of Yahweh is
evident in a number of ways, as in the direct divine speech of the Decalogue,[57]
in the motivation-clauses that ground exhortations in Yahweh's deliverance of
Israel from slavery (e.g. Lev. 25.55), or simply in his holiness (Lev. 19.2). And
we shall explore in due course the connection between the nature of the one
God Yahweh and the laws concerning Israel's political organization (Deut.
16.18–18.22).[58]

The law as given to Israel, then, is part of what marks Israel's special role in
the story of human origins. Yet law as such is by no means unique to Israel in the
ancient world. Just as the worship of Israel was in principle an expression of all
humanity's relation to God, so with law Israel participates in the wider world of
the organization of human society. Its law codes find many detailed similarities
with those of the ANE. Law, indeed, is somewhat like wisdom in this respect, a
dimension of the culture of the ancient world, assimilated into Yahwistic theology yet providing an interface with the broader culture of its time and place. The

---

56. E. Otto, recognizing this, even regards BC as having undergone Deuteronomic editing,
because of its preface in a law demanding the worship of Yahweh alone; Otto, 'Rechtsreformen in
Deuteronomium XII–XXVI und im Mittelassyrischen Kodex der Tafel A (KAV 1)', VTSup, 61
(1995), pp. 239–73 (271–2); also *idem, Wandel der Rechtsbegründungen in der Gesellschaftsgeschichte des antiken Israel: eine Rechtsgeschichte des "Bundesbuches" Ex XX 22–XXIII 13*
(StudBib, 3; Leiden: E. J. Brill, 1988), e.g. pp. 1–3. This is a striking reversal of the classic critical
theory which saw the differences between Exod. 20.24–25 and Deut. 12.1–5 as a ground for distinguishing the older Pentateuchal traditions from D.

57. This aspect of Israel's law has been recognized since Albrecht Alt identified apodictic law
(typified by direct commands, such as 'You shall not…') as uniquely Israelite, in distinction from
the more commonplace casuistic type ('If…then…'). This so-called apodictic style occurs in some
laws outside the Decalogue, e.g. Exod. 22.17–21[EVV 22.18–22]. See Alt, 'The Origins of Israelite
Law', in *Essays on Old Testament History and Religion* (Sheffield: JSOT Press, 1989), pp. 79–132
(original 1934). Alt's definitions have been questioned, yet still have validity; see Levenson, *Sinai
and Zion*, pp. 47–8, and (in contrast) J. G. McConville, 'Singular Address in the Deuteronomic Law
and the Politics of Legal Administration', *JSOT* 97 (2002), pp. 19–36, esp. 20–3.

58. See below, Chapter 5. The OT laws have been described as having in themselves a
'democratic' tendency; Jean-Louis Ska, 'Biblical Law and the Origins of Democracy', in William
P. Brown (ed.), *The Ten Commandments: The Reciprocity of Faithfulness* (Louisville, KY: WJK,
2004), pp. 146–58.

distinctiveness of Israelite law, as of its wisdom, lies less in the individual components that make it up than in its contexting within the narrative of Yahweh's rule and Israel's consequent responsibility to enact justice.

What, then, is the connection between law as a function of Israel's role and law as a broad phenomenon in ancient culture? The Old Testament's answer to this lies in the connection it sees between Israel's laws and God's creation order. The link is made, for example, in Psalm 19 and in the *Yahweh malak* Psalms (Psalms 93, 96–99, see Ps. 93.5; 97.8; 99.6–7). In the last-mentioned, God's judgement of the nations is paralleled with his gift of law to Jacob/Israel (cf. 99.1–2).[59] If law is a widespread phenomenon and Israel shares much of its practice with the world around it, this has its roots within the creative purpose and judgement of Yahweh, and it is properly placed in that context. Israel as an arena within which Yahweh rules testifies to his purposes for all creation, and its laws play a part in this. It is for this reason that nations will in due course be depicted as admiring the wisdom of Israel and the justice of its laws (Deut. 4.6–8). To Yahweh's role as king may be added his role as judge, though the two are interconnected. In Israel's acceptance of its covenantal status lies the germ of its political responsibility of rule and judgement which it will assume in the land.

Law and God's Justice/Judgement
The connection between God's purpose in creation for the whole world, Israel's law and its incipient political responsibility may be considered in the light of the theme of justice-righteousness (*tsedaqah*) which was so important in the story of beginnings in Genesis. There we found a thread connecting the 'righteousness' of Noah and Abraham and the exemplary judgement on Sodom. In that sequence God was distinguishing between just and unjust in a series of actions. The judgement on Sodom was a demonstration of justice-righteousness (*tsedaqah*) and an action of 'judgement' (*mishpat*, Gen. 18.25). In the gift of the law to Israel, this story of judgement enacted continues.

Israel's laws, as we have seen, are given in the context of God's action of deliverance and re-creation. In Israel's law, God's justice is closely related to his active judgement. It is crucial to an understanding of the narrative that the deliverance of Israel from Pharaoh's house is at the same time an act of judgement against Pharaoh. The cry of Israel that God hears, and which moves him to respond (Exod. 2.23–25), recalls the cry that came to him because of the oppressions of Sodom (Gen. 18.20–21). The condemnation of Pharaoh is pronounced, ironically, by himself, when he says to Moses and Aaron, near the end of the sequence of trials:

> This time I have sinned (חטאתי); the LORD is in the right (יהוה הצדיק, *hatsaddiq*), and I and my people are in the wrong (הרשעים, Exod. 9.27).

59. O'Donovan drew attention to these Psalms, where the laws given to Israel are part of an affirmation of God's just judgement in the world, within which his revelation to Israel has a purpose of testimony; *Desire of the Nations*, pp. 33–4. In connection with Ps. 93, he speaks of 'Yhwh's throne and its transcendence over the chaotic energies of nature and (by implication) of history' (p. 33).

The terminology is that of the law court (Exod. 23.7–8). Pharaoh expresses in this moment (of insight or pretence) the true nature of the issue between him and God. The conflict is about God's purpose to enact justice in the world. Pharaoh's persistent refusal of this leads to God's overwhelming act of judgement on him, and to the creation of a new moral and legal environment in Israel.

There is an evident connection between what God demonstrates in his judgement on Pharaoh and the responsibility laid upon Israel in respect of its law. For they are not just to obey a code, but to undertake for a process in which justice would regularly be done. This is clear in Exod. 23.6–8, which is less a law than a command or exhortation that the judges should not pervert justice. Falseness in the performance of law is to be abhorred because it can lead to the judicial killing of the 'tsaddiq' (v. 7, together with the נקי, 'innocent', v. 7). Justice must not be skewed by any sort of special pleading, not only to the disadvantage of the poor but even to their advantage (v. 3; cf. Lev. 19.15). And here the close connection between the judgement required of the judges and the judgement of God himself appears, for he declares that *he* will not acquit the guilty (or 'regard the wicked as righteous', לא־אצדיק רשע). He thus declares not only that it is always his decision to acquit the righteous but also that he will condemn as wicked those who abuse their judicial responsibility. God's action in upholding the righteous while condemning the wicked runs through his sentence on Pharaoh into the process of right judgement established in Israel's system of law.

A further illustration of the close affinity between the exodus and law is found in Leviticus 19. Drawn from the so-called Holiness Code (Leviticus 17–26), the chapter opens with the grounding of all that follows in the basic command that Israel should be holy as Yahweh is holy (19.2), and then supports this with the repeated declaration, 'I am the LORD your God' (or shorter variations; 19.4, 10, 12, 14 etc.). The chapter is well known for its apparently unsystematic juxtaposition of civil and religious laws (e.g. vv. 5–10, 29–30), and so illustrates well the premise that God's authority is exercised over all of Israel's life, even going beyond surface action to the heart (19.18). But it is the connection between God's character and the action required of humans that is most striking. And in the culmination of the chapter the appeal to the character of God turns again to the judgement enacted in the exodus. This justifies not only a call to Israel to 'love the alien as yourself' (v. 34, already noticed above), but also a duty of scrupulous honesty in commercial dealings (vv. 35–36). In these commands concerning measures the divine imperative regarding justice and righteousness addresses the ordinary routines of life. Dishonesty in trade is regarded as 'doing injustice in judgement' (*mishpat*, v. 35).[60] The term עול ('injustice') is used for serious perversion of right and truth, the antithesis of God's own justice and righteousness (Deut. 32.4, where God is 'faithful' and righteous, *tsaddiq*). Elsewhere, those who do עול are an 'abomination' to God (Deut. 25.16; cf. also Pss. 7.4 [EVV v. 3]; 82.2; Prov. 29.27). The strength of the term in v. 35 is attested by the occurrence of the same expression a few verses earlier (Lev. 19.15), in connec-

---

60. The translation here follows Hartley, *Leviticus*, p. 303.

tion with the legal process itself, where judges are warned against 'doing injustice in judgement', again under the rubric of God's declaration, 'I am the LORD' (v. 36). The sense of 'justice' according to God's character should not be lost from Lev. 19.35–36. KJV's 'Ye shall do no unrighteousness in judgement, in meteyard, in weight, or in measure' is quaint, but closer to the mark than NRSV's 'You shall not cheat in measuring length...'. The same is true of the honest measures in v. 36, where the term *tsedeq* occurs four times as the qualifier. While the modern translation 'honest' is defensible, KJV's 'just' once again brings out the contextual nuances more clearly. The collocation of *mishpat* and *tsedeq* ('justice' and 'righteousness') in these verses calls attention to the character of God displayed in his whole activity in judgement and salvation, and now imposed on Israel as an obligation in its judicial practice and its daily affairs.

Still in H, the well-known law of 'jubilee', providing for the return of property to families who have been forced to forfeit the use of it to creditors, marks a further link between the person of Yahweh and the laws of Israel. The jubilee provision is embedded in an extended application of the Sabbath-principle to the practices of agriculture and property-holding, which were closely linked and fundamental in an agrarian society. The Sabbath-day of Gen. 2.1–3; Exod. 20.8–11 is now broadened to a Sabbath-year, 'a Sabbath of complete rest (שבת שבתון) for the land', in which preparations for the following year's crop are forbidden (Lev. 25.2–5). The fiftieth year is the jubilee, a further year of sabbatical rest after seven cycles of seven, with the added implication of the return of people and land, forfeited through debt, to their families (25.8–12). The sabbatical rest for the land and the return of families to land are conceptually connected, since in each reposes a claim that Israel's life consists in Yahweh's gift and blessing, and not in the self-regarding exaction of the land's benefits. As the land is not to be sown in the seventh year, so the creditor is not to 'oppress' his neighbour when land is changing hands for money (Lev. 25.14; the 'oppression' or 'cheating' in this case recalls that in 19.33, a key text on the treatment of 'aliens'). Both infringement of the Sabbath and the use of land for profit at others' expense would negate the underlying principle that the land and its benefits are the gift and blessing of God. A departure from the Sabbath-jubilee principle into the mere commercial exchange of land for profit would obscure the clear vision of this reality. This is why the Sabbath-jubilee laws call forth God's declaration: 'The land shall not be sold in perpetuity, for the land is mine; with me you are but aliens and tenants (גרים ותושבים)' (25.23). In this remarkable rhetorical thrust, Yahweh goes beyond the otherwise frequent saying that the people were aliens (*gerim*) in Egypt and so should treat aliens among them well (though this is itself important and we will return to it shortly); rather, he is saying that Israel's status is properly that of 'alien' (*ger*), even in the land in which he is settling them. In fact, the affirmation 'for the land is mine' (כי־לי הארץ) carries a distinct echo of God's statement at the beginning of the Sinai encounter, when he proclaims his choice of Israel as his 'special possession...a kingdom of priests and a holy nation' (Exod. 19.5–6), and explains 'for all the earth is mine' (כי־לי כל־הארץ). We have met the double possibility of *'erets* as 'earth' and as 'land' already (in the echo of Gen. 1.28 in Josh. 18.1). The affirmation 'the land/earth is mine' is used to illumine God's purpose in acting for Israel in exodus and covenant and now also to explain how Israelites should treat each other, and the land as means of life, in their regular relationships. Once again, God's laws are rooted in his actions. The analogy between 'earth' and 'land' is also a further suggestion that what is displayed in Israel has its meaning against the canvas of the wider world. And the association of jubilee and Sabbath makes another link between the laws of Israel and the creation. These affinities are carried through into the final chapter of H, Leviticus 26, where the picture of blessing as the consequence of covenant-obedience has paradisal overtones (Lev. 26.3–6), where Sabbath-keeping is an essential aspect of such obedience (v. 2), and where the withdrawal of the people from the land in the exile is portrayed as a mechanism to allow the land to 'enjoy its sabbath years as long as it lies desolate' (vv. 34–35).

We have now seen that the giving of laws to Israel is integrated into the story of God's action in the world whose purpose is the establishment of justice and righteousness. The gift of law to Israel, within the covenant at Sinai made prior to the occupation of land, is part of the furtherance of that purpose. Law is not an abstract concept, but an obligation laid upon Israel to perform justice in accordance with its relationship with God.[61] In its calling to be 'holy as Yahweh is holy' it is even to exhibit the character of God (and so the idea of the 'image of God', with its implications of human 'royal' rule, is close at hand in the laws, at least in H, as it was in the depiction of Israel's worship). The dynamic nature of the practice of law explains why in the Pentateuchal narrative one single law code does not suffice. The law codes do not aim at a notional comprehensiveness or timelessness. The collection of distinct law codes (principally BC, H and the deuteronomic code), whose relationship to each other is unsystematic and not articulated, corresponds to the obligation on Israel to practise law as part of its covenantal commitment to realize justice in its corporate life. Justice cannot ultimately be measured against adherence to any particular set of laws, since all such bear the marks of their time and place. Canonically, the untidiness of this concatenation of codes has the effect of emphasizing the obligation to seek justice itself.[62] Not only is Israel expected to do justice, but it is charged with responsibility for ensuring it is done, a responsibility which has a political character. We see this when judges are enjoined to act justly, and when Israelites generally are taught to think of the spirit of the law, and so not to hate their neighbours, or even bear grudges against them, but to love them (Lev. 19.17–18), and when law becomes in effect exhortation to mercy and generosity (Lev. 25.35–38).

The gift of law to Israel, embedded in covenant, has the imprint of both privilege and vocation. Its law illustrates the contingency of Israel's situation, for they are bound to manifest the justice that God intended from creation. The laws may

---

61. Cf. O'Donovan, *Desire of the Nations*, p. 39.

62. It is therefore misguided, I think, to suppose that any one of the codes is intended to supersede another, as B. M. Levinson has argued for the deuteronomic code in relation to BC; *Deuteronomy and the Hermeneutics of Legal Innovation* (New York: Oxford University Press, 1998).

even be said to have an eschatological quality, because they reach beyond the limit of legal process to the human will and so to places that law cannot control (as Leviticus 19 illustrates).[63] The particularities of the codes, therefore, embodying norms that are sometimes quite alien to a modern readership (such as the assumptions about slavery which are entangled with the laws of jubilee, Lev. 25.44–46), have an intrinsically penultimate status, case-studies in the realization of justice in a particular society. Such particularities are inevitable, being placeholders for other particularities in the only possible kind of universal vision.

With law, as with worship then, due account should be taken of the way in which it is given to Israel, that is, between the deliverance from Egypt and the occupation of land. It is significant, once again, that the location of the law-giving is outside the promised land and prior to the formation of permanent institutions. Israel's laws are received independently of its possession of land or of any particular form of statehood or political organization. Law in Israel has no function in sanctioning any particular national or political *status quo*.

3. *Israel's Nationhood*

The foregoing raises the question of how the destiny of the nation Israel relates to the larger divine plan for humanity. There is no doubt that the story marks off Israel from other nations. It is chosen out of them in a series of choices that go back to Abraham and are enshrined in covenants. Israel becomes Yahweh's 'treasured possession' (Exod. 19.5), is separated from Egypt and destined to be given a land from which other nations will be expelled for the purpose (Exod. 23.23–33). The question is whether this privilege of Israel is for its benefit alone or has another purpose.

It will be clear that the view presented here favours the latter perspective. In particular it challenges the interpretation that sees the exodus-tabernacle sequence as an apologia for a political ascendancy in Persian Yehud. Mullen's conviction that the texts served the needs of a specific group, rather then expressing anyone's actual beliefs, determines his reading of them.[64] Thus, his understanding of the wilderness setting for the origins of law and worship serves a typology whereby the wilderness generation, barred from entering the land (Numbers 13–14), corresponds to the 'people of the land' who had not gone into exile, in distinction from the returned exiles who now constituted the ruling party.[65] The tabernacle's evocation of creation motifs serves only to legitimate the priestly hierarchy.[66] I have argued in contrast that the close relationship between Israel's origins and the origins of the world and humanity tends in the opposite direction, to cast Israel in an exemplary role with a function within the story of humanity. Israel's standing as a 'holy nation, kingdom of priests' (Exod.

63. Cf. R. J. Bauckham, *The Bible in Politics* (London: SPCK, 1989), pp. 28–9.
64. Mullen, *Ethnic Myths*, p. 251 n. 3.
65. Mullen, *Ethnic Myths*, pp. 266–7.
66. Mullen, *Ethnic Myths*, p. 252.

19.6) belongs to the people as a whole (not just the hierarchy[67]). And the location of the covenant-making outside the land, prior to the formation of permanent institutions, tends to make such institutions contingent and to place them under scrutiny, rather than confer unqualified legitimacy on them.

Indeed, the specifically political character of Israel begins to emerge in the exodus-Sinai narrative, not only in the sphere of legal responsibility that we have already observed, but also in the conception of the people itself. For this people is not defined in a narrowly ethnic way (despite the bonds with Abraham, Isaac and Jacob proclaimed in the story of Moses, Exod. 3.15; 6.3); rather, it is a 'mixed crowd' that leaves Egypt (Exod. 12.38). The new society is defined by its separation from Egypt and its allegiance to Yahweh, marked initially by its projected celebration of Passover, in which an 'alien' residing in the land (*ger*) may participate on the same footing as a 'native of the land' (הארץ האזרח), since there is 'one law' (אחת תורה, *torah*) for each (12.48–49). This is subject only to his desire to do so and his submission to circumcision. The equal standing of native and alien in relation to law and worship runs through Exodus–Numbers (cf. Exod. 12.19; Lev. 16.29; 17.15; 18.26; 19.34; 24.16, 22; Num. 9.14; 15.29–30). Aliens enjoy full participation in the worship life of the people, and the benefits as well as the rigours of its law. The rationale for this inclusive policy lies in Israel's own former status as 'aliens' in Egypt; Israel is even to 'love the alien as yourself' for this reason (Lev. 19.34). Moses names his first son Gershom (including the element *ger*, 'alien'), because 'he said, "I have been an alien residing in a foreign land"' (Exod. 2.22; 18.3). The foreign land in this case is probably Midian, whereas the idea more regularly recalls the period in Egypt. Yet the memory of Moses' sojourning in Midian adds to the importance of the theme, Midian resembling Joseph's Egypt in its hospitality to the stranger. Such a rationale for the inclusion of the alien tells against the idea that the application of the law to him lies in a theology of holiness, that is, in the intrinsic holiness of the land.[68] The alien, after all, is not compelled to join fully in Israelite life. But the openness of Israel to him is an expression of its political character, namely its conscious rejection of the Egyptian politics of enslavement.

A further indicator of the political nature of Israel lies in Moses' fraternization with Midianites. Not only does Moses marry the Midianite Zipporah (as Joseph had married the Egyptian Asenath), but her father Jethro (otherwise Reuel, Exod. 2.18, and Hobab, Judg. 1.16) plays an important part in Israel's political development. Jethro joins in thanksgiving to Yahweh for all he has done for Israel, confesses that Yahweh is greater than all gods, and even leads Aaron, Moses and all the elders of Israel in an act of sacrificial worship (Exod. 18.9–12).[69] This

67. *Pace* Mullen, *Ethnic Myths*, p. 258; see above, n. 28.

68. Here too I disagree with Mullen, who thinks the inclusion of the alien along with the Israelite 'emphasizes that Israel's identity was inextricably tied to the land', *Ethnic Myths*, p. 244, citing Lev. 24.16–21, pp. 243–4 (he has, mistakenly, 23.16–21).

69. Jethro's worship of Yahweh led in former times to the so-called Kenite hypothesis, in which the origin of Yahweh-worship was found among the Kenites. Jethro-Hobab is called a Kenite in Judg. 1.16, where his descendants are said to have gone up with the people of Judah into the wilderness of Judah (cf. Judg. 4.11, 17; 5.24).

subordination of Moses to a non-Israelite, who nevertheless adopts or has adopted the worship of Yahweh, is remarkably discordant in a narrative about the formation of an *Israelite* people of Yahweh. Furthermore, Moses accepts Jethro's counsel on the judicial administration of Israel, giving up sole responsibility for judging disputes and instituting a devolved judiciary, in a move that anticipates the more elaborate provisions in Deuteronomy (Exod. 18.13–27, cf. Deut. 1.9–18; 16.18–17.13). The devolution of judicial and administrative responsibility can be traced through Numbers and into Joshua (cf. Num. 34.16–29; Josh. 19.5, where the distribution of the land of Canaan to Israel is undertaken by Joshua, Eleazar the priest, and tribal and family leaders).

4. *Conclusion*

God's purpose to bring into being a human society that lives according to justice and righteousness in his creation is carried forward by means of his chosen people Israel. Out of the collision between the claims of Pharaoh and Yahweh arises the assertion of Yahweh's kingship, grounded in the creation, in his triumph over Pharaoh's chaotic regime, in the nature of this as a judgement, in the creation of a new sphere within which Israel recognizes his rule, and in his laws which reflect his justice. The election of Israel has as its counterpart Yahweh's perspective that 'all the earth is mine' (Exod. 19.5). Israel before Yahweh in worship, and as 'kingdom of priests' (Exod. 19.5), represents humanity in its vocation to rule responsibly in the earth. Yet it is to be fully formed as a nation among nations, and the exodus-Sinai narrative begins to establish Israel as such. In this context it will exercise its specifically political responsibilities, to function as a people administering and implementing Yahweh's law.

These responsibilities of the nation Israel will be fleshed out more fully in the following chapter. By this stage it has the following elements. It is provided with a memory of its origins embracing its ancestry since Abraham's emergence from Mesopotamia, its experience of deliverance from slavery in Egypt, and its covenantal bond made with Yahweh at Sinai, giving it a sense of its identity and an ideological and cultural heritage. It is given a belief in its legitimacy, by virtue of its formation in an act of divine judgement and salvation, supported by law. It is supplied with an undergirding faith, in Yahweh–God, creator of the world, redeemer and ruler of Israel, and the object of its worship. And it is on its way to possessing a territory.[70] The story has stood still at Sinai while the means of its sustaining a life in close proximity to God are carefully articulated. But at Num. 10.11 the Sinai phase ends and the people move off, organized around the tabernacle for the march on the the promised land, Yahweh in their midst now as warrior. The stage is set for the transition into the promised land, and its entry to its full heritage as a nation.

---

70. For these as the elements in the political constitution of the nation see O'Donovan, *Desire of the Nations*, pp. 36–49. They are preliminarily identified as 'salvation' (ישועה), 'judgement' (משפט), 'possession' (נחלה), and 'praise' (תהלה, p. 36). Elsewhere they are expressed as 'power, right and tradition' (p. 46).

The march on Canaan continues some of the elements seen in the approach to Sinai. The people again show reluctance to be the vehicles of Yahweh's mission. Yet his purpose prevails in a narrative which has aspects both of demonstration to the nations and conflict with opposing powers. This is evident in the words of the non-Israelite prophet-diviner Balaam, summoned by King Balak of Moab to utter a curse on Israel.[71] Balaam knows this cannot be done because God has determined to bless them. The counterplay of blessing and curse points directly back to God's promise to Abraham: 'I will bless those who bless you and the one who curses you I will curse' (Gen. 12.3a). These words are echoed first by Balak, when he attributes to Balaam the power to do what God has in fact reserved to himself to do (22.6), and then several times directly negated by Balaam, finally in an almost exact repetition of God's words to the patriarch (23.8, 20; 24.9).[72] In the context of Balaam's testimony to Yahweh's irresistibility, and closely connected with the exodus-deliverance, comes another direct affirmation of his kingship (Num. 23.21).

Part of the great transition of Numbers is the passing from one generation to the next. Not even Moses or Aaron would reach the land, because they were judged to have failed to honour God at the waters of Meribah (Num. 20.12–13). As Moses finds a successor in Joshua (27.15–23), so does Aaron in his son Eleazar (20.22–29). It is the new generation that is the subject of the second census in the Book of Numbers (Numbers 26), where it is expressly stated that none of those numbered in the first census was counted in this one (26.64–65). This is the generation that will gather at Moab to hear Moses declaim the speeches recorded in Deuteronomy, and finally cross the Jordan under Joshua.

Finally Numbers tells of the last stages of the movement towards the land of promise (chs 27–36). The topics of land-possession, inheritance and victory over enemies become an increasingly louder drumbeat. The section begins and ends with the matter of inheritance of property by daughters when there are no sons (27.1–11; 36.1–12). Mahlah, Noah, Hoglah, Milcah and Tirzah, the daughters of Zelophehad, contend for their father's inheritance, their petition is granted, and the ruling acquires the status of 'a statute and an ordinance' (27.11). Here as in both the previous sections of the book, law and statute continue to be enacted as new issues and needs are perceived. But the preparation for landedness dominates. Joshua is appointed to succeed Moses (27.15–23); a war is waged against Midian as revenge for their seduction of Israel at Peor (ch. 31); and two and a half tribes, Reuben, Gad and the half-tribe of Manasseh, become the first to receive their 'inheritance' when they are settled to the east of the Jordan in the lands taken in war from the Amorite kings Sihon and Og (ch. 32). This harbinger of greater victories to come plays an important part in establishing the unity of Israel. In the view of Numbers, the two and a half tribes occupy 'the land of Gilead' which is distinguished from 'the land of Canaan' (32.29–32). Moses

---

71. As Fretheim sees this, 'no Israelite, including Moses, has standing enough left to bring them [the promises] to expression', T. E. Fretheim, 'Numbers', in John Barton and John Muddiman (eds.), *Oxford Bible Commentary* (Oxford: Oxford University Press, 2001), pp. 110–34, here p. 112.

72. The verb for 'curse' in Num. 24.9 is אָרַר, whereas it is קָלַל in Gen. 12.3.

initially compares their petition to stay in Gilead with the rebellious spirit of their 'fathers' when they allowed themselves to be disheartened by the gloomy report of the spies and suffered dire consequences (32.7–15) However, their request is granted on condition that they participate with their fellow-Israelites in the war for the land of Canaan. The incident is important in determining the unity of both people and land. The topic of 'inheritance' is central, and the declaration of the Transjordanians as they accept the terms imposed by Moses is crucial for the meaning of the Book of Numbers: 'We will not return to our homes until the people of Israel have inherited each his inheritance' (32.18 RSV[73]).

The book closes with a description of the march by stages to the plains of Moab (ch. 33), an anticipation of the determination of the land's boundaries and its division for the tribes (ch. 34), the appointment of cities for the Levites and cities of refuge (ch. 35), and a return to the theme of family inheritance (ch. 36). In these chapters the language and thematics of Deuteronomy and Joshua begin to be heard clearly. In 33.50–56 we already learn of God's command to Moses to instruct the people to drive out the inhabitants of Canaan and destroy their worship-places as the necessary prelude to settling in and dividing the land, thus anticipating one of the characteristic requirements of Deuteronomy (7.1–5; 12.1–5) in language that is also reminiscent of that book.

The final words of Numbers fully adopt the deuteronomic style, closing the book with the summarizing: 'These are the commandments and the ordinances that the LORD commanded through Moses to the Israelites in the plains of Moab by the Jordan at Jericho' (36.13). The stage is set for the speeches of Moses in Deuteronomy.

---

73. In this way, the RSV conveys the insistence on the idea of inheritance by rendering both the verb (נחל hith.) and the noun (נחלה) rather literally. NRSV has 'until all the Israelites have obtained their inheritance', which dampens the thematic stress, and misses the sense that each Israelite has an inheritance within the whole.

Chapter 5

A POLITICAL NATION: DEUTERONOMY

I have been arguing that the Pentateuchal narrative unfolds God's purpose that the created order should manifest justice and righteousness, and that Israel is the chosen means, in an imperfect world, by which this should come about. With Deuteronomy, the narrative comes to the moment at which the nature of Israel and its mission is explored most extensively and profoundly. At the core of this exploration is the issue which the present study aims primarily to address, the relationship between a God who commands and the political responsibility of human beings. The aim of the chapter is to show how the divine purpose for creation is encapsulated in a vision for the nation Israel. It will be argued that in that vision Deuteronomy contains a charter for nationhood (distinct from 'nationalism'), that within this notion of nationhood there is a concept of political responsibility both of the body politic and of the individual, and that the portrayal of Israel as a nation is subordinate to the larger idea of exhibiting the divine purpose for a whole created order that is marked by God's own qualities of justice and righteousness.

1. *The Book of Deuteronomy*

The Book of Deuteronomy has traditionally been recognized as a distinctive part of the Pentateuch on the grounds of its language, style and theology.[1] In terms of the Pentateuchal narrative, it represents a long pause on the plains of Moab, where according to Numbers Israel had arrived after its forty-year wait in the wilderness (Num. 33.49). In terms of narrative progression it makes only a small contribution. It tells how, after Moses' farewell speeches to Israel which constitute the bulk of the book, a covenant is made in Moab in addition to the covenant at Sinai (Deut. 28.69 [EVV 29.1]).[2] It prepares the people for a further covenant-renewal to take place at Mt. Ebal near Shechem after they have entered the land of Canaan (Deut. 27.1–8), a ceremony whose performance is eventually narrated in Josh. 8.30–35. It records the commissioning of Joshua as Moses' military suc-

---

1.   It was the only Pentateuchal book that roughly corresponded to one of the source-documents ('D') in classical Old Testament criticism. See for example S. R. Driver, *Introduction to the Literature of the Old Testament* (Edinburgh: T&T Clark, 3rd edn, 1892), pp. 65–77. On the question of the date and composition of the book, see above, Chapter 2.

2.   In my view the Moab covenant is not exactly a new covenant, distinct from Sinai/Horeb, but a new realization of that covenant; McConville, *Deuteronomy*, p. 409, cf. p. 401.

cessor in the Tent of Meeting (Deut. 31.7–8, 14–15, 23). Most significantly, it tells that Moses wrote down 'this law' (or *torah*, הַתּוֹרָה הַזֹּאת, 31.9), referring presumably to the words of Moses recorded in Deuteronomy, directs that it be read solemnly before the whole assembly of Israel every seven years at the Feast of Tabernacles (31.10–11), and that it be deposited ('this book of the law') alongside the ark of the covenant in the Tent of Meeting (31.25–26). It closes with an account of Moses' death on Mt. Nebo, from which he was able to see the land that he would never enter (34.1–8). To this extent the book makes certain necessary contributions to the story. Moreover, in style and theme it is not wholly new. The theme of the imminent occupation of Canaan was sounded in the latter chapters of Numbers, often in language reminiscent of Deuteronomy (e.g. Numbers 32). There are more remote anticipations of the book in Gen. 15.12–21 and Exod. 23.23–33. A 'deuteronomic' influence on the composition of the Pentateuch is now widely recognized in critical scholarship.[3]

Even so, Deuteronomy is in a sense self-contained and unique. Unlike the other books of the Pentateuch, it is marked out as a 'book' and given a special role in the ongoing worship life of the community (31.9–10, cf. 17.18).[4] Its well-known formal resemblance to ANE treaties and law codes also points to its integrity as a work. In terms of the Pentateuchal narrative moreover, there is a change of pace and focus. The change of pace is observable as a marked difference between narrative time and real time. The action of the book could have taken place within a single day,[5] yet the narrative slows almost to a standstill. This formal feature of the book emphasizes the significance of the moment at which Israel has arrived, on the point of possessing what has long been promised, not only since Sinai/Horeb, but since the first encounter between Yahweh and the patriarch Abraham. It is a time for retrospect, self-examination and preparation. All of this is embedded in the discourse of the book.

Its retrospective and resumptive aspect is evident from the opening words, with its cursory rehearsal of place-names, and its parenthetical allusion to the relatively short distance from Sinai/Horeb to Kadesh-barnea, an ironic comment on the long time it actually took (Deut. 1.1–2). In this way, the opening verses signal not only the geographical situation of Israel, but also the moral issue that has surfaced on the journey. The first three chapters continue the retrospect, retelling the setback following the spies' mission, the initial failure to take the land with its consequence in the exclusion of the Horeb generation from it, details of the route around Edom, Moab and Ammon, and the preliminary success against

3. See for example, E. Blum, *Studien zur Komposition des Pentateuch* (BZAW, 189; Berlin: W. de Gruyter, 1990).

4. The 'book of the law' cannot be quite identical with Deuteronomy, since the former is referred to in the latter. Yet the reference is in a sense a self-reference, since the contents of the two overlap so much, and since the logic of the narrative requires that the 'book of the law' have an identifiable written form, and it is Deuteronomy that most closely conforms to this. The point is discussed penetratingly in J.-P. Sonnet, *The Book Within the Book: Writing in Deuteronomy* (BIS, 14; Leiden: E. J. Brill, 1997).

5. Cf. N. Lohfink, 'Zur Fabel des Deuteronomiums', in G. Braulik (ed.), *Bundesdokument und Gesetz: Studien zum Deuteronomium* (HBS, 4; Freiburg: Herder, 1995), pp. 65–78 (65).

the Amorite kings, Sihon and Og, (Deuteronomy 1–3). There follows an extensive reminiscence of Horeb, initiated in the long self-contained address in ch. 4
with its strong emphasis on the divine commands (the 'ten words', 4.13) and the
prohibition of images. This is continued in ch. 5 which gives the Decalogue
again (5.6–21) in a form slightly modified from Exod. 20.1–17. The fundamental
requirement of loyalty to Yahweh, at the heart of this here as in Exodus, is then
elaborated in the chapters that follow, with the confession of faith in Yahweh's
oneness (the Shema) in a prominent position (6.4–5), followed by the typically
deuteronomic command to drive out the Canaanite population and destroy all
vestiges of non-Yahwistic religion (ch. 7). In its sequence from the encounter at
Sinai/Horeb to the pronouncement of specific laws Deuteronomy differs from
Exodus in introducing hortatory material between the two (in chs 6–11). Part of
this consists of Deuteronomy's version of the Golden Calf incident (Deut. 9.13–
10.11), here placed before the law code rather than after as in Exodus (Exodus
32). The law code itself (chs 12–26) is partly based on the Book of the Covenant
(BC), notably in beginning with a law about the place of worship (ch. 12), but
also differs in many respects.

Deuteronomy, therefore, creatively recapitulates events and themes that have
already been met in the narrative. Its traditional name (literally 'second law') is
based on the ancient Greek misreading of the Hebrew of Deut. 17.18 ('a copy of
this law'). The name is not inappropriate to the reflective second look that the
book gives to the formative events of Israel's life, yet this is by no means a mere
recapitulation. Almost everything that is repeated from the earlier narratives
appears in a new and distinctive form. The differences are in principle capable of
various explanations, and historical and redaction-criticism have attempted to
supply these. However, the Book of Deuteronomy is clearly not merely the result
of a haphazard growth, but always has the vigour and creativity of independent
argument. By its nature it seems to assert the need for this, as if the givenness of
the divine *torah* has a necessary correlative in hermeneutic and application.

Finally, the book takes as its theme nothing less than the whole sweep of
Israel's history, set within the perspective of the creation.

a. *Humanity, Land, and the Creation*

As we have seen earlier,[6] Deuteronomy can be read as the strongest statement of
Israel's election, an argument for Israel's separateness from and superiority over
all other nations. However, when read as part of the Pentateuchal narrative beginning with creation, it can be seen to fit within the story of the divine purpose that
began there. Deuteronomy's vision takes in the full scope of created time and
space.

This creation setting appears from the argument in Deuteronomy 4, which
brings together the two themes of God's word to Israel (vv. 1–14) and his
prohibition of images (vv. 15–24). The prohibition of images in 4.15–19 echoes
the Second Commandment (5.8–10), but elaborates it in such a way as to recall

---

6. See above, Chapter 2.

the description of creation in Genesis 1. In fact the order in Gen. 1.14–27 is roughly reversed here: the human creation (implied in 'male and female', v. 16), animals, birds, creeping things, fish, the sun, the moon and the stars.[7] The idea of humanity as 'image of God' is not explicitly stated, but the allusion to Genesis 26 strongly suggests it. The status of humanity as 'image' of God is now directly related to the prohibition of images of God, which in turn is based on the fact that no form of God was visible at Horeb (vv. 15–16). Covenant with Israel grows out of creation.

The theme of image-prohibition develops into a discourse about the oneness of God. If Israel makes images to worship they will be exiled to a place where the gods are no gods (4.25–28), and this affirmation is reinforced with an argument that returns to the theme of creation (vv. 32–40). The argument takes as its scope all of time 'ever since the day that God created human beings on the earth' (v. 32).[8]

There Yahweh's actions in saving and forming the people of Israel are depicted as unparalleled in the history of the world, in order to demonstrate that there is none besides him (vv. 35, 39). The deliverance from Egypt and the expulsion of other nations from Canaan (vv. 37–38) serve the same purpose. Even the gift of land to Israel 'for all time' (כל־הימים, v. 40) bespeaks his unrivalled sway over all that exists. Yahweh reigns alone in heaven and earth (vv. 36, 39).

The evidence in Deuteronomy 4 that the election of Israel should be read as part of God's creative purpose is suggestive for the interpretation of other features of the book. The analogy between the land of Canaan and the earth is hinted at in several places, notably in Deuteronomy 8. Here God's acts in sustaining Israel through the barren wilderness are depicted as the result of his creative word, and intended that Israel should know that humanity (*'adam*) does not live by bread alone (8.3). There follows a description of the land in 8.7–10 that is framed by the phrase ארץ טובה ('a good land', *'erets*, vv. 7, 10), echoing the 'good earth' with its rich produce in Gen. 1.11–12; 2.4b–6. It is a well-watered land, where water springs up from under the earth, its plenty signalled by a rich vocabulary of water, including the term תהמת (v. 7), the plural form of *tehom*, 'deep' (Gen. 1.2), that occurred in Exod. 15.5, 8, there too with connotations of the creation.[9] This is 'the earth' under blessing, yielding its wealth without undue labour (cf. 6.10–11), and so putting into reverse the curse of the ground in Gen. 3.17–19, imposed because of a broken command. In depicting the land as a place of life, Deuteronomy follows Exodus in contrasting it both with the wilderness and with Egypt. The wilderness appears even more strongly here as a place of death (Deut. 8.15, cf. Exod. 15.2–25, Num. 21.5–6), and Egypt is remembered not only as the house of slavery but as a place of disease, in contrast to the land

---

7. M. Fishbane calls the allusion to the human creation in Gen. 1.26 a case of 'aggadic exegetical adaptation'; *Biblical Interpretation in Ancient Israel* (Oxford: Clarendon Press, 1985), pp. 321–2 and n. 19. See also McConville, *Deuteronomy*, p. 108.

8. למן הים אשר ברא אלהים אדם על־הארץ The four words ברא, אלהים, האדם, and ארץ are all used in Genesis 1. ברא, 'create', is used only here in Deuteronomy–Kings.

9. See above, Chapter 4.

where there would be only health and human fertility (Deut. 7.14–15, cf. Exod. 15.26). In characterizing Egypt in this way Deuteronomy knows and challenges the people's misguided craving to return there, recorded in Exodus and Numbers (Exod. 16.2–3; 17.3; Num. 20.2–5). Indeed, Deut. 8.8 ironically evokes Num. 20.5, where the aggrieved Israelites lament the absence of grain, figs, vines, pomegranates and water in the wilderness, as they contrast the barren place with fruitful Egypt. In the rhetoric of Deuteronomy, the land that awaits Israel has all this and more.[10] The portrayal of it as bountiful and disease-free borders on the paradisal. The typology of life-giving land versus the deathliness of both wilderness and Egypt parallels that of Genesis, where the good earth stands over against the Chaos overcome by God's creative word, and also the earth as it was reduced to disorder as a result of human disobedience to divine command.

Through Israel, therefore, Deuteronomy shows the life of a nation as a microcosm of humanity (*'adam*) about to enjoy the blessings of the earth (*'erets*). All is set within the covenant, the means by which the basic problem of human existence exposed in Genesis 3–11 is to be overcome. The covenant with Abraham comes to maturity in Deuteronomy, the descendants of the patriarch having endured its lengthy servitude and seen God's judgement on its tyrannous overlords (Gen. 15.13–16). And the creative purpose is now embraced within the Mosaic covenant, which offers the means by which humanity/Israel may enjoy the paradisal blessings. This is why the Abrahamic and Mosaic covenants both play major roles in the book, and also why Mosaic command is set within the context of creation concepts, as in the artful splicing of *torah* exhortation and image-prohibition in Deuteronomy 4.

b. *Israel, Torah, and Justice-Righteousness*
The status of Israel as Adamic representative in the land/earth represented by Canaan is subject in the first instance to the covenant of Sinai/Horeb and the Mosaic command which is the substance of the re-realization of Horeb at Moab. But behind these stands a more general imperative which we have been observing since Genesis, namely the absolute requirement to enact righteousness and justice (*tsedeq/tsedaqah* and *mishpat*) in the earth.

The basis of the righteousness imperative in Deuteronomy is the ascription of it to God himself in the Song of Moses with the epithet *tsaddiq* (Deut. 32.4).[11] He is also said to execute justice (*mishpat*) for the orphan and widow (10.18), and in 33.21 we read of Gad that he 'executed the justice (*tsedaqah*) of the LORD'. Deuteronomy, therefore, is in line with the concept, observed earlier, that justice-righteousness is rooted in God and part of the Old Testament's conception of the created order. Justice-righteousness surfaces in three further important ways in

---

10. It echoes in some respects Egyptian claims about its land, for example in the 'Instruction to King Merikare' and 'Sinuhe'; see M. Lichtheim, *Ancient Egyptian Literature 1*, pp. 103–4 and 226–7 respectively. The Joseph narrative (Gen. 37–50) portrays Egypt as a place known for its bounty, albeit disrupted by famine.

11. The term *tsaddiq* is predicated of God (Elohim and Yahweh) also in Pss. 7.10, 12[9, 11]; 11.7; 119.137; 129.4; 145.17; Jer. 12.1; Lam. 1.18; Dan. 9.14; Zeph. 3.5.

the book. It occurs first in a passage that is telling for its view of the moral and natural order, Deut. 6.24–25.[12] The context is the address following the confession of Yahweh's oneness in the Shema (6.4–5), in which the teaching of future generations is commanded, and the passage in question is part of an answer to be given to the child who asks about the meaning of the deuteronomic laws (v. 20). After recalling the miraculous deliverance from Egypt to fulfil the promise of land given to the ancestors, the parent's answer turns to the place of the laws and commands. The instruction to obey these frames vv. 24–25, and inside the frame occur in parallel two phrases expressing the purpose and consequence of law-keeping, namely 'for our lasting good' (לטוב לנו כל־הימים) and 'it will be righteousness for us' (RSV; וצדקה תהיה־לנו). The paralleling of 'good' and 'righteousness' in the inner part of the structure expresses the nature of the order of reality. In this context *tsedaqah* is best understood as the quality of justice-righteousness that belongs to a society functioning in conformity to the divine purpose in creation.[13] Once again, it is commandment-keeping in covenant that enables the condition of *tsedaqah* to be realized. The phrasing of the expression ('it will be righteousness to/for you') merits comment, because it seems to denote a decision of God to recognize Israel's obedience as producing the condition of justice-righteousness.[14]

The second important usage is the application of the term *tsaddiq* to the laws and statutes themselves (Deut. 4.8), constituting the *torah* that Moses was teaching Israel. This is the most direct evidence that the laws are seen as expressing and conforming to both the character of God and the created order. It is significant that the wisdom of Israel is seen and acknowledged by the nations because of the justice of its laws (4.6).

Third, *tsedaqah* may be predicated of human beings, and must be established within society by means of the legal process. This is stated emphatically at the beginning of the section of Deuteronomy that deals with the offices in Israel (Deut. 16.18–20). Here, the judges (*shophetim*) and officers are obliged to 'judge' (or perhaps 'rule',[15] the people according to 'righteous judgement' (*mishpat tsedeq*, v. 18); justice (*mishpat*) is not to be perverted, because that would frustrate the cause of the 'innocent' (*tsaddiqim*); rather, Israel must rigorously pursue justice-righteousness (*tsedeq tsedeq*, v. 20).

It follows from these initial observations about justice-righteousness in Deuteronomy that the divine purpose of establishing it in the created order is pursued by means of the commission to Israel to enact it in the land which is a

---

12. This passage was observed by H. H. Schmid, *Gerechtigkeit als Weltordnung*, p. 124.

13. In my commentary I translated the phrase 'we shall be held righteous' (*Deuteronomy*, p. 137; cf. NRSV 'we will be in the right'), tending to give the phrase the sense of legal acquittal as in Deut. 25.1. The intention then was to stress the sense of being considered righteous (see next note). I have followed RSV's more straightforward translation on this occasion, to highlight the objectivity of *tsedaqah* as a condition established (as also explained in *Deuteronomy*, p. 146).

14. It therefore recalls what is said of Abraham in Gen. 15.6, as observed in Ch. 3; cf. Ps. 106.31.

15. The verb is ושפטו, related to *mishpat* ('justice', 'judgement'), and *shophet*, ('judge').

microcosm of the whole earth. However, the project is always under the shadow
of the possibility of its non-realization. The peculiar characteristic of Deuteronomy is that while it proposes Israel as the vehicle for the implementation of the
project, and lays out at length what is required for its success, it also accuses
Israel of a deep-rooted unsuitability for it. The Pentateuchal story prior to Deuteronomy has prepared us for this with its narratives of the people's resistance, in
their desire to return to Egypt and their apostasy with the Golden Calf at the
moment of covenant-making. In that context they were repeatedly called a 'stiff-
necked' (or 'stubborn') people (Exod. 32.9; 33.3, 5; 34.9). The issue confronted
was whether God could continue to go with them, and it was resolved by God's
decision to be gracious and the renewal of the covenant (the point of Exod. 34.1–
9). In Deuteronomy, therefore, there is no longer a question about whether God
will accompany Israel into the land, for the whole book is predicated on his purpose to do so. Yet the accusation of 'stubbornness' is actually heightened here.
The deuteronomic Golden Calf discourse (Deut. 9.6–10.11) has less the force of
a dramatic crisis than a rehearsal of past failures in a pattern of behaviour (e.g.
Deut. 9.22–24). Israel is not only 'stubborn' (Deut. 9.6, 13), but persistently 'rebellious' (9.7; the phrase, ממרים הייתם, expresses habitual action).

Moreover, the rebelliousness of Israel goes to the heart of the issue of justice-
righteousness (*tsedaqah*). In the rhetoric of Deuteronomy which articulates the
unique chosen status of Israel there have been a number of qualifications. They
were chosen not because of their great numbers but simply because God loved
them (Deut. 7.7); their election has been attended by the discipline of the wilderness years, and warnings about the dangers arising from the comfort and
plenty of a rich land, which could result in their death (8.11–20). In this rhetoric
there is neither intrinsic qualification for the mission, nor unconditional guarantee
of perseverance. And in the prelude to the Golden Calf discourse they are now
denied the right to consider themselves 'righteous'. God is giving them the land,
not because of their righteousness (*tsedaqah*), but because of the wickedness of
the other nations (9.4–5). Nor are they even moderately righteous, but actually
characterized by 'stubbornness, wickedness and sin' (9.27). They are therefore
the very opposite of *tsaddiq*, exactly like the nations who are being driven out of
the land on the grounds of their wickedness. The discrepancy between Israel's
ideal destiny and reality could hardly be more stark, nor its tenure of Edenic
Canaan more insecure.

The tensions between the prospects of success and failure run through Deuteronomy. They have often been explained by appeal to redactional layers which
differ in the relative priority they give to the aspects of promise and law. However, the discourse of Deuteronomy as we know it can be explained rhetorically
and theologically. The portrayal of Israel's moral shortcomings is not intended to
vilify Israel, but rather stresses both the grace of God in their life and the moral
nature of the project. Indeed, the project is not defined by the destiny of Israel
as such, but by the realization of a people on earth characterized by 'justice-
righteousness'. For Israel is here called to be something that, in the deuteronomic
perspective, it has not yet been. The systematic repudiation of Israel's intrinsic

qualities to conform to the divine purpose prepares in one sense for the miracle of its ultimate adaptation to such a role, which always remains prospective (whether in Deuteronomy or in other parts of the Old Testament, such as the Prophets). Yet it is essential that it is characterized first as ill-equipped for its role. This is done, not by mere calumny, but by setting the portrayal within a story. The story is told at one level within Deuteronomy itself, since it both rehearses a past that includes salvation and unfaithfulness, and anticipates a future in which both the blessings and the curses of the covenant come to pass in turn, the lens shifting from the time before entry to the land to a time after its loss and a vision of potential re-possession on the grounds of radical change (Deut. 30.1–10). And it is told by the narrative of Genesis–Kings in which the deuteronomic 'end' of blessing and perdurance is overtaken by a different 'end', a conclusion in exile, with only a prayer that Israel's enemies might have mercy on them there (1 Kgs 8.46–51), and the ambivalent sign of an exiled king of Judah admitted to the Babylonian king's table (2 Kgs 25.27–30). The tension between the potential ultimate fulfilment of Israel's destiny in Deuteronomy and the end of Genesis–Kings in non-fulfilment is part of the dynamic of prophetic openness that operates in the work. In other terms it is what prevents the nationhood of Israel from being portrayed as 'primordial', a concept to which we shall turn shortly.

2. *The Politics of Deuteronomy*

An understanding of the role of Israel in the story of the divine purpose for humanity has been an essential prelude to an analysis of the politics of Deuteronomy. While Deuteronomy and Genesis–Kings leave the destiny of Israel open, it nevertheless aims to display what Israel as righteous nation would be. The concept of righteous nation, therefore, is projected in a sense apart from the specific history of Israel in its Old Testament horizon, though it is enmeshed with that history. Critical scholarship feels this tension when it hesitates between casting Deuteronomy as a real political programme, usually in support of King Josiah's reform, and as a post-exilic utopian work of imagination, impossible to put into practice.[16]

a. *Deuteronomy and the Concept of Nationhood*
The idea that Deuteronomy embodies a view of peoplehood is long-established in Old Testament studies, at least since von Rad's early work, in which he pointed to the close interconnections between its tenets of one God, one people and one

---

16. The view of Deuteronomy as utopian is taken, for example, by L. Perlitt, 'Der Staatsgedanke im Deuteronomium', in S. E. Balentine and J. Barton (eds.), *Language, Theology and the Bible: Essays in Honour of James Barr* (Oxford: Oxford University Press, 1994), pp. 182–98, and N. Lohfink, 'Die Sicherung der Wirksamkeit des Gotteswortes durch das Prinzip der Schriftlichkeit der Torah und durch das Prinzip der Gewaltenteilung nach den Ämtergesetzen des Buches Deuteronomium (Dt 16,18–18,22)', in H. Wolter (ed.), *Testimonium Veritati* (FS W. Kempf; Frankfurt: Knecht, 1971), pp. 143–55; English edn, 'Distribution of the Functions of Power: the Laws Concerning Public Offices in Deuteronomy 16:18–18:22', in D. L. Christensen (ed.), *A Song of Power and the Power of Song* (SBTS, 3; Winona Lake: Eisenbrauns, 1993), pp. 336–52.

place.[17] The origins of this concept of the unity of the people, corresponding to the belief in one God, was traditionally associated with the reform of King Josiah, narrated in 2 Kings 22–23 and 2 Chronicles 34–35. The 'book of the law' discovered in the temple during Josiah's renovations (2 Kgs 22.8) was identified with 'this book of the law' by which Deuteronomy refers to the speeches of Moses that largely compose it (Deut. 31.26, cf. 28.59, 61; 31.9). As Josiah's reform was seen as a kind of nationalistic repudiation of Assyrian rule, Deuteronomy became the instrument of such nationalism.[18] Aniconic Yahwism came to be seen as the official religious sanction for the independence ideology promoted by the political ascendancy in Jerusalem.[19]

In my view, however, the nature of Deuteronomy's view of nationhood requires an analysis that does not pre-judge its relationship to Josiah's reform.[20] In a reading of Deuteronomy as a constituent part of Genesis–Kings I think it important to comprehend it first as the final book of the Pentateuch, rather than under the influence of its supposed role in Josiah's reform.[21] Our reading of Kings will follow in due course.

Von Rad's triad of land, people and worship offers a starting-point for discerning a theory of nationhood in Deuteronomy. However, in terms of a programme for nationhood it lacks essential dimensions. One important pointer towards a more satisfactory analysis is Oliver O'Donovan's use of Old Testament Israel as the basis for his political theology. As we saw above, O'Donovan finds four key concepts in the biblical story of Israel, salvation or 'victorious deliverance', judgement or 'judicial discrimination' (*mishpat*), possession, or 'community-possession', and praise.[22] This is fruitful because in its 'victorious deliverance', it emphasizes the importance of the memory of constitutive events in a people's consciousness. It underlines the close relationship between land

17. G. von Rad, *Das Gottesvolk im Deuteronomium* (BWANT, 47; Stuttgart: W. Kohlhammer, 1929), p. 50. The association of Deuteronomy's confession of one God, its distinctive polity, and its command to worship God at a single place, is already found in Josephus, *Antiquities of the Jews* 4.199–201; see Yehoshua Amir, 'Josephus on the Mosaic "Constitution" ', in H. Graf Reventlow, Yair Hoffmann and Benjamin Uffenheimer (eds.), *Politics and Theopolitics in the Bible and Postbiblical Literature* (JSOTSup, 171; Sheffield: JSOT Press, 1994), pp. 13–27 (15).

18. E. W. Nicholson, *Deuteronomy and Tradition* (Oxford: Blackwell, 1967), p. 11.

19. N. Lohfink, 'The Cult Reform of Josiah of Judah: II Kings 22–23 as a Source for the History of Israelite Religion', in P. D. Hanson (ed.), *Ancient Israelite Religion: Essays in Honor of Frank Moore Cross* (Philadelphia: Fortress, 1987), pp. 459–75; B. M. Levinson, *Deuteronomy and the Hermeneutics of Legal Innovation* (New York: Oxford University Press, 1998), p. 63.

20. I have argued in a number of places that Deuteronomy's concept of polity is actually at odds with that of the reform, e.g. in 'Law and Monarchy in Deuteronomy', in Craig Bartholomew, Jonathan Chaplin, Robert Song, Al Wolters (eds.), *A Royal Priesthood? The Use of the Bible Ethically and Politically* (SHS, 3; Grand Rapids: Zondervan/Carlisle; Paternoster Press, 2002), pp. 69–88; 'King and Messiah in Deuteronomy and the Deuteronomistic History', in John Day (ed.), *King and Messiah in the Old Testament* (JSOTSup, 270; Sheffield: Sheffield Academic Press, 1998), pp. 271–95.

21. This is a case, therefore, of giving priority to 'the world of the text' over the supposed 'world behind the text'; see above, Chapter 1.

22. O'Donovan, *Desire of the Nations*, p. 36. See above, Chapter 4, n. 70.

and people (in his 'community-possession', otherwise 'inheritance'), and the way in which the metaphorical language surrounding landedness suggests reflection on the manner in which land is held.[23] In 'judgement', which he notes might just as well be identified with *tsedeq* ('justice-righteousness') as *mishpat*,[24] he identifies that leading concept that we have found to illuminate the divine purpose since the beginning of the Pentateuchal story. While in his view 'judgement' is essentially performance, it is also related to Israel's idea of law, which 'remained an avowed testimony to the experience of Yhwh's past judgements'.[25] I have argued somewhat differently that the judgement implicit in law has roots already in the divine nature and purpose made known in creation and primaeval history.[26] And in praise is recognized the rule of God as the proper purpose of the people's life.

O'Donovan pursues his study on a broad Old Testament canvas on which Deuteronomy is not particularly foregrounded.[27] Yet we have observed all these elements in our overview above of the character and themes of that book. Israel is a people on a journey to a land, with which its identity and destiny will be closely bound up. God's imminent gift of this land to this people is one of the features that marks the distinctive style of Deuteronomy. In its intermediate state between slavery and landedness, Israel is regularly urged to keep alive the memory of its origins (e.g. Deuteronomy 8). It is also bound by covenant to keep the laws promulgated by Moses ('statutes – *mishpatim* – and ordinances'), which are directed expressly towards life in the land (Deut. 12.1). And at the heart of its life will be the worship of Yahweh its God, a culmination of the purpose of the exodus which was at first that the people should worship Yahweh in the wilderness (Exod. 5.1; 7.26 [EVV 8.1]); that purpose is now re-directed to Israel's new mode of existence in the land, the importance of the theme now disclosed by the dominance, especially in the law code, of the command to 'seek the place that the LORD your God will choose out of all your tribes to put his name there as its dwelling-place'.[28] The 'place' as sanctuary and the 'place' as land are closely related (as in Deut. 26.9), so that tenure of land and worship of Yahweh are interdependent. Indeed all five topics, people, land, law, memory and worship, are intertwined. And together with the rhetorical nature of the dis-

---

23. O'Donovan, *Desire of the Nations*, p. 41.
24. O'Donovan, *Desire of the Nations*, p. 36.
25. O'Donovan, *Desire of the Nations*, p. 39.
26. See further below, Chapter 10, on this.
27. He documents his unifying idea of the rule of Yahweh particularly from Psalms and the Prophets. In my own appreciative response to his thesis I argued that Deuteronomy merited a higher profile in the analysis than it received. I differed also on the relation of Deuteronomy to Josiah's reform; 'Law and Monarchy in Deuteronomy', and his response, also in Bartholomew *et al.* (eds.). *A Royal Priesthood?*, pp. 89–90. The volume consisted of papers given at a Scripture and Hermeneutics Seminar in Cheltenham, which took *The Desire of the Nations* as its topic, and at which O'Donovan responded to all the papers.
28. This translation differs from NRSV in making the dwelling-place refer to the name in line with Deut. 12.11. I account for it in McConville, *Deuteronomy*, pp. 209, 211. It should not be taken to mean that the name dwells at the place in distinction from Yahweh himself, however; pp. 221–2.

course itself, which recognizes and addresses the responsibility of Israel, both communally and individually, to maintain the common life, they form the essential substance of the book.

Many of these themes feature too in modern discussions about nationhood. A. D. Smith has in one place defined a nation as 'a named *human population* occupying *a historic territory* and sharing *common myths and memories, a public culture*, and *common laws and customs* for all members' (emphasis added).[29] The definition lacks the specific connotation of O'Donovan's 'judgement', though it may be present in an attenuated or implicit form. However, in the same study Smith also demonstrates the importance of religion in the self-consciousness of peoples, even if it is frequently present in secularized forms. The dimensions of community, territory, history and destiny belong to the 'sacred foundations' of nations.[30] That is, in a sense of nationhood these dimensions are not simply taken as phenomena, but are religiously legitimated, whether in a memory of 'salvation in a supra-empirical cosmos' or according to a functional analysis of religion in society.[31] Such foundations of national identity, moreover, do not result in static forms. On the contrary, national identity is defined as 'the maintenance and continual reinterpretation of the pattern of values, symbols, memories, myths and traditions that form the distinctive heritage of the nation, and the identification of individuals with that heritage and its pattern.'[32]

These definitions chime with the features of deuteronomic theology and discourse that we have been noticing. Nor is this accidental, since, as Smith, Hastings and others have argued, self-conscious nationhood has roots early in the Christian era, and these roots grew in the soil of the biblical story of Israel.[33] Steven Grosby has made important contributions to exploring these roots in the Old Testament literature, in particular discerning the emergence of genuinely national and universal ideas of peoplehood and land from the 'primordial', exclusive and sacral.[34] In doing so he has drawn extensively on Deuteronomy, as we shall see below.

---

29. A. D. Smith, *Chosen Peoples* (Oxford: Oxford University Press, 2003), p. 24.

30. Smith, *Chosen Peoples*, p. 31.

31. Smith, *Chosen Peoples*, pp. 24–8. The former understanding of religion he calls 'substantive', while the functional understanding is associated with Dürkheim.

32. Smith, *Chosen Peoples*, pp. 24–5; and see p. 265 n. 5, for a criticism of static interpretations.

33. Hastings, *The Construction of Nationhood*. Smith and Hastings both take issue with what they call 'modernism' in theories of nationhood, e.g. Hastings, pp. 1–2, citing Eric Hobsbawm, *Nations and Nationalism Since 1780* (Cambridge: Cambridge University Press, 1990). Smith thinks of nations as 'willed communities', in deliberate opposition to the 'imagined communities' of the modernist Benedict Anderson, in his *Imagined Communities: Reflections on the Origin and Spread of Nationalism* (London: Verso, 1983); see Smith, *Chosen Peoples*, pp. 19–24. Hastings broadly supports Smith, although he characterizes his approach as 'sociological', and thinks there are traces of modernism in his work despite his dissatisfaction with it; *Construction of Nationhood*, p. 8.

34. Steven Grosby, *Biblical Ideas of Nationality Ancient and Modern* (Winona Lake: Eisenbrauns, 2002). See also Kenton L. Sparks, *Ethnicity and Identity in Ancient Israel* (Winona Lake: Eisenbrauns, 1998).

At this point we recall that Deuteronomy has been criticized precisely on the grounds that it has fostered dangerous nationalistic ideologies.[35] However, it is important in this connection to try to distinguish between several closely related concepts, namely 'ethnicity', nation and nationalism, even though historically they are interconnected,[36] and definitions are somewhat contested.[37] 'Ethnicity' is a narrower concept than 'nation', consisting essentially in a shared cultural identity and perhaps a spoken language, while the nation draws in the extra dimensions of a territorial claim and an aspiration to political autonomy.[38] Nationalism is not simply identical with the sense of being a nation, but rather implies a belief in a certain privileged status for the nation which may be pursued even at great cost to other nations or groups.[39] For Smith, nationalism comes about when traditional belief systems and symbols have been employed in order to mobilize nationalistic sentiment and politicize ethnic groups, or, put in theological terms, when the people itself has become the object of worship.[40]

For a number of modern exponents of the idea of the nation, therefore, biblical Israel provided its prototype. Whether biblical Israel may be held responsible for nationalism should await further analysis of the relevant texts, not least the narrative of Israel, which records its shortcomings when measured by biblical standards.

b. *Deuteronomy as 'Constitution'*

A number of recent analyses have pointed to the political character of Deuteronomy. S. D. McBride gave an important lead when he argued that the *torah* in Deuteronomy, which already Josephus had taken as a *politeia* in his demonstration of the priority of Jewish political thought over Roman, should be understood as 'an Israelite "polity", or "political constitution"'.[41] Deuteronomy's repeated reference to a written *torah* within it he takes to indicate Deut. 4.44–28.68:[42] '"This Torah" is covenantal law, the divinely authorized social order that Israel must implement to secure its collective political existence as the people of God.'[43]

35. See above, Chapter 2.
36. Hastings, *Construction of Nationhood*, p. 1.
37. Julian Rivers notes the discrepant usages of the terms 'nation', 'nationalism' and 'nation-state', and points among others to Ernest Gellner's thesis that nations are the product of nationalism, rather than the reverse (as in Smith, Hastings); Rivers, 'Nationhood', in Michael Schluter and John Ashcroft (eds.), *Jubilee Manifesto* (Leicester: IVP, 2005), pp. 122–37 (123–4). Gellner is also cited by Hastings among those who take the 'modernist' view; Hastings, *Construction of Nationhood*, pp. 8–9.
38. Hastings, *Construction of Nationhood*, p. 3. Rivers notes how 'ethnicity' is played down in the biblical idea of nationhood; 'Nationhood', pp. 127–8.
39. Hastings, *Construction of Nationhood*, pp. 3–4. Hastings explains nationalism in relation to statehood, suggesting that it implies the inherent right of a nation to statehood.
40. Smith, *Chosen Peoples*, pp. 42–3.
41. S. Dean McBride, 'Polity of the Covenant People: the Book of Deuteronomy', *Interpretation* 41 (1987), pp. 229–44, repr. in Christensen, (ed.), *A Song of Power*, pp. 62–77, cited here (65).
42. McBride, 'Polity', pp. 62–4.
43. McBride, 'Polity', p. 66.

For McBride, the 'outer frame' of Deuteronomy serves to introduce and con-
clude the 'polity proper', with illustrations of the consequences of success or
failure in keeping it, and preparations for Moses' succession, in both Joshua and
the *torah* itself.[44] The substance of the constitution is the 'statutes and laws'
promulgated by Moses which in Deuteronomy stand on an equal footing with the
Decalogue.[45] Their address to 'all Israel' by the speeches of Moses has the effect
of empowering all Israelites politically. McBride, accepting from Josephus the
idea of a 'constitutional theocracy', argues that while the laws have their origin
in the divine will they are not mere impositions of that will, such as might be
found in divine decrees elsewhere in the ANE.[46] Rather the political responsibility of the individual Israelite is secured by means of this persuasive address. The
political character of the constitution is guaranteed above all by the section concerning the judicial system (16.18–17.13), which stresses that responsibility for
the maintenance of social justice is the obligation of all Israelites. The law of the
king (17.14–18) even anticipates the modern constitutional principle that the
executive 'neither makes the law of the land nor stands above it'.[47] The pervading
purpose of the constitution is the protection of the life and dignity of all members
of the community equally.[48] In sum, the deuteronomic *torah* is 'a social charter
of extraordinary literary coherence and political sophistication…the archetype of
modern western constitutionalism'.[49]

The idea that Deuteronomy embodies a 'constitution' has been adopted by a
number of others also. Crüsemann, writing about the sovereignty of the people
and a 'political constitution', refers mainly to the provisions in Deut. 16.18–
18.22.[50] He too observes the limitations imposed upon the king, and the political
recognition of the whole people by means of the second-person address. Also
taking a cue from Josephus, he uses the term 'theocracy as democracy', but
qualifies 'theocracy' since Deuteronomy knows nothing of an authoritarian
priestly rule. The people as such are supreme in the political sphere, subject not
to authoritarian powers but only to a law given in the distant past in an action
of God that also established their freedom. The leading role of the principle of
justice, and the judiciary, together with the limitation placed on the monarchy,
are decisive features in Deuteronomy's radically innovative politics. For these
reasons he ventures a formulation of Deuteronomy's politics in modern terms:
'The sovereignty of the people underlying the law compels us to speak of something like a democracy'.[51] U. Rüterswörden, C. Schäfer-Lichtenberger and
N. Lohfink have also found a 'constitution' ('Verfassungsentwurf') in Deuter-

---

44. McBride, 'Polity', pp. 68–9.
45. McBride, 'Polity', p. 72.
46. McBride, 'Polity', pp. 70–1.
47. McBride, 'Polity', p. 74. Cf. Josephus, *Antiquities* 4.223; and Amir, 'Josephus', p. 16.
48. McBride, 'Polity', pp. 75–6.
49. McBride, 'Polity', p. 77.
50. Crüsemann, *The Torah*, pp. 234–49.
51. Crüsemann, *The Torah*, pp. 246–7. For democracy and the deuteronomic law see also Ska,
'Biblical Law'.

onomy. The latter two have in addition identified in Deut. 16.18–18.22 a 'separation of powers', following Montesquieu and Locke, on the grounds that the several offices of judge, king, priest and prophet have separate roles and are independent of each other.[52]

The most important and extensive recent attempt to characterize the politics of Deuteronomy comes from J.-M. Carrière. Carrière's main concern is with the nature of the individual's political responsibility and action. He too begins with Josephus in *Contra Apion*, and finds a distinction between the forms of political organization (*politeuma*) and the 'political order' ('l'ordre politique', *politeia*). The latter goes beyond forms to 'the sum of the conditions that determine the citizen's attitudes and actions'.[53] In Josephus' terms, this means that political order (*politeia*) aims at *eusebeia*, that is, a manner of life characterized by godliness.[54] It is in this respect that politics and religion share common ground. Like McBride, he recognizes that Josephus' concept of 'theocracy' is not such that the divine will is imposed directly on the individual.[55] Rather, the 'theocratic' idea belongs properly in the realm of 'political organization' (*politeuma*). That is, while power and political 'leadership' are *attributed* to God, this does not mean that God actually possesses such power and leadership.[56] Rather, the effect of attributing these to God is that they are not attributed to any particular individual or institution.[57] With that proviso, political activity belongs within the human sphere. In particular, Carrière is interested in the construction of the individual as political subject, understood as the way in which he or she relates to laws and institutions, what constraints and convictions come into play. He freely uses the concept of 'citizenship', and with it the notion of a nation ('peuple'), to charac-

52. C. Schäfer-Lichtenberger, *Josua und Salomo: eine Studie zu Autorität und Legitimität des Nachfolgers im Alten Testament* (VTSup, 58; Leiden: E. J. Brill, 1995), pp. 52–85, 103–6; *idem*. 'Der deuteronomische Verfassungsentwurf: Theologische Vorgaben als Gestaltungsprinzipien sozialer Realität' in Braulik (ed.), *Bundesdokument und Gesetz*, pp. 104–18; U. Rüterswörden, *Von der politischen Gemeinschaft zur Gemeinde. Studien zu Dt 16,18–18,22* (BBB, 65: Frankfurt: Athenäum, 1987), pp. 89–90; Lohfink, 'Distribution of the Functions of Power'. See also B. Halpern, *The Constitution of the Monarchy in Ancient Israel*, (HSM, 25; Chico, CA; Scholars Press, 1981), pp. 226–33.

53. '…le politique ne désigne pas seulement l'organisation concrète des institutions, mais aussi l'ensemble des conditions qui determinent les attitudes et les actions des citoyens', J.-M. Carrière, *La théorie du politique dans le Deutéronome* (ÖBS, 18; Frankfurt: Peter Lang, 1997), p. 28.

54. He bases this judgement on Josephus' argument in *Contra Apion 2* in distinction from *The Antiquities of the Jews 4*, where the term *politeia* was used more narrowly of the ordering of the deuteronomic laws; Carrière, *La théorie du politique*, pp. 22–9, esp. p. 28.

55. Cf. McBride, above, n. 44.

56. Carrière is guarded about the relationship between religion and politics. He declines an *a priori* assumption that the theory of politics in Deuteronomy is essentially 'religious', and aims in the first instance to understand it in sociological terms; *La théorie du politique*, p. 18. He notes that Deuteronomy's politics may be conceived as in a sense 'secular' (p. 18), citing also Y. Amir for a similar view; 'θεοκρατία as a Concept of Political Philosophy: Josephus' Presentation of Moses' πολιτεία', *SCI* 8-9 (1985/88), pp. 13–27 (*La théorie du politique*, p. 31).

57. Carrière, *La théorie du politique*, pp. 28–9. Carrière translates Josephus' ἀρχή with both 'le principe' and 'le leadership', and ἀνατίθημι with 'attribuer'.

terize this political status of the individual.[58] In such a relationship between the individual and political forms lies 'the emergence of the political' ('l'émergence du politique'). Liberation from traditional concepts of power, thus in Deuteronomy liberation from Egypt, is of the essence of this.[59]

Carrière finds the 'constitutional project' ('projet constitutionnel') strictly in Deut. 16.18–18.22,[60] which he locates within Deut. 4.44–28.68 because the latter is widely accepted as a major redactional unit.[61] His method, however, is not redactional or historical. Rather, he wants to examine the 'architecture' of the text as it stands, believing that this is essential to understanding the political concepts it contains.[62] In his analysis of Deut. 16.18–18.22 he highlights four 'institutions' in turn, namely the judiciary (16.18–17.13), the monarchy (17.14–20), the priesthood (18.1–8) and prophecy (18.14–22), and then traces through these the underlying concepts of the land as 'structured space', the citizen subject to the law, and law itself. I have found his thesis largely persuasive, as will be clear from the remainder of the present chapter. I differ from him mainly in relation to the setting of Deuteronomy within Genesis–Kings, which attracts almost no attention from him.

3. *The Constituents of a Political Theology*

We have now observed how Deuteronomy has been thought to have affinities with modern concepts of nationhood and of political categories such as the 'constitution' and citizenship. It is time to look more closely at how these may be discovered in Deuteronomy itself. We will consider in turn land, people, law and institutions, following the order of Deut. 16.18–18.22. It is not possible to keep these completely separate; indeed it is in their interrelationship that their meaning lies. Nor can we confine our enquiry to Deut. 16.18–18.22 alone.

a. *Land*
As we have seen, the concept of a people called to enact justice in a land is one of Deuteronomy's major contributions to the portrayal of the divine project for

---

58. In this respect he takes a lead from Crüsemann, who thinks the second-person address in Deuteronomy confers political freedom on free land-owning males; Crüsemann, *The Torah*, pp. 220–1; Carrière, p. 47. He prefers this concept of citizenship to Lohfink's 'separation of powers', pp. 48–9.

59. Carrière, *La théorie du politique*, pp. 18–19, 31.

60. Carrière, *La théorie du politique*, pp. 40–1. With this phrase he translates Lohfink's 'Verfassungsentwurf', and accepts it provisionally, acknowledging its modern provenance. In limiting the 'constitution' to 16.18–18.22 he expressly differs from McBride.

61. Carrière, *La théorie du politique*, p. 17.

62. He does not reject redactional or historical approaches as such, and recognizes that there must be a historical matrix for the emergence of political ideas. However, for a redaction-critic like A. D. H. Mayes 'the fundamental characteristic of Deuteronomy is linguistic'; Mayes, 'On Describing the Purpose of Deuteronomy', *JSOT* 58 (1993), pp. 13–33 (25). He chooses instead to focus on 'the world of the text', citing Ricoeur (cf. above Chapter 1); *La théorie du politique*, pp. 14–17. And he finds the study of Rüterswörden, though ostensibly germane to his interest, largely irrelevant to it, because of its strong redactional orientation (p. 41).

the creation in Genesis–Kings. We now look more closely at what is denoted by 'land' in the book.

There is no single designation for 'land' in Deuteronomy. Typical are both *'erets* and *'adamah,* each capable of designating it in its full extent. Land in Deuteronomy is an extension of territory, bordering other territories. This was already established in Num. 34.1–15, where 'the land of Canaan', Israel's 'inheritance' (34.2) was marked out to the north, south, east and west. The borders will be more fully described in the book of Joshua, where tribal boundaries are also established. Within Deuteronomy, the delimitation of the land is clear in a number of ways: from the description of their approach to it, when they are required to recognize the territorial integrity of neighbouring Edom, Moab and Ammon (Deut. 2.1–25); from the rudimentary descriptions in 11.24 and 34.1–2, and from the prominence of the River Jordan as an eastern boundary, highlighted by the special conditions under which the two and a half tribes of Reuben, Gad and half-Manasseh were permitted to settle on its eastern side (3.12–22, cf. Numbers 32). The land is not only delimited but unified, an effect of the repeated requirement to establish a place chosen by Yahweh at which all the tribes should worship (12.5, 11, 14 etc.). Land, therefore, is a bounded land that belongs to the people as such.[63]

The land is qualified in ways that express its relation to both God and people. Above all, it is that which Yahweh 'gives' to Israel, a point that is made in a frequently recurring formula.[64] This ideological justification for Israel's possession of it not only points to the origins of Israel in covenant with Yahweh, but should be understood in the context of Deuteronomy's rejection of arbitrary, self-aggrandizing power.[65] Yahweh's ownership of the land is the logical precondition of its narrative and themes. As Sandra Richter has demonstrated, the formula of the placing of the name of Yahweh at the central sanctuary (12.5 etc.) has the effect of establishing his claim to the land.[66] The claim corresponds not only to the promise to Abraham (invoked in 1.8), but also to the removal of Israel from

---

63. Grosby, *Biblical Ideas of Nationality*, pp. 23–4.

64. The formula of the gift of the land was characterized by G. Seitz as 'historicizing introductions to the commandments' ('Gebotseinleitungen'); G. Seitz, *Redaktionsgeschichtliche Studien zum Deuteronomium* (BWANT, 93; Stuttgart: W. Kohlhammer, 1971), pp. 95–6. They are: Deut. 6.10; 7.1; 8.7; 11.29, 31; 12.29; 17.14; 18.9; 19.1; 26.1; 27.2.

65. It was in this respect that Schwartz found the OT's monotheism to have left 'its deepest, most lasting, and undoubtedly its most troubling political legacy'; *The Curse of Cain*, p. 39. Her judgement is understandable in view of abuses of Deuteronomy, but should be qualified by attention to the force of it in its ancient context.

66. Richter, *The Deuteronomistic History*. Richter thus challenges the common view of the 'name-theology' advocated by M. Weinfeld, T. Mettinger and others, that it is an instrument of a theology of the divine presence, which holds that Yahweh dwells only in heaven, and that the 'name' is a kind of representative hypostasis at the sanctuary; Weinfeld, *Deuteronomy and the Deuteronomic School*, pp. 192–6; T. Mettinger, *The Dethronement of Sabaoth: Studies in the Shem and Kabod Theologies* (ConBot, 18; Lund: C. W. K. Gleerup, 1982). See also Peter Vogt, *Deuteronomic Theology and the Significance of Torah: A Reappraisal* (Winona Lake: Eisenbrauns, 2006). I have also argued against this view in McConville and J. G. Millar, *Time and Place in Deuteronomy* (JSOTSup, 179; Sheffield: Sheffield Academic Press, 1994), pp. 89–139.

the spiritual-geographical realm of Egypt in order to bring them into another space in which his rule would be undisputed. Yahweh's ownership of the land, therefore, is both geographical and spiritual, the place in which Israel might mature into its destiny, and the divine creative purpose might be fulfilled. The point of the gift-formula is not only that Yahweh has given the land to Israel and to no-one else, but also that it is Yahweh who has the right to give, and not any individual, certainly not a foreign tyrant, or even a domestic one. Deuteronomy thus has affinities with the prophetic critique of possession in an oppressive, acquisitive sense. Its attitude is echoed in narrative in the story of Ahab and Naboth's vineyard (1 Kings 21).[67]

Israel's land is not only received as a gift, it is 'inherited' from Yahweh. The idea of the land as an 'inheritance' (נחלה) was introduced along with the boundary description in Num. 34.2 (cf. 36.2). It now occurs in Deut. 4.21, 38; 32.9 and nine times in the law code (12.9; 15.4; 19.10, 14; 20.16; 21.13; 24.4; 25.19; 26.1), always in parallel with the gift-formula (with the exception of 32.9). (In 4.21 it also corresponds to the characterization of Israel as Yahweh's 'inheritance', cf. 9.29.) The metaphor is essentially familial, and in Numbers it occurs most often in that context (Num. 18.23–24; 26.62; 27.7; 36.7–9). In Joshua it typically refers to tribal inheritances (Josh. 17.14; 19.49), though the land as a whole is also sometimes designated in this way (Josh. 13.6–7; 23.4). In Deuteronomy it appears in this sense principally in respect of the Levites (10.9; 12.12; 14.27–29; 18.1–2, but cf. 29.7[8]).

This essentially family metaphor is thus applied in Deuteronomy predominantly to Israel as a whole. It expresses the fact that their right to occupy the land derives from their relationship with Yahweh. But more importantly this application of the family metaphor to the whole people suggests a movement from the familial to the political sphere.[68]

It is balanced by the idea of 'possession' (ירש, ירשה). (The two terms come together in e.g. 26.1: '...the land that the LORD your God is giving you as an inheritance to possess'). 'Possession' signifies Israel's legal right to the land as distinct from other nations. Sometimes 'the nations' are the object of the verb (qal or hiphil), which may be translated 'dispossess'.[69] The LORD's 'dispossessing' these nations is an act of judgement on the grounds of their abhorrent practices (18.12). Conversely, Israel's possession is contingent on doing justice. It is significant that the call to do justice in 16.18–20 comes at the beginning of the section on the political institutions. The contingency of continuance in the land

---

67. Cf. Carrière, *La théorie du politique*, pp. 221–2.

68. Carrière, *La théorie du politique*, pp. 222–4. Carrière notes the relative preponderance of the familial sense of 'inheritance' in the historical books following Deuteronomy and thinks this is the typically deuteronomistic usage as opposed to the deuteronomic. Yet the 'national' sense also occurs in those books (e.g. 1 Sam. 10.1; 26.19; 2 Sam. 14.16; 20.19; 2 Kgs 21.14). In some cases the senses of the people and the land as the inheritance are difficult to distinguish. We shall return to the relationship between tribal and 'national' inheritance in relation to Joshua.

69. Lohfink, however, thinks the hiphil is related to a root רוש, impoverish, destroy; 'Die Bedeutungen von hebr. jrš qal und hif', *BZ* 27 (1983), pp. 14–33.

upon doing justice is clear in 16.20. This concept of 'possessing', like that of inheriting, is applied to the whole people and the whole land. Lohfink, observing that שׁרי (qal, with personal object) likewise has its origins in family affairs, finds in its larger reference an expansion from the familial to the national level.[70] Israel's 'possession', therefore, implies a legal title to the land it has inherited.[71] It does not merely occupy, but it possesses as of right. Legal possession, finally, is the basis on which Israel 'dwells' or 'settles' (ישׁב) in the land. This term also often appears in tandem with other terms (e.g. 17.14, '...when you have come into the land, and *taken possession of* it and *settled* in it...'). The 'settling' anticipates duration. When the land has been given and inherited, Israel has a legal title to it, which opens on to the future.

The land as bounded territory requires further examination, in terms of its internal structuring. In Carrière's terms it is 'structured space' ('un espace structuré').[72] This may be expressed as the relation between the centre and the distributed locations of Israel,[73] a relationship already postulated by the land as continuous and bounded. The contrast between the centre (the chosen place of worship, 12.5 etc.) and the towns of Israel (always 'gates' in Deuteronomy, 12.17) is well known. The relationship between them is the subject of several of the laws concerning worship. Deuteronomy 12 regulates what is proper locally and centrally in respect of sacrificial and non-sacrificial slaughter of animals; Deut. 14.22–29 has a similar provision regarding the tithe. The relationship between centre and locations is one of mutuality, however, not opposition, a point that is not always recognized in formulations of deuteronomic 'centralization'. This is often conceived as an assertion of the rights of the Jerusalem hierarchy over rival sanctuaries and priesthoods, and sometimes as the superimposition of a statist centralism on a more traditional, patriarchal or tribal type of political organization.[74] In my view the deuteronomic programme as it bears upon the relation between centre and localities is quite different. While Yahweh's name is memorialized at a particular chosen place (the 'centre'), it is nevertheless the whole land that is sanctified by his possession of it. This is why guilt can be brought upon the land by idolatrous and sinful behaviour (Deut. 24.4), and also why the land and the central place are virtually identified in the pregnant use of מקום ('place') in Deut. 26.9.

The relationship between centre and locations may be illustrated by a comparison of two further texts. At Horeb, after the giving of the Decalogue, the people have demanded that Moses henceforth act as mediator between God and themselves. God says to Moses:

70. Lohfink, 'Bedeutungen', esp. p. 33.
71. Carrière, *La théorie du politique*, p. 218.
72. Carrière, *La théorie du politique*, pp. 201–40.
73. In political anthropology, the counterpart of the centre is sometimes designated the 'periphery'; Edward Shils, *Center and Periphery: Essays in Macrosociology* (New York: St. Martin's, 1975). The use of the term is challenged by D. A. Knight on the grounds that it diminishes the political significance of locations outside the political centre; Knight, 'Political Rights and Powers in Monarchic Israel', p. 99. I have consequently preferred 'distributed locations'.
74. The latter is the view of Knight, 'Political Rights and Powers'.

God and Earthly Power

> If only they had such a mind as this to fear me and keep my commandments always, so
> that it might go well with them and with their children for ever! Go, say to them
> 'Return to your tents'. But you stand here by me, and I will tell you all the com-
> mandments, statutes and ordinances, that you shall teach them (5.29–31).

The key element here (besides the anticipation of the need to keep God's laws in
perpetuity) is the relationship of tension between the 'centre' (Moses staying
'here by me') and the locations (Israel returning 'to their tents'). The latter phrase
is precisely echoed in 16.7b, where the celebrants of Passover are instructed, on
the day after the Passover feast, to 'return to their tents'. There as here, I think, a
relationship in principle is established between the centre and the distributed
locations of Israel. Deuteronomy's Passover law is carefully constructed to articulate this relationship of tension.[75] That is, the centre and the distributed locations
are both distinct from and yet continuous with each other; for example, there is
to be no leaven 'in all your territory'; the location of the special assembly (עצרת)
on the final day is undetermined.

The mutual and inclusive relationship between centre and locations within
boundaries has been well expressed by Grosby (who uses the term 'periphery'):

> ...the jurisdiction of the center was believed to have been such that it should appro-
> priately encompass the periphery. Indeed the center designated the periphery as its
> periphery; and the periphery recognized the center as its center...[The boundaries] are
> regarded by members of the society contained within them as determining or properly
> determining the appropriate extent of the life-giving, life-sustaining, and life-ordering
> power (Deut 30:20) of the trans-local communion (Josh 22:25) of the territorial
> possession.[76]

The connection of the locations of Israel to the chosen place means that all places
are related to each other in a coherent whole. The corollary of our observations
about land in Deuteronomy is that it envisages a move away from locality as the
decisive territorial horizon, towards extensive territory held in common by a
people. This takes us to the next category.

b. *People*

People and land are closely associated in Deuteronomy as we have seen. And
just as the land is unified rather than reflecting tribal divisions, so it is with the
people. Tribal distinctions are hinted at only *sotto voce*. The united people Israel
belongs within the unified land Israel, the term applying equally to both. This
concept too is found already in Numbers 34 in conjunction with the description
of the land's boundaries, in the phrase 'children/sons of Israel' (בני ישראל,
Num. 34.2, 13, 29).[77] In Deuteronomy, the metaphor of 'brotherhood' reinforces

---

75. I have argued this more fully in 'Deuteronomy's Unification of Passover and Massot', *JBL*
119 (2000), pp. 47–58.

76. Grosby, *Biblical Ideas of Nationality*, pp. 87–8.

77. This idea of Israel as a unity also underlies texts in which the land is distributed to tribes,
e.g. Josh. 3.7, where 'all Israel' (כל־ישראל) occupies land, as prelude to land-division; cf. 'all the
sons/children of Israel' (כל־בני ישראל), Josh. 3.1; 'all the nation' (כל־הגוי), 4.1; 'the people'
(העם). 'All Israel' is depicted as acting together in other ways also, e.g. 4.14; 7.25.

the solidarity of the whole people, as when the Transjordanian tribes are permitted to settle only after they have helped their 'brothers, the children of Israel'
(אחיכם בני־ישראל) to take possession of the land west of Jordan (Deut. 3.18–
20). The 'brotherhood' of all Israelites is a powerful motivating factor in the
ethical discourse of the book, undergirding the obligations to release debts and
slaves in due course, in order to restore the disadvantaged to full participation in
the social, economic and worshipping life of the community (Deut. 15.1–18).
The king too must be 'one from among your brethren' (17.15, RSV).

The language of unity, sonship ('sons of Israel') and brotherhood, is once
again based in family metaphors. In the former case it is rather more than metaphor, since the narrative of origins portrays Israel precisely as descended from
the patriarchs. In some interpretations, the familial-genealogical aspect of the
identity of Israel predominates. Kenton Sparks takes the brotherhood metaphor to
portray ethnicity as extended kinship, and so to furnish evidence of a general
kinship-ethnicity theory (which he attributes to P. L. van den Berghe): 'Deuteronomic "brother-theology" was a deliberate attempt to extend the natural affilia-
tions of kinship beyond the immediate family to fellow Judeans and Israelites'.[78]
Grosby thinks in contrast that transitions from kinship notions of collectivity to
properly national ones leave traces of the former, indicating what he calls 'the
inexpungeability of the primordial'.[79] In Deuteronomy, the memory of Abraham,
Isaac and Jacob is in the service of its theology of covenant and oath, signifying
its origin in a decision of God, and also its vocation to enact justice and righteousness. We have seen in both Genesis and Exodus that the constitution of Israel
across the generations and at key moments (the exodus itself) was open to non-
Israelite strains, indeed that the patriarchal concern for marriage within the
extended family could not be sustained. The retreat of the tribal divisions of
Israel in the rhetoric of Deuteronomy confirms this effacing of the 'primordial'.
Israel is perpetuated here by adhering to its confession of Yahweh alone, and its
teaching of the formative events of Israel and the laws and teachings given by
Moses from generation to generation.

For these reasons, in the case of the people as of the land, we are justified in
seeing a move away from traditional, tribal constructions of collective belonging
to the idea of a 'trans-tribal people'.[80] In Carrière's terms it has transcended
'parenté' (kin-relationship).[81] Israel is not a collection of clans related by kinship.
Nor by the same token is it modelled on Empire (which, for Grosby, is based on
a hegemony rooted in a family and a locality). In Deuteronomy it is the people as
such that is 'elect' (7.6; 14.1a); they do not derive their status from the prior
election of a king.

---

78. Sparks, *Ethnicity and Identity*, pp. 328–9; P. L. van den Berghe, *The Ethnic Phenomenon*
(New York, Elsevier, 1981).

79. Grosby, *Biblical Ideas of Nationality*, p. 21.

80. Grosby, *Biblical Ideas of Nationality*, p. 24.

81. Carrière, *La théorie du politique*, p. 393; cf. Schäfer-Lichtenberger, *Josua und Salomo*,
p. 225, on Joshua's non-familial succession.

c. *Law and justice*

In the administration of the law the theme of justice-righteousness (*tsedeq/ tsedaqah*) comes into the foreground. The judges are charged: 'Justice, justice (*tsedeq tsedeq*) you shall pursue' (Deut. 16.20: 'Justice and only justice', RSV). We recall that in Deuteronomy *tsedeq/tsedaqah* is attributed to God and the laws in themselves (32.4; 4.6–8 respectively), and described the right ordering of society as a whole (6.24–25). Judges are charged with making the divine justice a reality by responsible action in judicial practice.

The practice of law relates both to the whole land and to the whole people. Its validity as a 'law of the land' is evident in programmatic texts, in which the law is expressly required to be kept in the land (6.1–3; 12.1), and texts like 21.1–9, where the location is by definition anywhere in the land and where the judicial apparatus is seen in terms of its geographical jurisdiction (cf. 19.1–3). Its validity is not just a matter of extent, however, but once again relates to the inner structure of the land. The practice of law is located *both* in the 'gates' *and* at the chosen place (16.18; 17.8–13). This two-sidedness is an aspect of the relationship between the localities of Israel and the centre which we have noticed already. The resort to the central court is not to be thought of as an 'appeal' procedure; rather it is for consultation, and illustrates the coherence of the application of law throughout land and people. As Grosby puts it: 'The law is the vehicle by which the periphery participates in the center, and through which the nature of that participation is determined (Deut. 17.8–13)'.[82]

As the law applies throughout the land, so the responsibility for administering it lies with the people as a whole. This I take to be the significance of the address to the 'Thou' in 16.18, since the person addressed there is clearly distinct from the judges themselves.[83] In that place Israel as a whole is instructed to appoint judges in the localities. How such a responsibility might be conceived in practice is unclear. But a point of principle is being established. The structure of responsibility for law is as follows: *Yahweh's torah* is given by *Moses* to *the people*, who delegate its operation to chosen members of the community.

The resort to the central court for 'hard' cases is explicable in the context of the law as the responsibility of the whole people, and applicable uniformly to the whole people. The finality of the court's decision (17.10–13) illustrates *this* rather than a hierarchical view of the society (i.e. in which the priest's word is in itself beyond contradiction; note that the court brings together priests and 'judge', 17.9, in a synergy that is never explained, but which seems to emphasize the importance of the function over the office-bearer). That is, the law is itself final. Refusal to obey it brings the ultimate punishment (17.12). The process at the high court is the means by which the finality of the *torah* is actualized in the life of the people.

With the administration of the law we begin to see what is involved in the individual functioning as a member of Israelite society. The judicial activity to

82. Grosby, *Biblical Ideas of Nationality*, p. 112. He also uses the term *lex terrae* of the deuteronomic law, expressing its validity by definition throughout the bordered land; p. 87.

83. I have argued more fully for this in 'Singular Address in the Deuteronomic Law'.

which some Israelites are appointed involves deliberation and responsible action. The givenness of the law as divine command does not have the effect of pre-empting every decision. On the contrary it calls for the making of judgements. Judgement here carries the sense of the careful weighing of a case as well as the connotation of God's justice, or indeed his judgement. The judge of cases seeks to establish what is just on the basis of God's 'justice-righteousness' (*tsedeq*). In this responsible action of the citizen, the concept of the legal process in Deuteronomy may be said to transcend the casuistic.[84]

d. *Institutions and Citizenship*

In our consideration of law and justice we saw that political responsibility in Israel lay in principle with the people as a whole. We can now explore more carefully how the individual Israelite was expected to relate to the political institutions of the nation. The departure point, I think, is the use of the singular address. The singular address in Deuteronomy is directed at times to Israel as a whole, yet equally, at other times, to the individual Israelite. The dual possibility of the singular is neither untidy nor merely rhetorical, but of the essence. That is, the responsibility of 'all Israel' falls on individual Israelites by virtue of their being 'Israel'. This is nowhere clearer than in 15.1–18, where the individual's obligation towards the fellow-Israelite is grounded in the fact that he ('thou') had been a slave in Egypt – though in fact he had not (15.15).[85] Carrière observes similarly that the singular address applies variously to the judge and to the larger entity that is responsible for the judge's appointment.[86]

The reason for this rhetorical nuancing lies, I think, in the relation between individual Israelites and the institution. For Carrière (rightly), the key element in the operation of the institutions is the *responsible action* of the individual (or in his terms, the *citizen* – i.e. the individual in political capacity). The citizen participates in what is incumbent on the institution.[87] That is, he or she is not merely subject to the law, submissively and without choice,[88] but bears responsibility for its interpretation and practice. The institutions require that the citizen uses judgement and makes decisions. The nature of the decision-making emerges from an examination of what precisely is laid upon the actors in connection with each institution. In legal cases it involves making enquiries ('searching', 17.4), hearing evidence, coming to a verdict based on justice, and either carrying out a sentence or not.[89] In this capacity for responsible decision lies what Carrière calls a 'political quality'. It is evident not only in the realm of justice, but also that of prophecy, where both prophet and hearer are required to make decisions, facing

84. Carrière, *La théorie du politique*, p. 372.
85. McConville, 'Singular Address', pp. 26–7.
86. '...the Thou seems to occupy different positions successively and according to points in the development of the law... The Thou is at once distinct from the judge (local or central) and at the same time in his place' (author's translation); Carrière, *La théorie du politique*, p. 378, cf. pp. 348–9.
87. Carrière, *La théorie du politique*, p. 248.
88. Carrière, *La théorie du politique*, p. 278.
89. Carrière, *La théorie du politique*, p. 269.

an unknown future, based on a capacity to listen, know and judge.[90] The priest for his part exemplifies the right disposition and action of the 'citizen' in choosing to go from the locality to the central place; the king acts as 'model citizen' in his meditation on the *torah*.[91]

What is the aim of this legislation in political terms? As we have noticed already, it is not a political treatise. Rather it seeks to call and enable the individual to act in the political sphere. This sphere may be defined as that which belongs to the people at a high level of organization, which accounts, in Deuteronomy's discourse, for the role of the central place, and the journey there from the locality. The emergence of politics lies in the reflection on the relation between the particular and the totality, the discovery of what Carrière calls 'l'autre du particulier' (that which is other than the particular).[92] Essential to Deuteronomy's political concept, therefore, is the transcendence of the local and particular. Such transcendence can be observed in relation to all the institutions: regarding law and justice, in a transcending of casuistic law; regarding land, in a transcending of the local; regarding citizenship, in a transcending of the familial; regarding the king, in a transcending of slavery.[93]

4. *The Succession to Mose*s

A description of the political provisions of Deuteronomy is incomplete without attention to its notion of the succession to Moses following his death. Even Moses is prevented from becoming the holder of political power absolutely.[94] Indeed, his death is by no means incidental to the narrative (Deuteronomy 34), but is a crucial part of the picture.[95] Israel enters into its full inheritance without Moses. Who or what, then, takes his place? In fact Moses is succeeded perfectly by no one person or agency, but rather in part by several.

First, he is succeeded by the written *torah*.[96] Moses 'teaches' the *torah* and mediates it to Israel, an effect heightened in Deuteronomy because it places the laws after the Decalogue clearly within the realm of Moses' teaching. But after Moses this role devolves on no individual, rather on the *torah*, the 'book of the law'. The self-consciousness of Deuteronomy as 'book' has been well described by Sonnet.[97] It is the provision for a 'book of the law' that ensures that the teaching role of Moses continues. The responsibility for the activity to continue is guaranteed by the people, in assembly (Deuteronomy 31). It is the supremacy

---

90. Carrière, *La théorie du politique*, p. 271.
91. Carrière, *La théorie du politique*, pp. 272–3.
92. Carrière, *La théorie du politique*, p. 368.
93. Carrière, *La théorie du politique*, pp. 372, 386, 393, 400. On transcending the familial, cf. Schäfer-Lichtenberger, *Josua und Salomo*, p. 225.
94. Carrière, *La théorie du politique*, pp. 403–6.
95. Denis Olson has made this case persuasively in *Deuteronomy and the Death of Moses* (OBT; Minneapolis: Fortress Press, 1994).
96. As Joachim Schaper has put it, Moses' grave is not known, but the *torah* is known everywhere (paper given at SBL, 2004).
97. Sonnet, *The Book Within the Book*.

of the *torah* in Israel's life above all that mitigates the concentration of power in any one person or agency.

Second, Moses is succeeded by the institutions. This is adumbrated at the outset, in Deut. 1.9–18, where Moses' specifically judicial functions are dispersed among tribal leaders. The topic of the judicial function in Israel is then resumed at 16.18, for the time after the occupation of the land, with its establishment of a local and central judiciary, all under the aegis of 'Israel'. Moses' priestly and prophetic roles are also carried on in separate institutions.

Third, Moses is succeeded by Joshua.[98] This is a unique 'succession'. Joshua has been Moses' 'assistant' (מְשָׁרְתוֹ, Exod. 24.13) from an early point in the story. The nature of the relationship is undefined,[99] but is in any case not familial. The succession of Moses by Joshua is therefore specifically non-dynastic and non-nepotistic. Joshua is not entirely like Moses. (He is, for example, in a different relationship to the *torah*). And he himself is succeeded by no one. Indeed, Joshua succeeds for a specific, defined purpose, and his task complete he recedes into the anonymity of his local 'inheritance', in common with other Israelites (Josh. 24.28–30).

The significance of Joshua as successor is thrown into relief by the course of the story *after* Joshua, which may be seen as designed to show precisely the dangers of 'dynasticism'. This danger is not confined to kings. Rather, each of the institutions treated by Deuteronomy comes under scrutiny in its turn in the story that follows. Samuel, as judge of Israel, echoes 'the judge who is in office in those days', Deut. 17.9. His attempt to install his sons after him (1 Sam. 8.1–3) runs right against the grain of the deuteronomic provision, which places a limitation on the particular judge's jurisdiction. At the same time, their corruption demonstrates with great clarity the seriousness of Deuteronomy's concerns. Priests fare little better, with the story of Eli.[100] And the dynastic succession of kings leads to disastrous results. One could say that the books of Joshua to Kings are structured so as to illustrate the dangers which Deuteronomy strives to obviate. I will attempt to demonstrate this in due course (in chs 7–9, below).

5. Conclusion

I have argued that Deuteronomy expresses powerful political ideas that are rooted in the experience and memory of Israel. Its political thought involves an organizational aspect, since it provides for roles and offices, procedures for law and worship, an assembly of the whole people, and the relation of these together. However, the genius of its thought does not lie in the organizational provisions

---

98. The role of Joshua will be explored further in the following chapter.

99. The term מְשָׁרֵת 'assistant', is often used of priestly service, but does not seem to be so limited when applied to Joshua.

100. The dynastic character of the priesthood – 'Aaron and his sons' – is not challenged either in Deuteronomy or in Samuel, but Eli is accused of 'honouring his sons above the LORD' (1 Sam. 2.29), and is replaced by 'a faithful priest' and *his* house. Even here dynasticism brings no special guarantees that transcend the need to fulfil the priestly role of honouring God.

themselves. Josephus' distinction between *politeuma* and *politeia* may be recalled here. Where the former was organizational, the latter referred to 'the sum of the conditions that determine the citizen's attitudes and actions'.[101] Those conditions include the Israelite's participation in a people that shares a memory of deliverance from slavery, the provisions for the worship of the God who delivered them, and the pervasive presence of *torah* throughout the corporate life. These were the factors that could operate to produce a consciousness of the kind of political responsibility of all Israelites that the laws both presuppose and aim to nurture. The forms of political organization themselves might change (and the narrative after Deuteronomy testifies to such change), but would (or should) be constrained by a sense of Israel's essential nature and vocation. Deuteronomy itself does not merely lay this out as a thesis, but participates in it, by virtue of its appeal to the memory, its rhetorical character, and its moral force.

I have argued too that the politics of Deuteronomy enshrine a concept of nationhood, whose main tenets are expressed in and through its laws. This concept is not 'nationalism', but rather Deuteronomy furnishes elements of what it means to be a 'nation', a point that is incipiently developed in relation to nations other than Israel (Deut. 2.1–23). The main aspects of this related to its understanding of the tenure of land, of peoplehood itself, of law and of the role and responsibility of the individual within society. Far from legislating for nationalistic exclusivism, the relationship between Israel and Yahweh in Deuteronomy is part of its thorough rejection of religious and political tyranny, since the required loyalty to Yahweh operates against the concentration of power and liberates the citizen for participation and responsibility.

The power of the ideas of Deuteronomy to transcend their original home in ancient Israel was noticed with reference to a few examples from the reception history of the book. For example, we observed the close relationship between it and the notions of democracy that were appealed to in the seventeenth century. It is significant that the deuteronomic law was used in situations of ideological conflict, in a way that is true to the character of Deuteronomy itself, and indeed to its invitation to hermeneutical re-appropriation.

The subjection of the whole life of a nation under God leads, not to tyranny, but to a wholly different type of society. It may be defined by its vocation to manifest qualities that transcend itself, summed up as justice-righteousness. As such it stands in direct contrast to a 'primordial' conception of nationhood. It is a *political* nation, in the sense that its members are dignified with the responsibilities of citizenship. The nationhood imagined in Deuteronomy describes the freedom that precisely repudiates the 'slavery' of Egypt. Biblical monotheism has sometimes led to violent, exclusive attitudes and societies. But it need not do so, and better readings of it tend in a different direction, allowing its enlightened social vision to become ethically significant in different times and places from ancient Israel.

---

101. See above, at nn. 53, 54.

Chapter 6

POSSESSING LAND: JOSHUA

1. *Reading Joshua-Kings Politically*

After Deuteronomy we have reached a crucial junction in the primary history. Canonically speaking, *torah* gives way to Prophets, or Pentateuch to Historical Books. The formative Mosaic phase of Israel's life has ended and we turn to the life of Israel after Moses. Israel's commission has been given; it now sets out on its campaign.

It is important, therefore, to focus briefly again on the nature of the commission. Its ultimate context is the divine purpose that justice-righteousness should be realized in human society on earth. Israel is the chosen vehicle, called to nationhood under God as a provisional realization of that purpose. To this end it is brought into political space defined by its rejection of the chaotic rule of Pharaoh. The land of Israel becomes a microcosm of the earth as it ought to be inhabited and governed. Israel representatively offers worship to Yahweh alone, its laws reflecting his universal justice. Finally, it is mandated to exercise political power in relation to Yahweh's ultimate rule, and his *torah*. This last aspect was elaborated chiefly in Deuteronomy.

Joshua–Kings is formally projected as a single, continuous narrative by means of the links between the books found in their opening words (Josh. 1.1; Judg. 1.1; 1 Kgs 1.1). Its subject-matter flows out of all that has been prepared in Genesis–Deuteronomy, and tells the story of Israel's partial accomplishment of its mission. In pursuit of this, they enter the land that God gives them, they undertake to live within its boundaries according to the *torah*-law (Joshua 24), and in due course they establish religious and political institutions, with a centre first at Shiloh then at Jerusalem. The history unfolds in the theatre of the surrounding nations, on occasion eliciting recognition from these of Yahweh's rule in history (as in the case of Rahab, Joshua 2), but more typically illustrating the ongoing conflict at a profound level, with Israel's religious-political loyalties constantly contested between Yahweh and Baal, *torah* and the hierarchical and oppressive tendencies depicted of Canaan and Assyria. This last conflict comes to a head in Josiah's discovery of the 'book of the law' (2 Kgs 22.8), which contrasts especially with the Assyrianizing rule of Manasseh, and the religious apostasy associated with it (2 Kings 21).

An important running theme of Joshua–Kings is the manner in which Israel seeks to exercise the responsibility of political life and leadership in relation to

Yahweh's supreme rule as 'judge' (Judg. 11.27) and 'king' (Judg. 8.23; 1 Sam. 8.7). Israel is ruled successively by Joshua in association with priestly and tribal leaders, by judge-deliverers, and by kings, first in a united kingdom, then in two divided ones. In the heart of the story is the contention over the transition from rule by 'judge-deliverers' to rule by a king (1 Sam. 8.4–9), which connects expressly with the law of the king in Deut. 17.14–20. As throughout Genesis–Deuteronomy, the political concern is embedded in a religious one, namely the imperative to worship Yahweh alone (1 Kgs 8.60–61), itself a function of the mission of Israel to be a witness to the nations. At its simplest, the narrative portrays a history in which the synthesis projected by the *torah* is variously and partially enacted, and finally dissolved. In the absence of loyalty to Yahweh the connection between people and land is broken, and with it the possibility of political nationhood envisaged by the *torah*.

In the narrative of Joshua–Kings, the political vision is entangled with the actuality of Israel's life as it unfolds in a history. Interpreters have often sought the political orientation of the texts in connection with the conflict of political ideas encountered by Israel. Consequently, some have found strongly pro-monarchical ideology here, and others its converse in anti-monarchical protest. In what follows I will try to show that the political vision in the books is misread if one tries to force them in advance into apologia for one political agenda or another. Rather, they refrain from promoting any political programme as if it could be effective in itself. In the midst of an ever-changing political landscape, the narrative illustrates Yahweh's patience and grace in his dealings with Israel under all kinds of rule. At stake, however, is how far Israel can model the politics of God as portrayed in Genesis–Deuteronomy.

The following treatment of the books from Joshua to Kings will attempt to show how the main themes identified in our study so far are developed in each. The themes do not present uniformly in the various books, each having its own particular emphases. The treatments will accordingly vary in their organization and focus. However, in every case we shall consider how the main themes we have identified are developed, namely: a) the universal creation-horizon of the mission of Israel to establish Yahweh's justice on earth, b) the manner of the exercise of human power in relation to Yahweh's rule, and c) the progress of Israel itself as Yahweh's covenant-partner and a nation under *torah*.

2. *Towards Fulfilment of the Creation-Mandate*

The book of Joshua presents serious problems to the reader. In recording Israel's overcoming of barriers to land-possession, it appears itself as a barrier to acceptance of the deuteronomic vision. If Deuteronomy contains a formula for nationhood that is in principle valid for all humanity as God's creation, how does that square with this narrative, which relates the beginning of Israel's life in the land in a decree that all the present inhabitants of the land, by definition not Israelite, should be subject to a 'ban of destruction'?

I have offered an initial response above.[1] The story of Israel's disengagement from Egypt and its entry to Canaan is part of the primary history's extended controversy with the political claims of the superpowers of Old Testament times. The crossing of the Sea, and now the Jordan, has echoes of mythological confrontations between the god and Chaos. Chaos threatens in the political realm as well as the natural. The political propositions unfolded in Deuteronomy are therefore set against imperial claims to rights of dominion, and the controversy is dramatized in the narratives of exodus and conquest.

This kind of understanding implies a reading of the book that does not simply take it at face value, namely as a story of conquest legitimating Israelite possession of territory. One such reading is to regard its story of conquest and annihilation as metaphorical, a lightly coded message about rigorous faithfulness to Yahweh in a society that was in reality an ethnic and religious mix.[2] In my view, this resort to metaphor does not quite capture the book's strong political thrust. The themes of war, nationhood and land can hardly be elided from Joshua, and a metaphorical approach runs the risk of doing this. Joshua *is* the story of how Israel came to possess its land, and as such it is a necessary part of the narrative from Exodus to Kings.

However, to make sense of Joshua it is necessary to read it on different levels. In its character as an echo of the mythological conflict between God and Chaos it forecloses an interpretation of the book as a warrant for wars of dispossession. However, it is in fact the narrative of a war of dispossession, conceived in the terms of the realization (or not) of the deuteronomic programme for land-occupation. At this level, the reader is asked to accept provisionally the assumptions of the narrative, namely that it is right for Israel to expel the nations from Canaan. By the same token, failure to expel the Canaanites completely is a mark of failure to realize the project of covenantal obedience. In this perspective, the gap between the goal that Israel's possession of the land aims at and the reality achieved is stressed from the start.[3] In Joshua's words to Israel at Shechem: 'You cannot serve the LORD, for he is a holy God. He will not forgive your transgressions or your sins' (Josh. 24.19). This note concerning Israel's inability to keep the covenantal requirements joins that theme that has run through the story since the first account of the Golden Calf apostasy (Exodus 32–34), reinforced in Deut. 9.4–10.11, and sounded again in the Song of Moses (Exodus 32). The story of Joshua becomes the first instalment in an account that displays the discrepancy between Israel's vocation and its actual performance.

Joshua is, therefore, a victory over Chaos, affirming Yahweh's rule in the world and his resolve to liberate from tyrannical power. Correspondingly, the incompleteness of the conquest signifies the ongoing struggle to make this a reality, a struggle which will continue in the life of Israel after Joshua. But it also

1. In Chapter 2.

2. See, for example, Moberly 'Towards an Interpretation of the Shema', pp. 133–7.

3. Going somewhat further than this, Daniel Hawk sees a strong ironic undercurrent in Joshua, which deconstructs an ostensibly nationalistic project: *Joshua* (Berit Olam; Collegeville, MN; Liturgical Press, 2000).

functions to account for realities of life in the land. Land is indeed possessed, yet Israel must co-exist with other entities which do not share the same fundamental commitments. There is a kind of political realism in this. Individual stories, notably that of Rahab to which we turn in a moment, enshrine these ambiguities.

a. *Fulfilment and Non-Fulfilment*
In Joshua, fulfilment of the commands and promises proffered in Deuteronomy is held in tension with their non-fulfilment. In the story viewed as one of fulfilment, Israel enters the land that Yahweh promised to give, overcomes enemies, in large measure possesses it, and settles in it. Yahweh is 'with' Joshua in this, as he was with Moses (Deut. 31.7; Josh. 1.5, cf. Exod. 3.12), and his leadership is a model of faithfulness to Yahweh and obedience to *torah* (1.8; 24.15b). In places, the possession of land is portrayed in ways that suggest unqualified success (11.23; 18.1; 21.44–45). This picture of complete possession has a significant function, since it affirms a realization of God's purpose for his people, even if that realization should prove to be not yet. The glimpses of fulfilment have in effect something anticipatory about them.

Indeed, the prospect of Israel's possession of land contains a close echo of another prospect, namely the creation-mandate to 'subdue the earth' (Gen. 1.28). We recall the semantics of 'land/earth' (*'erets, 'adamah*) in Hebrew, such that 'land' and 'earth' always lie conceptually close, since the two terms can both apply to each,[4] depending on context. Josh. 18.1 is one of those texts that depict the land as completely possessed. There, the 'whole congregation of the Israelites' assemble at Shiloh and erect the Tent of Meeting. The terms used hark back to the Pentateuchal narrative on a broad canvas.[5] Most strikingly, this is a first realization of the deuteronomic command to 'seek the place that the LORD your God will choose, out of all your tribes, to put his name there as its dwelling-place' (Deut. 12.5). In this cameo of fulfilment, not only is the land possessed, but Israel is constituted as the assembly of Yahweh's covenant people united in his worship at a single sanctuary that corresponds to their integrity as a people. The importance of Shiloh in this respect is further emphasized in the story in Joshua 22, when the Transjordanian tribes are suspected of defecting from the tribal federation because they have erected an altar at the Jordan. The issue there turns on whether their altar is a fully-fledged place of worship, or in contrast a memorial to the full inclusion of those tribes in Israel (Josh. 22.22–29). Shiloh continues, in the story of Israel's early days in the land, to be the only place that counts as a worship-centre for the whole people (Judg. 18.31; 1 Samuel 1–3). It also enters the biblical record in Jeremiah, where it is remembered, in Yahweh's words, as the place 'where I made my name dwell at first' (Jer. 7.12).

To this picture of Israel entering upon its destiny as God's people in God's land is now added the phrase: 'The land lay subdued before them'. At one level

---

4.   We recall the Edenic overtones of the bountiful descriptions of the land in Deuteronomy: Deut. 8.7–10; 11.9–12.

5.   The terms used (עדה and קהל) draw on Priestly and deuteronomic strands respectively; the Tent of Meeting appears across the Pentateuchal strands, more in P than in Deuteronomy.

this asserts that the land of Canaan is fully possessed. But because 'land' can also connote 'earth', and because the word translated 'subdued' here is the very word by which God commissions the first humans to 'subdue the earth' (כבש, Gen. 1.28), it is strongly implied that Israel's possession of Canaan – itself realized only in anticipation – is an earnest of yet another possession, the realization of humanity's mandate to 'have dominion' over the creation. This intimation of an eschatological destiny of humanity lends to Joshua an aspect of provisionality that goes beyond the deferred hope of Israel's own full possession of Canaan.

However, the account has much on the debit side. Against the texts that announce a complete possession must be placed those which convey the opposite impression. The basic discrepancy is signalled by Josh. 13.1, with its surprising information that in Joshua's old age much land remained to be taken, in spite of the categorical notice in 11.23. It continues with the repeated admissions that the various tribes were not able to occupy their assigned territories fully (13.13; 15.63; 16.16. 17.12–13, cf. 19.40–48). The picture in these texts coheres with the beginning of Judges, where, after the death of Joshua, the war against the Canaanites still requires to be undertaken (Judg. 1.1). The dissonance was at one time considered as a discrepancy between Joshua and Judges, but in reality it exists within Joshua. Redactional-critical accounts find divergent strands in the composition of the book, representing more and less positive accounts of the possession of the land, and attitudes to the fact of Yahwistic Israel's cohabitation with non-Yahwists.[6] Theologically, however, it is likely that such divergent views have been allowed to stand together in order to affirm both that the land has been given by Yahweh, the victory over the forces of Chaos definitively won, and that due possession of land remains a project, in an ongoing struggle to realize the divine order on the earth.

b. *The Creation Mandate, and Political Realism*
The purpose of an Israelite nation to dispossess Canaanites and occupy the land purely and exclusively encounters a difficulty at the outset. A new expedition of spies finds itself dependent upon the inside knowledge and good graces of Rahab, a Canaanite prostitute, who protects the Israelites from the king of Jericho (Joshua 2). In familiar deuteronomic terms, she confesses faith in the God of Israel and his project to give them the land, and asks to be spared along with her family when the city falls (2.9–13). The prominence of this episode in the narrative corresponds to its significance, yet it resists a simple reading, having many of the ambiguities noted above. In terms of the conflict with chaotic power, Israel fails in its purpose by sparing Rahab. The very circumstances in which

---

6. The modern classic is R. Smend, 'Das Gesetz und die Völker: ein Beitrag zur deuter-onomistischen Redaktionsgeschichte', in H. W. Wolff (ed.), *Probleme biblischer Theologie: Festschrift Gerhard von Rad* (Munich: Chr. Kaiser, 1971), pp. 494–509, translated as 'The Law and the Nations: a Contribution to Deuteronomistic Tradition History', in G. N. Knoppers and J. G. McConville (eds.), *Reconsidering Israel and Judah* (SBTS; Winona Lake: Eisenbrauns, 2002), pp. 95–110; see also G. Mitchell, *Together in the Land: A Reading of the Book of Joshua* (JSOTSup, 134; Sheffield; Sheffield Academic Press, 1993).

Israelite spies become helplessly dependent on this Canaanite prostitute are in themselves disconcerting. If Yahweh has determined to give Canaan to Israel according to deuteronomic promise, how is it that their success in taking it depends on making a deal with Rahab not to give the game away to the king of Jericho (Josh. 2.12–14)? Rahab, as Canaanite and prostitute, is doubly estranged from the ideal of an uncontaminated Israel, standing pointedly for the temptation to apostasy, in spite of her confession of faith in Yahweh.[7] The deuteronomic injunction to 'utterly destroy them, make no covenant with them, and show them no mercy' (Deut. 7.2–3) is disarmed already on the threshold. When Rahab is spared, together with all in her house, we are told: 'Her family has lived in Israel ever since' (Josh. 6.25), and this without indication as to whether they became assimilated Israelites, let alone Yahwists. The sparing of Rahab is a setback in the contest with the forces of Chaos.

At the realistic narrative level, the encounter with Rahab illustrates the difficulties and compromises of political life. Israel seems to be drawn inexorably into its entanglement with her. Her very confession of faith in Yahweh the God of Israel, in a voice very similar to the dominant voice of the narrative (Josh. 2.9–11), is part of this entanglement. Can it be taken at its face-value, or is it the ingenious ploy of one who sees which way the wind is blowing and changes allegiance judiciously? In terms of the larger narrative context, the confession rings true. As the soothsayer Balaam knew that he could not oppose the forward march of Israel (Numbers 22–24), so does this Canaanite. We do not need to resort to the grim device of supposing that any Canaanite could escape the coming massacre by converting to Yahwism. In Rahab we see again that Yahweh's purpose is recognizable even to non-Israelites as one that has ramifications beyond Israel itself. If the story of Rahab is from one angle a defeat, from another it re-affirms the creation horizon of Yahweh's purpose in his deliverance of Israel.

As a story of politics, it is also multivalent. First, it speaks of the compromises entailed in political realism. Historically, Israel was never alone in the land, but the peoples of Israel and Canaan commingled, as did the religion of Yahweh with that of other gods. The story of Rahab testifies to this fact of Israel's life. It too can be put positively, however, showing that those who are not Israelite by descent may yet participate in Israel. Obliquely, the story of Rahab throws the accent from ethnicity on to politics. The inhabitants of the land won by Israel are and will be a 'mixed multitude', like those who came out of Egypt (Exod. 12.38). The equation of nationhood with ethnicity, which we found to be negated by the political vision of Deuteronomy, is precluded here too.

This reading is borne out by Joshua's treatment of the Gibeonites (Joshua 9). In this case the subterfuge lies more visibly on the surface. There is no confession of Yahweh, nor pretence of assimilation. Rather, Israel is caught between the obligations of the ban on one hand and the covenant with Gibeon on the

---

7.   For Hawk the confession can be read as an entrapment of the already compromised Israelites; *Joshua*, pp. 41, 44–6.

other, even though they have been duped into making it. The Gibeonites, living alongside them, illustrate the ambivalences of the life of Israel as a nation, their subjugation as servants of the Yahweh-sanctuary an ironic memorial to the imperfect equation between people (as ethnicity) and land. The story is a further illustration of the realities of politics, where decisions and compromises may be neither wholly good nor wholly bad.

There is in Joshua no 'end of history' in a nationalistic triumph. In the story that unfolds from Deuteronomy to Samuel, the expected 'rest' is postponed until the greater victories of David, who subdues the Philistines and takes Jerusalem (2 Sam. 7.1). But even that introduces a new phase which brings its own complications; there too, the end is not yet.

Joshua's enigmatic pronouncement that Israel 'cannot serve the LORD' (Josh. 24.19) is illuminated in part by the entanglement of Israel with Canaan. Such entanglement carries with it on one hand an implication of imperfect attachment to Yahweh, which will be fully exposed in the sequel in Judges. Israel's historic calling, to be a nation that witnesses to other nations, stands over this reality, though remaining an unrealized ideal. Meanwhile, a realistic story still unfolds, in which the possibilities involved in political power continue to be aired.

2. *The Exercise of Power*

However, the relationship between Deuteronomy and Joshua is complex and not mere negation. Both the promises and the obligations stressed at length in Deuteronomy find a real continuity here. With all the qualifications we have entered, the land is possessed and distributed to the tribes, so that at least in principle the project of establishing the people in the land, bound by *torah*-constitution, goes forward. If there is no nationalistic triumph nor 'end of history' here, there remains a question of how Israel is depicted as organizing itself as a nation. And there is a positive beginning here, not least that in Joshua Israel occupies a bordered land, according to the deuteronomic mandate; it is not a recipe for unlimited expansion in the Assyrian fashion.

But we turn now to consider how far Joshua puts into practice the deuteronomic charter for the administration of Israel.

a. *Joshua in 'Constitution'*
The figure of Joshua himself is crucial to the politics of the book of Joshua. Our understanding of the book, and its contribution to the political vision of Genesis–Kings, depends to a large extent on how Joshua himself is understood. He is in certain respects like Moses, judges and kings, by virtue of his leadership of Israel, his conquests and his imposition of *torah*. But in what way does Joshua represent a political ideal? In particular, is he a type of future kings, as supposed in the 'Josianic' model of interpreting Deuteronomy–Kings?

We look first at the resemblances between Joshua and Moses. His appointment to lead Israel after the death of Moses (Num. 27.12–23) suggests a certain correspondence between this succession and Eleazar's succession to Aaron. Each leads

Israel miraculously across a body of water (Reed Sea, Jordan, 4.23); each leads in the conquest and distribution of the land (Josh. 12.1–6 and 13.8–33 recall Moses' role east of the Jordan). Each is entitled to the allegiance of all the tribes, as shown by the Transjordanians' pledge to obey Joshua just as they had obeyed Moses (Josh. 1.16–18). Moses writes his words in the 'book of the law' (Deut. 31.9), and Joshua reaffirms this as his own rule and that of the people (Josh. 1.7–8; 8.32); in doing so, he is even associated with the writing in a certain sense (Josh. 24.25–26, cf. Exod. 17.14).[8] And he receives the personal assurance from Yahweh 'I will be with you' (Deut. 31.7; Josh. 1.5), as Moses did (Exod. 3.12). Because of such resemblances, Weinfeld believed Moses and Joshua stood at the head of a line that led to David and Solomon and to the kings following them. Citing Josh. 1.7–8; 8.30–35; 22.5; 23.6, he says. '…it seems that the Dtr could not conceive of the implementation of the moral law contained in the "book of the *torah*" in the absence of the monarchy or of a quasi-regal figure like Joshua'.[9]

As for Joshua and Josiah, both are charged to think and act according to *torah*, Joshua when he assumes the leadership (Josh. 1.7–8) and Josiah according to the deuteronomic law of the king (Deut. 17.18–20).[10] Each will have success as a result: Joshua possesses the promised land by conquest, and Josiah repossesses the lost northern territory (at least symbolically). Each leads in great acts of covenant renewal (Josh. 8.30–35; 24; 2 Kgs 23.1–3). Each celebrates a Passover (Joshua, the first in the land, Josh. 5.10–12; Josiah, the first since 'the days of the judges', 2 Kgs 23.22[11]), and warns against contamination of true Yahweh worship with that of foreign gods. In addition, Yahweh's charge to Joshua is like David's to Solomon (1 Kgs 2.2–4). These resemblances can hardly be accidental, and are widely attributed to a redactional purpose to highlight them.[12]

In spite of such similarities, Joshua is not quite like either Moses or Josiah. As Schäfer-Lichtenberger has shown, the Joshua narratives from Exodus to Joshua carefully subordinate him to Moses. Characterized from the beginning as his 'servant' (משרת, Exod. 24.13), he is commissioned by Moses before Eleazar and 'all the congregation' to lead the people in war (Num. 27.16–23). Moses, indeed, is to invest him with '*some* of your authority' (מהודך, v. 20), as if to emphasize that he will succeed Moses only in a limited way and for a specified purpose, namely to lead the people into the land.[13] His role is military, and his relation to

---

8. See Schäfer-Lichtenberger, *Josua und Salomo*, pp. 109–10, 116. See also R. D. Nelson, *Joshua* (OTL; Louisville: WJK, 1997), pp. 21–2.

9. M. Weinfeld, *Deuteronomy and the Deuteronomic School*, pp. 170–1.

10. Nelson observes that the phrase 'a copy of the law' in Josh. 8.32 occurs only here and in Deut. 17.18, in the 'law of the king'; Nelson, *Joshua*, p. 119.

11. No celebration of the Passover is recorded in DtrH between Joshua and Josiah.

12. For Marvin Sweeney, Joshua 1 and 23 are the product of redaction designed to establish the analogy between Joshua and Josiah (partly following Smend, eg on 1.7–9), Sweeney, *King Josiah of Judah: The Lost Messiah of Israel* (Oxford: Oxford University Press, 2001), p. 135. Nelson's thesis owes more to the concept of a Josianic edition of DtrH.

13. Schäfer-Lichtenberger, *Josua und Salomo*, pp. 140–62 (157). Schäfer-Lichtenberger thinks that Joshua becomes more independent in P (p. 141), but that nevertheless he always remains subordinate to Moses in the tradition.

the *torah* is different from Moses', in that, while Moses concludes the Moab covenant, Joshua will be bound by the *torah*-constitution.[14] Nor does Joshua have the
same independence in his authority that Moses had. While both leaders 'cause
[part of Israel] to inherit' land (נחל, pi.),[15] Joshua does so in conjunction with
Eleazar the priest and 'the heads of the fathers' houses of the tribes of the Israelites' (Josh. 14.1; 19.51),[16] in accordance with Num. 34.16–29.[17] Similarly in 21.1,
'the heads of the families of the Levites' come to these same authorities to claim
their special type of inheritance. Furthermore, when Joshua is mentioned in this
connection, it is invariably Eleazar who is named first.[18]

Joshua's final act in the story of land-distribution involves a role-reversal in
which 'the Israelites' give (נתן) an inheritance (נחלה) to Joshua (19.49).[19] And,
his work done, he goes to Timnat-Serah, 'in the hill-country of Ephraim', and
settles there, one Israelite among many (19.50). While Joshua still has work to do
(chs 20–24), there is a provisional climax of the book here (19.49), because it is
the last word on the distribution to tribes in itself (apart from the summarizing
19.51).

In this sequence Joshua's role in the distribution is clearly limited. Joshua is
subordinated to Eleazar, and both are bound into 'a college of tribal representa-
tives'.[20] Joshua's role in the 'giving' of land is therefore qualitatively different
from that of Moses. Schäfer-Lichtenberger draws the important inference: 'Viewed
in this way, Moses the monocrat has no successor *as monocrat*'.[21] We shall see
too that Joshua's succession is not merely limited, but determined by the larger
deuteronomic vision of authority in Israel after Moses.

b. *Joshua a Royal Figure?*
If Joshua is like Moses only in a limited way, does he, as many have thought,
typologically foreshadow the kings, especially Josiah? The narrative from Joshua
to Kings is often thought to be subordinate to a redaction that promotes the
programme of the Josianic reform. For R. D. Nelson, Joshua is 'a thinly dis-
guised Josianic figure'.[22] Here too, however, the match is by no means perfect.[23]

---

14. Schäfer-Lichtenberger, *Josua und Salomo*, pp. 173–5.

15. Josh. 13.32 (Moses); 14.1–2; 19.51 (Joshua).

16. The composition of the body of leaders with whom Joshua supervises the distribution is
expressed slightly differently in these two texts, but presumably designates the same group of people.
The translation here follows NRSV.

17. The verb in Num. 34.29 is נחל pi., and probably also in vv. 17–18 (*contra* MT).

18. Num. 32.28; 34.17; Josh. 14.1; 17.4; 19.51; 21.1.

19. This usage, נתן plus נחלה, is as in 13.8, when it is applied to Moses.

20. Schäfer-Lichtenberger, *Josua und Salomo*, p. 163 ('ein Kollegium von Stammesvertretern').

21. 'So betrachtet, hat der Monokrat Moses als Monokrat keinen Nachfolger', Schäfer-Lichtenberger, *Josua und Salomo*, p. 163.

22. R. D. Nelson, 'Josiah in the Book of Joshua', *JBL* 100 (1981), pp. 531–40 (540). In his recent
commentary he describes him as 'a royal figure, one who particularly resembles Josiah', *Joshua*,
p. 21.

23. The thesis that Joshua is a royal figure can hang on slender exegetical threads. Josh. 8.32 is a
case in point, in which Joshua writes on the stone altar on Mt. Ebal 'a copy of the law of Moses,

The constitutional tendencies just observed provide an initial caution, as does the fact that Joshua conspicuously refrains from bequeathing his authority to any successor, but in retirement takes his place quietly among the rank and file of Israel. The Book of Joshua, moreover, has nothing to say explicitly about kingship, and indeed has been found to tell against it. The covenant-renewal in Josh. 24, for example, can be read as an assertion that God alone is 'king' in Israel, and not a human king.[24] For Konrad Schmid, Josh. 24 'allows everything that follows, especially the period of the kings – at least in principle – to appear in a negative light'.[25]

Hesitations about seeing Joshua as a type of Josiah are borne out by a consideration of his actual typological profile in Joshua–Kings. Given his prominence in the crucial phase of settlement in the land, it is astonishing to find that after Judg. 2.21 he is mentioned only once more in Judges–Kings (at 1 Kgs 16.34). At times, indeed, he even seems to have been overlooked. In several texts in Samuel–Kings the achievement of Joshua might have attracted notice but has not. In Samuel's recollection of the formative events in Israel's life in 1 Samuel 12, Joshua is twice conspicuously absent. In v. 8, Moses and Aaron are credited with both the exodus and the conquest, in contrast to Josh. 24.5, where their work is limited to the exodus. And in v. 11 the next phase after Moses and Aaron is recalled and includes a number of judges up to Samuel himself and once again Joshua does not appear. Somewhat later, Joshua is again unnoticed in the account

which he had written'. In Nelson's interpretation, the phrase 'which he had written' refers to a copy of the law which *Joshua* had written, in obedience to Deut. 17.18, a concept which thus portrays Joshua as a royal figure: 'Joshua is here portrayed as a royal figure leading a ceremony of covenant renewal' (*Joshua*, p. 119). Nelson notes the textual doubt about the phrase אשר כתב ('which he had written', NRSV), and thinks that its omission in LXX[B] was not original in OG, because 'The reference to Joshua's obedience to Deut. 17.18 was not understood and dropped as awkward' (p. 116). However, it seems strained to find a reference here to Joshua's having made his own copy of the law, and preferable to take the phrase to refer to *Moses*' having written the law. Noth, for example, deleting the phrase 'which he had written', as a poorly integrated gloss, says that it wants to relate the following 'before the Israelites' to Moses, not Joshua; Noth, *Josua* (HAT 1/7: Tübingen: Mohr, 1953), p. 50. Hawk, without emending, points to the passage's strong focus on Moses rather than Joshua; *Joshua*, pp. 131–2. Moreover, Nelson's interpretation, that the phrase refers to a writing that *Joshua* did, in obedience to Deut. 17.18, is not persuasive, since Joshua's writing of the 'copy of the law of Moses' appears to refer to the act of writing publicly on the stones, rather than to a personal copy that he had already written. There is no other indication that Joshua did such a thing; and Nelson's idea that Joshua is here 'reproducing his own personal copy of the law on the stones' (*Joshua*, p. 119) goes beyond what the text can bear.

    24. Konrad Schmid, as we have noticed, finds that Joshua rounds off a phase in the narrative of Genesis–Kings which he calls 'salvation-history' ('Heilsgeschichte'), while Judges–Kings then represent its opposite, 'judgement-history' ('Unheilsgeschichte'). He observes a link between Deut. 33.5 and Josh. 24.1, which implies that the insistence on Yahweh's kingship in the former text is carried into Josh. 24. The location of the ceremony in Shechem makes the scene a kind of anti-type of the later enthronement of Rehoboam there (1 Kings 12). And the motif of 'serving' (עבד) Yahweh strikes a polemical note against the 'serving' of kings; Schmid, *Erzväter und Exodus*, p. 212 and n. 248. This is reminiscent of the conflict over Israel's 'service' between Yahweh and Pharaoh in Exodus; see above, Chapter 4.

    25. Schmid, *Erzväter und Exodus*, pp. 211–12 (author's translation).

of Solomon's forced levy of the nations that Israel could not drive out of the land (1 Kgs 9.20–22). And finally, in connection with Josiah's Passover, it is said that 'no such Passover had been kept since the days of *the judges*', where the only Passover recorded in the narrative is that of Joshua (Josh. 5.10–12). The typology of leadership suggested by this evidence is that Yahweh dealt first with Israel through Moses and Aaron, then with judges (including Samuel), and finally with kings. Joshua finds no place in it.[26]

In the book of Joshua itself, and the opening chapters of Judges, Joshua is included with the faithful generation that had grown up in the wilderness (Josh. 24.31; Judg. 2.7–10), and so distinguished from the generations that were born in the land.[27] Joshua thus stands both with Moses' generation, which did not see the land, and the succeeding one that did. Joshua–Judges has a distinctive typology, therefore, when compared with Samuel–Kings. But here too his significance is confined largely to the narrative in the book that bears his name. Joshua has no strong typological significance for the story beyond that book.

c. *Israel Under Torah*
If Joshua is not a mere type of something else (such as kingship), does he represent something distinctive in the life and governance of Israel? If not monarchy, then what? The 'exilic' readings take us in a certain direction. The monarchic experiment is over; Israel must now find new ways of being Israel. The post-exilic community finds its identity in a hostile world by telling the stories of its past. To say this, however, leaves much open. Does the negative judgement on kingship mark a turning away from what in Dietrich's terms are all forms of state-controlled existence? He writes: 'the author of [Deut. 17.18–20] does not care about the realities of the control of a state…he who wants kings only in the context envisaged here in fact does not want kings'.[28] And this is taken to mean no mode of existence as a state. Or should we look for actual political models? The ingredients in Joshua – law, land, people – would encourage this.[29]

---

26. A possible redactional answer is to suppose a pre-deuteronomic tradition in which Moses and Aaron were the conquerors, not Joshua; noted in R. P. Gordon, *1 and 2 Samuel* (Exeter: Paternoster Press, 1986), pp. 127–8, 342; cf. R. W. Klein *1 Samuel* (WBC; Waco, TX: Word Books, 1983), p. 116.

27. This faithful generation is the same as that which was too young to fight at the time of the exodus, or was born in the wilderness (Num. 14.29; Deut. 2.14; cf. Josh. 5.4–7), Joshua and Caleb being an exception to this (Num. 14.30). It is thus the same as the new generation of Deuteronomy, which enters into covenant at Moab (Deut. 26.16–19).

28. W. Dietrich, 'History and Law. Deuteronomistic Historiography and Deuteronomic Law Exemplified in the Passage from the Period of the Judges to the Monarchical Period', in A. de Pury. Thomas Römer and Jean-Daniel Macchi (eds.), *Israel Constructs its History: Deuteronomistic Historiography in Recent Research* (JSOTSup, 306; Sheffield. Sheffield Academic Press, English language edition, 2000), pp. 315–42 (342).

29. There is some strongly political language among those who find anti-monarchical tendencies in DtrH, e.g. Françoise Smyth: 'the king is dead, long live the new people…!', 'When Josiah has Done his Work or the King is Properly Buried: a Synchronic Reading of 2 Kings 22.1–23.28', in de Pury *et al.* (eds.), *Israel*, pp.343–58, (358). See also p. 348 n. 2, where she points to the *people* as the celebrants of Josiah's Passover.

What indications are there in Joshua? Certainly the Canaanite kings appear in an unfavourable light. It is striking that the resumptive ch. 12 offers us a catalogue of *kings* conquered by Moses and Joshua, and it is possible that this is more than a list of conquered Canaanites, but implies a critique of a kind of political organization. The Rahab narrative is another example, where the King of Jericho is easily duped, and the readiness of Rahab to collaborate with the invader may indicate a 'populist' sympathy. Nelson thinks it 'a typological antiestablishment story'.[30] And his terms are highly political: 'The landless gain land (the word itself is used seven times) and a marginal group traced back to a prostitute acquires a future. The Rahab clan and the peasant class in Israel, both at odds with centralized power structures, would each have had a reason to enjoy this story'.[31] If such an orientation is indeed present, it could be explained as a relic, unrepresentative of the book's dominant view, the story functioning simply as an explanation of foreign or non-Yahwistic elements among Israelites. So we need to look further, and take a different tack. What organization of Israel does the book exhibit?

In answer to this question, we look again at Joshua in relation to other agents. We have already observed that, in the distribution of the land, Joshua operates alongside the priest Eleazar and the heads of the tribes (in this respect unlike Moses). Two distinct authorities thus join Joshua the military leader in the central action of the book, the 'causing to inherit', namely the religious and the tribal authorities. Can we find further evidence for the limitation of Joshua's authority, and (more importantly) for a developed concept of authority in Israel? Two passages are important, Joshua 9 and Joshua 24.

We have considered the Gibeonite episode above for its angle on the imperfect realization of Israel's possession of the land. It is also interesting, however, for the manner of the Israelites' negotiation with the Gibeonites (Joshua 9), well known for its shifting agents on the Israelite side. The story is heralded with a note about the kings in various parts of the land who gathered 'to fight Joshua and Israel' (v. 2). Then we have 'Joshua and the Israelites' (v. 6), 'the Israelites' (v. 7, 17–18), 'Joshua' (v. 8), 'the men' (MT) or 'leaders' (הנשׂיאים following LXX) (v. 14), 'the leaders of the congregation' (נשׂיאי העדה) (v. 15, 18), 'they' (v. 16), and 'all the congregation' (v. 18).[32] These are at times in close proximity (v. 15, 'Joshua' and 'the leaders of the congregation'), so that the distinctions can hardly pass unnoticed or be accidental. In fact, the agents act in relation to each other: '*the congregation*' enters into dialogue with '*the leaders*' (v. 18). *Joshua* made peace, but the *leaders* swore an oath (v. 15). The *leaders* decide to let the Gibeonites live (v. 21); but *Joshua* condemns them to be 'hewers of wood and drawers of water' (v. 23); however, *Joshua* saves them from the Israelites (v. 26).

Can we make sense of such variety among the agents? Some have seen it as a result of the tradition shifting the blame for the failure to implement the ban.

30. Nelson, *Joshua*, p. 45.
31. Nelson, *Joshua*, p. 45.
32. There is some textual uncertainty, perhaps reflecting early confusion over the various terms (e.g. v. 14).

Nelson observes this,[33] but he finds no satisfying explanation in these terms. It is not clear, in any case, that this is an 'embarrassed' narrative. Rather, it exhibits an established strain in the book, in which Israel does not drive out the inhabitants, and is arguably not alone in implying blame for this (cf. Rahab). So can we simply read it as it stands, to see if it tells us something about the structure of Israel that is presented as natural or desirable? Joshua exercises authority in conjunction with the 'leaders'. He sometimes acts as spokesman, at other times not, and he is finally the enforcer. The people are variously 'the Israelites', 'the congregation', and perhaps 'the men'. They seem to have their own voice and capacity to act. Joshua has to save the Gibeonites from 'the Israelites' (v. 26). This approach can be maintained more or less straightforwardly. The division Joshua-leaders-congregation is rational, and their respective parts in the action are more or less separately defined.[34] This fits with a pattern in the book which is also exemplified by the agents who distribute the land (Joshua, Eleazar, the 'heads of the tribes'). The same pattern may be found in the ceremonies in Josh. 8.30–35; 24.

Josh. 8.30–35 tells of the assembly of Israel at Shechem held in fulfilment of the command in Deuteronomy 27, with the law written on a stone altar, and the ceremony of blessing and curse. The passage is important because it represents Israel's commitment to the ongoing place of the law in its life (in its characterization of what Joshua writes as 'a copy of the law of Moses' [משנה תורת משה] it stands close to Deuteronomy 31 as well as Deuteronomy 27). But it is also important for its concept of the structure of Israel. Here a difference from Deuteronomy 27 is significant. In Deuteronomy 27 the two groups drawn up on Mts Ebal and Gerizim are composed of the tribes of Israel, while the Levites declared the covenantal curses (Deut. 27.12–14). In the ceremony in Josh. 8.30–35 Israel is portrayed, not according to its tribes, but in such a way as to highlight both the totality of the people and its individual and varied membership. It is 'the Israelites' on whom the responsibility for *torah*-obedience is laid (8.31); 'all Israel' stands as witness to the ceremony (v. 33), and then its composition is displayed as 'alien as well as citizen, with their elders and officers and judges' (v. 33), and again: 'all the assembly of Israel, and the women and the little ones, and the aliens who resided among them' (v. 35 NRSV].

There are several debts to Deuteronomy here, notably Deuteronomy 31.[35] This comes over in the individuation of Israel (cf. Deut. 31.11–12, 28), and in the name used for the 'assembly' (קהל), v. 35 (cf. Deut. 31.12, 28[36]). The covenant renewal in Deuteronomy 29 also supplies an interest in Israel as a totality of individuals (Deut. 29.9–10[10–11EVV] (Josh. 8.35 interestingly omits the phrase

---

33. Nelson, *Joshua*, p. 123.

34. One has to suppose that it makes sense that the speaker in the negotiation may be either 'Joshua' or 'the Israelites'.

35. 'DH has characteristically understood the whole event in terms of the public reading of the law in Deut. 31.9–12' (Nelson, *Joshua*, p. 118).

36. The form of קהל is verbal in these texts.

'those who cut your wood and those who draw your water' from Deut. 29.10[11] – the story of that is going to come next in Joshua!). And the 'elders, officials and judges' require comment (8.33). The 'elders and officials' are in Deut. 31.28, but the combination of 'judges and officials' comes from Deut. 16.18.

The narrative voice here has clearly reflected on passages in Deuteronomy that point to the shape of Israel's future organization. The *torah* has a unique place in that, but so too has the composition of the people. The regular reading of the law (Deuteronomy 31) is done in the context of the seven-yearly 'assembly' of the whole people. The judges and officials have their place in deuteronomic thought, as we have seen, within a carefully elaborated 'constitution', in which various agencies find a distinctive role (judge, priest, prophet), and which accommodates but does not require a king. 'Assembly', *torah* and officials all participate in the succession to Moses as the means by which Israel's life should be authoritatively led. In the ceremony at Ebal and Gerizim, Joshua presides over an event that symbolizes an Israel that can continue without Moses – and now also without himself.[37]

We consider finally Joshua 24. Joshua's covenant renewal is more focused on the people as such than on the individual who presides.[38] Josh. 24.1 (with its verbal links to Deut. 33.5, noted above), pictures Joshua gathering 'all the tribes of Israel' to Shechem (again), and summoning 'the elders, the heads, the judges, and the officers of Israel'. This list is an inclusive description of the leadership of Israel, juxtaposing classes of leader previously named together only at 23.2 (though 8.33 is close; the term 'leader' itself, נשׂיא, does not appear here.) Yet the address that follows is to 'all the people'. The impression is of the people in its internal organization and authority structures.

The role of Israel is highlighted by the structure of the narrative, which is carried forward by a dialogue between Joshua and the people. Joshua makes the covenant on their behalf (24.25).[39] Yet, the effect of the whole narrative is to emphasize that it is the people who enter the covenant. Joshua is rather elusively both of the people and apart from them. In his second-person address to them he seems to stand apart (e.g. 'you [pl.] cannot serve the LORD', v. 19). At times in the rhetoric he is with them, but then it is simply as one of them ('as for me and my household, we will serve the LORD', 24.15). This is close to saying 'I've done all I can', and the terms point to the composition of Israel as 'households'. We are a long way from Josiah here!

The outcome of the event is that Joshua sends the people to their 'inheritances' (and so their 'households'); he dies, and is buried on his ranch in Ephraim where he has already received his own inheritance, just like other Israelites. At the end of the book, Israel has concluded a covenant with God, and Joshua,

---

37. Note too that in the case of the accidental homicide, the accused eventually stands before the 'congregation' (עדה) for judgement (משפט, *mishpat*, Josh. 20.6), the only occurrence of this term in the sense of 'judgement' in the book).

38. There is a striking contrast with Josiah's covenant renewal (2 Kgs 23.1–3), where the ceremony centres strongly on the actions of the king.

39. The Hebrew is לעם, meaning ' "for" or "on behalf of" Israel'; Nelson, *Joshua*, p. 277.

without successor (except for 'judges'), has left them to it. The death of Joshua is as eloquent at the end of this book as was that of Moses in Deuteronomy. The issue is whether *Israel* will be faithful to the covenant. The terms in which this is framed are deuteronomic, not least in the deuteronomic view of time (v. 7. 'your eyes saw what I did to Egypt'; but also v. 6, 'your ancestors' – so the conflation of generations is explicit in the text). This concept of Israel as reliving in all generations its first entry into covenant is crucial in Deuteronomy. (Horeb, of course, is not mentioned here; yet the concept of Joshua 24 is similar to that of Deuteronomy 29, where the covenant at Moab is a re-realization of Horeb. As Moab, so Shechem.) We are back to 'succession', and the only projection beyond Joshua is of an Israel led by 'elders, heads, judges, officers', and presumably priests (Eleazar is not forgotten; 24.33).

3. *The Nation Possesses its Land*

We have seen so far that the story of Israel entering the land of Canaan is an earnest of humanity's 'subduing the land' according to the creation mandate, and that Israel begins to be a nation duly occupying land and committed to living in it under the *torah* of Yahweh. Does it therefore match up to the political vision outlined in Deuteronomy?

Deuteronomy, as we saw in the preceding chapter, gives us a programme for the existence of a 'nation' in its land. Land was a territory *in extenso*, bordered, and defined not by familial possession, but rather in terms of a whole people. 'Inheritance', applied to the nation, was a family metaphor lifted out of the family sphere. The people in turn, a 'brotherhood' of 'all Israel', was an entity above the levels of family, clan and tribe, political in the strict sense. The complex relationship between the 'centre' and distributed locations expressed the connection of the localities in a coherent whole. The *torah*-law was valid for the whole people throughout the land, and was administered by institutions, within whose framework the individual Israelite played his or her role as citizen.

Is this system consistent with the picture in Joshua? Clearly it is not *elucidated* here; that is the province of Deuteronomy itself. In some ways there is clear agreement. The unity of Israel is expressed in the crossing of the Jordan, the military-liturgical march at Jericho, the covenantal ceremonies (chs 8 and 24), the studied inclusion of the Transjordanian tribes, the capacity for Israel to speak, whether through its 'leaders', or in its own voice (as in Joshua 9), and the concepts of the 'congregation' (קהל and עדה) and 'all Israel' (7.25; 8.33).

The unity of Israel is also maintained in terms of the notion of a central 'place'. In Josh 9.27 'the place that [Yahweh] should choose' is undetermined, but considered to be established in principle. This 'centre' is not identified in a fixed way with a single place in Joshua. Rather, both Shiloh and Shechem function to symbolize the unity of Israel. Shiloh because the Tent of Meeting is there (18.1; 22); Shechem, because it is the place appointed for covenant-renewal (Deut. 11.29–30; 27).

The *bounded land* is described in detail in the apportionment to the tribes. The *law* is the *torah* of Moses, promulgated 'for' all Israel (24.25), Israel adopting responsibility for obedience to it (Josh. 8.30–35; 24); and its 'reach' is the bor-dered land described in chs 13–19. The *institutions* appear, if not systematically (priest Eleazar; judges and officers, 24.1).[40] Joshua, as we saw, does not bear sole power.

The sticking-point may be on 'inheritance', for the usage in Joshua differs from that in Deuteronomy. Here, indeed, it is principally applied to the tribes (themselves in the background in Deuteronomy) and their separate and individual portions within the land, meticulously catalogued in chs 13–19. Is this a devia-tion from the unified concept in Deuteronomy? Such is the view of Carrière, who finds in Joshua a distinct usage, properly 'Deuteronomistic' (as distinct from 'deuteronomic'), in which 'inheritance' still means land assigned to a tribe or family, and therefore on his definitions not 'national'.[41] In fact he finds in the Historical Books a mixture of the 'Dtr' outlook,[42] and the idea of the 'inheri-tance' (נחלה) as the whole land (1 Sam. 10.1; 26.19), and concludes that this is evidence for the gradual emergence of the 'national' idea. Joshua is thus pre-cisely bracketed out of such a development. Carrière, citing 14.2, thinks Joshua manifests an idea according to which tribes receive 'the nearest land by God's gift'. 'Other groups, later, receive their inheritance too' (Dan, Judg. 18.1; Benja-min, Judg. 21.21, 24).[43]

But is the relationship between Joshua and Deuteronomy really as he claims? It is true that most occurrences of the verb 'inherit' (נחל qal: Josh. 16.4; 17.6; 19.9, 49[MT]) refer to the inheriting of individual tribes. However, in my view Josh. 14.1–2 should be read differently from Carrière. There it is the Israelites who 'inherit' (ואלה אשר־נחלו בני־ישראל); they do so 'in the land of Canaan', so that the whole people is set within the horizon of the full extent of the land; and in a piel usage of נחל, 'inherit', corresponding to the initial qal, Eleazar, Joshua and 'the heads of the families of the tribes of the Israelites' 'make them inherit' (אשר נחלו אותם). This precisely makes it an 'inheriting' of all the land on the part of all Israel, by the political authorities in Israel.

This passage, then, by no means suggests a piecemeal inheritance of disparate, proximate tracts of land. This is not a concept of land-possession according to which tribes take hold of the 'the nearest bit', but rather the several territories are apportioned by lot, in a systematic procedure by which the whole land came to be possessed by the constituent parts of Israel. This systematic picture takes account of the Transjordanian part of the whole land (14.2–4, following ch. 13), and also the fact that the Levites receive no 'inheritance', since Yahweh is their 'inheri-tance' (in accordance with Deut. 10.9; 18.2, as well as Num. 18.20. These texts, incidentally, require some such development as we find in Joshua 14–19). Finally, to make sure we get the point, 14.5 declares that 'the Israelites did as Yahweh commanded Moses, and allotted the land'.

---

40. Joshua himself has some affinities with the prophet. Yahweh speaks to him, and he is told not to fear, Josh. 1.9, cf. Jer. 1.17.

41. Carrière, *La théorie du politique*, p. 223.

42. This is represented, for example, by the Naboth story, 1 Kings 21, and the incident in which a woman of Tekoa is sent by Joab to David, 2 Sam. 14.16; Carrière, *La théorie du politique*, p. 224.

43. 'la possession de la terre proche du don par YHWH'; Carrière, *La théorie du politique*, p. 223.

As Josh. 14.1–2 introduces the section on the inheritances in Cisjordan, so 19.51 rounds it off. Here we have the individual 'inheritances' (הנחלת), together with the piel usage of the verb as in 14.1, in which Eleazar, Joshua and the tribal heads 'make the Israelites inherit'. And, in a precise echo of 14.5, 'So they finished dividing the land'. The all-Israel character of the entire event of the distribution is further reinforced by the fact that the 'making inherit' (often weakened in translation into 'distribution) happened 'at Shiloh, before the LORD, at the entrance to the tent of meeting'. The narrative of the inheritance therefore matches the claims about conquest in 11.23 and 12.7.[44]

It follows that Joshua conceives the inheriting of individual territories by the tribes *as* the inheriting of the whole land by Israel. They are one and the same. How should we think of this in relation to Deuteronomy? First, it is consistent with Deut. 10.9; 18.2, as suggested a moment ago. Second, the polarization between a 'deuteronomic' concept of 'inheritance' as relating to the whole territory and a 'Deuteronomistic' concept of it as relating to individual territories overinterprets Deuteronomy on the point. Deuteronomy exhibits both perspectives in Deut. 19.14, for example, where the 'thou'-address is directed to the individual and to Israel in such a way that the two cannot be separated.[45]

Moreover, the tribes do not disappear in that book, but merely retreat, to reappear, not least, in Deuteronomy 33. This chapter (which we have already found to link with Joshua – 33.5 with 24.1)[46] portrays Israel's possession of the land as a whole: it rehearses their common history (vv. 2–4), the giving of the law (v. 4), and portrays the people as an 'assembly' (קהלה, v. 4); it uses the telling phrase 'the totality of the tribes of Israel' (יחד שבטי ישראל, v. 5) in apposition to 'the heads of the people' (ראשי עם); it knows of Levi's responsibility to teach Yahweh's 'statutes' (משפטים) to Jacob, and his *torah* to Israel; it frames the poem at beginning and end with invocations of the united people, using the names Israel and Jacob, as well as the unusual Jeshurun (vv. 5, 26). On the other hand, the body of the poem portrays the possession of the land in its parts by the tribes. Here as in Joshua, therefore, the idea of possession of the whole land by

---

44. In fact, Carriere's polarization can hardly be found anywhere. The usage in Joshua has antecedents in Exodus–Numbers, in both JE and P texts. Here we find Israel, the tribes, individuals, the Transjordanians 'inheriting' (Exod. 23.30 – J; 32.13 – J; Num. 18.20, 23–24 (of the Levites *not* inheriting); Num. 26.55 (P - of each tribe inheriting a נחלה); Num. 32.19 (JE – of the Transjordanians inheriting their נחלה beyond Jordan; here the נחלה of Reuben and Gad is expressed as one); Num. 34.17–18 (29) (P) Joshua, Eleazar and the leaders will 'inherit' (נחל) the land 'for you' לכם (!). This last (34.17–18) is interesting because it puts the separate inheritings under the umbrella of Joshua, Eleazar and the tribal heads 'inheriting' the *land*. Moreover, it is this concept – Joshua together with Eleazar and heads of tribes – that is taken up in Joshua. It may be questioned whether the verbs in vv. 17, 18 are really qal, in view of the piel in v. 29). However, the qal may survive scrutiny because of the different syntax in vv. 17–18 compared with v. 29. These observations show that there is no obvious documentary development. Both JE and P have inheriting both as a whole and in parts.

45. This potential of the second-person singular address is typical of Deuteronomy; see McConville, 'Singular Address'.

46. See above, n. 24.

the whole people is held to be expressed by the possession of the parts by the parts. Deuteronomy 33 manifests the deuteronomic political vision *in nuce*. In precisely *this* context it exalts Yahweh as 'king in Jeshurun' (as I take 33.5). And it is practically an overture to the book of Joshua.

Finally, the convergence of perspectives in (Deuteronomy and) Joshua, the whole and the part, seems to me to be in keeping with the deuteronomic reckoning with the relationship between distributed locations and centre. Indeed it precisely works out that concept in the context of the narrative of possession of the land. This is the significance of placing the 'causing to inherit' at Shiloh, the location of the Tent of Meeting, the leading unifying symbol of land and people. For Israel to possess 'the land' *means* that, for example Judah, towards the boundary of Edom, possesses Kabzeel, Edur, Jagur – and so on (Josh. 15.21). The careful listing is a conferring of political significance on the obscure and remote. The same double focus on the land and its parts also explains the concern to splice the inheriting of land in Cisjordan with that in Transjordan under Moses (Joshua 13; 14.1–5). The narratives in Deuteronomy 1–3, therefore, together with the explanation about Levi's not inheriting 'with his brothers', create an expectation of precisely what we find in Joshua 14–19. In the book of Joshua, a *politeia* is worked out in practice.[47]

4. *Conclusion*

The book of Joshua begins to apply the political vision of Deuteronomy in practice to Israel as it now occupies its land. It shows awareness as it does so that the project has dimensions that go beyond the ambitions of a single nation, but rather partakes of the creational purpose that we have observed for God's chosen people since Genesis. When Israel gathers at Shiloh at the Tent of Meeting (18.1) we have an anticipatory glimpse of humanity's fulfilling of its creation goal of 'subduing of the earth', that is, ruling for the benefit of all creatures. The conflict with the Canaanites, on the surface contradicting the notion of a mission of Israel to the nations, is more profoundly a dramatization of the conflict with Chaos in the political sphere, in this sense resembling the confrontation between Moses and Pharaoh in Exodus. The journey from Egypt to Canaan manifests the action of Yahweh which places Israel in a land that is a microcosm of the earth, charged

47. The analysis offered so far has been based principally on forms of the verb 'inherit' (נחל). A study of other vocabulary confirms the picture. The verb ירשׁ qal is used to express Israel's possession of the whole land (1.11 [2×]; 12.1; 18.3; 21.43; 23.5; 24.8) and also the possession of parts of it by the tribes (1.15 [2×]; 19.47; 24.2). The same verb is used in the hiphil for Yahweh driving out the former inhabitants of the whole land (3.10; 13.6; 23.5, 9, 13), and also for tribes and individuals driving out (or failing to) the inhabitants of certain parts of it (8.7; 13.12, 13; 14.12; 15.14, 63; 16.10; 17.12–13, 18). This distribution also illustrates, incidentally, the close relationship between Yahweh's 'causing to possess' and Israel's 'possessing' (e.g. in 23.5). Again, the verb נתן, 'give', refers sometimes to Yahweh's giving of the whole land (Josh. 1.2–3, 11, 13–15) and sometimes parts of it (6.2; 8.1, 7, 18) and sometimes to Moses, Joshua or others 'giving' parts of it (1.14–15; 12.6–7; 13.8, 14, 13.15, 24, 29, 33; 14.3, 4, 12–13; 15.13; 17.4; 18.7; 19.49–50; 21.2, 3, 8, 9, 11, 12, 13, 21; 22.4, 7).

with keeping covenant, and by that means realizing his purpose of establishing his order in the political arena.

In the surface-level story of Israel, it renews covenant with Yahweh, and so takes its place as a nation among nations, having a distinct identity and ultimate loyalty. In the complex narrative of Rahab's assimilation, it at once raises questions about the completeness of victory, testifies to the inevitable compromises in the political sphere, and moves towards a strictly political concept of nationhood, rather than an ethnic one. In its portrayal of the way in which power is held, and the manner of its possessing the land, it conforms in large measure to the political pattern specified in Deuteronomy.

The figure of Joshua himself also fits into this pattern, as a 'constitutional' figure, neither quite like Moses nor like a king. Joshua leads Israel for a time, with a defined purpose. If he typifies anything it is what it means to be an Israelite. This 'servant' of Moses is fit to lead Israel into land because he was of the few who had faith to enter at the first attempt. He carries out his task in faithfulness to the law of Moses (to which, I think, he does not add); he does so in conjunction with the priest Eleazar, and the leaders of Israel according to its constituent parts; and his task of 'making inherit' complete, he withdraws to, and dies in, his own local 'inheritance' in the hill-country of Ephraim, without at any time showing an expectation that he should be succeeded by his own kin. The last word in the book is reserved for Eleazar, who is buried in *his* inheritance in the hill-country of Ephraim.

Joshua's achievement is to have delivered Israel into its land, with a sense of its historic unity in covenant with the one God Yahweh, and with a law that extends to the whole people in the whole land. Israel's law, which it reaffirms twice at Shechem, carries within it a vision for organization of the people which, as we have seen, carries 'constitutional' implications. We see the elements of a constitution beginning to operate in Joshua in the recognition of the several responsibilities of the leadership. It will be left to future generations to work out how it might come to take flesh. The pattern of leadership itself will be a central part of this development. But Joshua is not prescriptive of it. Rather, he creates the expectation that Yahweh will provide for leadership in ways that match the situations that Israel faces.

Chapter 7

THE THREAT FROM WITHIN: JUDGES

1. *Service or Freedom?*

With the book of Judges the sense of forward movement in Israel's story encounters a reverse. Gone is the notion of a complete possession (though as we saw
that was qualified even in Joshua); possession now becomes a matter of perpetual
struggle. And correspondingly, it exhibits a struggle within itself concerning its
ultimate loyalties, Yahweh or Baal. With Judges, then, the very possibility of
Israel's mission is at issue. Yet while it struggles to maintain its purposeful identity
over against the religio-politics of Canaan, it also engages with the nature of its
political existence in the crucial question of how it should be led and organized.

The book of Joshua, as we saw, was not wholly optimistic. The essential
problems anticipated there, namely Israel's imperfect grasp of the land, the hints
of compromise in the matters of Rahab and the Gibeonites, and the doubt sown
by Joshua himself over their continuing loyalty (Josh. 24.19), are now manifested
in their full maturity. In Judges 1, the hints of incomplete possession of the tribal
territories given in Joshua become a catalogue. The failure of the tribes to drive
out the Canaanites from their respective territories is a refrain in vv. 27–34.
Judah fares better but even it cannot dislodge 'the inhabitants of the plain', who
were equipped with iron chariots (1.19). The dominant concern in Judg. 2.1–3.6
is Israel's faithfulness to its covenant with Yahweh, and the danger of their
following other gods in his place in accordance with the religion of Canaan.
Indeed, they are now depicted as having already failed to keep the fundamental
requirement of the covenant that they should make no alliances with peoples of
the land but rather destroy the vestiges of their worship (Judg. 2.1–3; cf. Deut.
7.1–5).

The decisive turn for the worse after the death of Joshua is expressed programmatically in 2.6–10. This passage connects directly with the report of the
death of Joshua in Josh. 24.28–31, repeating the information that Joshua had sent
Israel to their respective 'inheritances', that Israel had 'served' (or 'worshipped',
עָבַד) Yahweh during the lifetime of Joshua and of the elders who outlived him,
and the notice of Joshua's burial in Timnath-heres.[1] Following the fresh portrayal

---

1. Timnath-Serah in Josh. 24.30. The similarity of Josh. 24.28–31 and Judg. 2.6–10 has led to
the supposition of editorial revision of an older Joshua–Judges story, in which an original ending has
now been re-applied so as to serve as the beginning of a new phase. It is also adapted to a theology of
the different epochs; Robert G. Boling, *Judges* (AB; New York: Doubleday, 1975), p. 72.

of Israel's incomplete possession of Canaan, and the note of their assimilation with Canaanites, it returns briefly to that perspective in Joshua according to which the land had been definitively taken. The notional possession of the land becomes the premise on which the story of the generations after Joshua is predicated. The new thing in this passage is that the faithfulness of Israel to Yahweh during Joshua's life is now contrasted with the unfaithfulness of the generations that followed. Whereas the older generation had 'served' Yahweh, the new generation did not 'know' him (v. 10). The story of Judges is a story of Israel's 'serving'. And after this programmatic statement, the people is said to 'serve' Yahweh on only one further occasion, in the Ammonite crisis (10.16). Otherwise the 'service' of Israel is repeatedly directed towards the god Baal and other deities (2.11, 13; 3.6–7; 10.6, 10, 13). In such contexts the serving of the foreign god is almost always accompanied by a negative counterpart, in which they 'forsook' or 'forgot' Yahweh, or 'did evil' in his eyes. Ironically there is a further 'serving', of the foreign kings Cushan-Rishathaim (a shadowy type of all Israel's oppressors) and Eglon, king of Moab (3.8, 14). Where foreign gods are served, so too are foreign tyrants. The fundamental political choice set before Israel in Exodus therefore re-emerges in Judges, with surrogates for the Pharaoh: will it choose slavery or freedom?

These opening chapters take a long, retrospective view of the story of Israel's covenant-keeping. The whole sweep of Israel under 'judges' (or 'deliverers')[2] is the subject of 2.16–23, and here again a pattern of Israelite unfaithfulness is reaffirmed, Yahweh in his compassion (v. 18, cf. Deut. 32.36) raises up a judge to deliver them, but they return chronically to their apostasy. This provides a way of thinking about the stories of crises and deliverances that follow (chs 3–16). As is now accepted, the pattern in the storyline is not simply cyclical, an alternation of success and failure.[3] Rather, the accent is on Israel's infidelity throughout, and rather than a cycle the pattern is one of persistent apostasy. In this important respect, the view of the so-called 'framework' (principally the theologically explicit sections in 2.1–3.6) corresponds to that of the stories of individual 'judges'. The underlying issue throughout the book is the propensity of Israel to abandon Yahweh and his covenant, and the corresponding fragility of its hold on the land lately possessed.

During the time of the judges, the land has periodic rest. But this respite is almost entirely due to Yahweh's compassion. In spite of the one occasion when Israel is said to have 'served' Yahweh (10.16), no period of faithfulness, nor of a commitment to justice and righteousness, is ever portrayed. It is not even explicitly said that when they cry to Yahweh they actually repent.[4] Instead, the accent

2. On the nature of the 'judges' in Judges see further below.

3. The idea of a cyclical pattern in Judges was given currency by G. von Rad's well-known distinction between editing techniques in Judges and Kings, which he thought hard to reconcile within a single work; *Old Testament Theology I*, pp. 346–7.

4. Israel is the subject of the verb םחנ, 'repent', only once, in Judg. 21.15, where they lament the hardship of Benjamin after the war against that tribe. Otherwise only Yahweh is subject of the verb, in the meaning of 'have compassion', Judg. 2.18. Israel weeps at Bochim, when Yahweh speaks words of judgement, and they sacrifice to him (2.4–5). But no lasting change is intimated.

regularly falls on the tendency to apostasy. It seems that the pattern of deliverance, apostasy and land loss is a metaphor for an Israel that is not conforming to its vocation of loyalty to Yahweh, rather than a portrayal of strict sequence.[5] Here is 'stubborn' Israel (Judg. 2.19), as represented at key moments in its covenant-making with Yahweh (Exod. 32.9; 34.9; Deut. 9.6; 31.27), and to which Yahweh responds in both judgement and mercy (the theme of Deuteronomy 32). In this context, the best that can be said of Israel is that they retain a memory of Yahweh as their God and deliverer, because it is to Yahweh that they turn in times of crisis. There are also glimpses of a Yahweh-piety in the episodes when he comes to people to call them to deliver or alert them to his plans (e.g. Judg. 6.11–27; 13).

Judges therefore, like Joshua, reflects on the danger to Israel of succumbing to the worship of foreign gods, and on the incomplete possession of the land. This reflection appears in the opening chapters in several ways. First, the continued presence of Canaanites is a punishment because Israel has failed to keep covenant; Yahweh revokes his promise, made repeatedly in Deuteronomy, that he would drive them out (Judg. 2.1–3). What begins as a consequence of Israel's disobedience becomes a punishment: the Canaanites will become adversaries,[6] and their gods a snare. In further developments, the partially revoked promise serves as a 'test' to see if Israel would in future keep the covenant (2.22),[7] and also so that the generations after Joshua might 'know war' (3.2).[8] The extended treatment of the incomplete possession closes in 3.5–6, as it opened in 2.2, with the accusation that Israel had failed to keep separate from Canaan.

2. *The Creation-Perspective*

In Israel's loss of confidence in Judges the divine mission to establish justice-righteousness in the world is evidently jeopardized. The very terminology of 'judging' in the book indicates a connection between that underlying theme and the present narrative.

We have already observed a continuation of the theme of opposition to political tyranny on the large scale, the threat from foreign oppressors to pre-monarchic Israel echoing not only the Canaanite kings of Joshua, but ultimately the Pharaoh of the exodus, whose tyranny was an eruption of Chaos in the politi-

5. Boling rightly says of 2.11–17, 'It is important to note that this is an introduction to the period as a whole; it does not imply a cyclical view of historical process'; Boling, *Judges*, p. 76.

6. Or 'thorns in their sides' (v. 3, ESV). The text is obscure; the translation 'adversaries' is indebted to LXX and Latin.

7. The logic of 2.21–23 can be construed in slightly different ways, depending on whether Yahweh's speech in v. 21 is continued into v. 22. If Yahweh's speech continues, the punishment becomes in turn a test of Israel (as ESV). NRSV in contrast closes Yahweh's speech at v. 21, and makes vv. 22–23 a summary conclusion, in which Yahweh *had* left the nations as a test in the first place. ESV is slightly preferable.

8. The several angles on the remaining Canaanites have been explained as different redactional strategies. Boling finds three redactional layers in ch. 2, two of them pre-deuteronomic: the oldest section in 2.20–23, and another hand in vv. 11–17. Verses 18–19 come from Dtr; Boling, *Judges*, p. 76. Cf. also pp. 78–79 on Judg. 3.1–6.

cal sphere. The exodus is expressly recalled in Yahweh's words: 'I brought you up out of Egypt', in the preamble and in the Gideon story (Judg. 2.1; 6.8).[9] There are other signs of continuity with the Exodus narrative. As Israel 'groaned' under their bondage in Egypt and 'cried to Yahweh' (Exod. 2.23), so they do under their new oppressors in Canaan (2.18; 3.9).[10] And in the same texts Yahweh responds to their appeal by acting to deliver, supported in one case with 'I am Yahweh', which frequently accompanies his actions of deliverance in Exodus.[11] In Judges, this claim of Yahweh on Israel's allegiance, with its far-reaching implications, is resisted by the appeal of Baal-worship in Canaan.

The story of deliverance in Exodus is inseparable from the divine intention to establish Israel in its land in justice and peace. And this is the background to the question about the nature of 'judging' in Judges, which is constituted not only by acts of deliverance from oppression, but by the establishment of just peace. The point emerges from a consideration of the words usually translated 'judge' and 'deliver' in Judges.

The Hebrew terms for 'judge' (the verb *shaphat* and the noun *shophet*) correspond to the term *mishpat*, which often occurs with *tsedaqah*, in the meaning (separately or in tandem) 'justice-righteousness'. The verb may mean 'judge', 'rule' or 'deliver', depending on context, and the noun has corresponding meanings.[12] While Deuteronomy provides for *shophetim* in a judicial function (Deut. 16.18), Judges tells of figures who are raised 'to deliver' Israel. (The noun *shophet* is applied to the judge-deliverers only in the theological introduction, in 2.16–19, and is otherwise reserved for Yahweh alone; 11.27). For this reason the hero-stories, in their putative early form, are sometimes referred to as a 'book of saviours'.[13] The semantic range of *shaphat* corresponds to political actuality, since administrative, military and judicial roles were closely linked in the ANE, and often embodied in the king.

The convergence of administrative, military and judicial roles in Judges can also be observed in the distribution of *shaphat/shophet* and the term usually translated 'deliver' (הושיע, *hoshia'*, a concept related to 'victory').[14] Othniel is introduced as a 'deliverer' (מושיע, *moshia'*) for Israel, from the oppression of Cushan-Rishathaim (3.9), and then it is said that he 'judged' Israel (3.10). The

9. The terms are the same as in Exod. 3.17; 33.1, i.e. עלה hi.

10. The echoes of Exodus are exact: their 'groaning' is נאקתם in Exod. 2.24 (cf. Exod. 6.5) and Judg. 2.18; and their 'crying' is זעק in Exod. 2.23 and in Judg. 3.9. Cf. Boling, *Judges*, pp. 6, 127. R. Smend also considered the possible 'historicity of Moses in the role of the first of the "major judges"'; *Yahweh War and Tribal Confederation* (New York and Nashville: Abingdon Press, 1970), p. 128.

11. Judg. 6.10, cf. Exod. 6.2–9, 29; 10.2; 12.12; 15.26.

12. In the case of Tola, NIV, for example, translates 10.2 as 'He *led* Israel twenty-three years…' Block, in his comment on the text, modifies this to 'governed'; Daniel I. Block, *Judges, Ruth* (NAC; Nashville: Broadman and Holman, 1999), p. 339.

13. In modern study this is attributable to W. Richter, *Die Bearbeitungen des 'Retterbuches' in der deuteronomischen Epoche* (BBB, 21; Bonn: Peter Hanstein, 1964). Cf. P. Guillaume, *Waiting for Josiah: The Judges* (JSOTSup, 385; London: T&T Clark, 2004).

14. Victory, it will be recalled, was one of the elements that for O'Donovan constituted Israel a nation; see above, Chapter 4, n. 70, and Chapter 5, n. 22.

'judging' in this case is closely analogous to the 'delivering'. It is preceded in v. 10 by the statement that 'the spirit of the LORD came upon him', which typically announces an empowering to do battle or other acts of great strength, as in the cases of Gideon, Jephthah and Samson (6.34; 11.29; 14.19; 15.14). And in fact it leads into the statement that he defeated the tyrant. Tola too arose to 'deliver' Israel, and then 'judged' them for twenty-three years (10.1–2). This 'judging' is attributed to the so-called 'minor judges', as well as to Jephthah and Samson (10.1–5; 12.8–15; 12.7; 15.20). Since no military feats are attributed to the 'minor judges', it used to be thought that their judging was the judicial sort, closely associated with Israel's earliest legal forms as attested in the biblical law codes.[15] However, the distinction between military and judicial activities cannot be maintained on the grounds of the two terms usually translated as 'delivering' and 'judging', because of the way they are used of Othniel and Tola. It follows that the 'judging' done by the minor judges, Jephthah and Samson may be the kind that involves protecting Israel militarily from enemies. Only in the case of Deborah, is it clear from the context that her judging is the sort that consists in settling disputes (Judg. 4.5).[16] Yet she too is called in addition to 'deliver' Israel.

The 'judging' that is done in Israel is an activity primarily of Yahweh, by which he decides issues between nations (Judg. 11.27). In the only occurrence of *tsedaqah* in the book, a plural form denotes the past 'victories' of Yahweh (Judg. 5.11). He is also the supreme 'deliverer' (Judg. 6.36; 12.3). The convergence of 'judging' and 'delivering' is best explained not by trying to distinguish between the terms, nor by appeal to underlying traditions, but by reference to the theme of the narrative from Genesis, that Israel should be freed from tyranny in order to become a people that exhibits justice and righteousness. For this reason Boling can see in Othniel's success against Cushan-Rishathaim an exemplary case, comprising the whole gamut of '(a) election (b) judging (c) victory and peace in Israel'.[17] By the same token he sees 'judging' as having the sense of mobilizing Israel for 'a Yahwist war', an understanding that works well in Judg. 3.10.

The consequence of these observations is that the judging in Judges is not reducible to one kind or another. Deborah's hearing of disputes among Israelites is of a piece with Othniel's defeat of the embodiment of the evil tyrant in Cushan-Rishathaim. The drama in Judges is a further instalment of the conflict between peace and righteousness on one hand and evil on the other, whether evil takes the form of external threats from enemies or internal threats from idolatry and the imitation of foreign oppression. The cosmic context of this struggle is seen in some of the language of the Song of Deborah, where river courses and even the stars in heaven participate in their defeat of Jabin and Sisera (Judg. 5.19–21). The peculiarities of Judges when compared with texts concerning the composition and constitution of Israel in Deuteronomy-Joshua appear in a different light when measured by the deeper-lying concerns that have been engaged since Genesis.

---

15. See Boling, *Judges*, pp. 7, 10–11, 186–7.
16. In this case the noun *mishpat* is used, not the verb *shaphat*.
17. Boling, *Judges*, p. 81.

Here as there, the leading character is Yahweh, 'the judge of all the earth' (Gen. 18.25), and the issue, how to translate his just rule into earthly reality.

3. *Israel in Judges: An Ideal Subverted*

Reading Judges as a sequel to the formation of Israel in Exodus–Deuteronomy, and the account of land-possession in Joshua, the reader is struck by the fact that the central provisions for Israel's life in the land, carefully prepared from Sinai and Moab to Shechem, are either absent from the picture given by Judges, or appear in the most negative way. Over all the absences lies the fact that there is no covenant-renewal in Judges. On the contrary, after the death of Gideon the Israelites worship the god Baal-berith (8.33), whose temple at Shechem becomes a centre of support for Abimelech (9.4), and finally a stronghold against him (9.46).[18] Shechem was the place of covenant-renewal in Joshua (Joshua 24), but now epitomizes the turn to Baal, and by the same token the deformation of political leadership. There is, finally, a recollection of the command not to make a covenant with the people of the land, only to observe that this had already been broken (Judg. 2.2).

As there is no covenant-renewal, neither is there any evidence of the substance of it, namely commitment to keep *torah*. The deuteronomic language of commandment appears only to reflect on disobedience to it (Judg. 2.2). As for priesthood, there is a memory in the story of Micah's priest that priests should be Levites, but priesthood is for sale to the highest bidder and the Levite in question is entirely venal (17.7–13; 18.17–20). Conversely, the provision for priests made repeatedly in Numbers, Deuteronomy and Joshua,[19] that they should have a foothold by right in the tribal territories of Israel, is also conspicuously absent, so that our Levite's venality corresponds to the institutional vacuum left by the neglect of religious and political rigour generally in Israel.

Correspondingly too, there is little evidence of the worship of Yahweh by all Israel at a place that counts as the central place of worship. In Joshua, as we saw, Shiloh appeared in that role, and was contended for as such (Josh. 18.1; 22). Shiloh is indeed the place where the 'house of God' is located for some extended (though unspecified) time (Judg. 18.31). But the fact is introduced almost in passing, only as an ironic comment on the Danites' idolatrous shrine, attended by the Levite they had captured from Micah. The reader is bound to wonder what kind of worship was cultivated at Shiloh. Is the Tent of Meeting – another absence – located in this 'house'? The question is sharpened by a further incidental note, that 'the ark of the covenant of God' stood at Bethel during the Benjaminite war (20.27). Why is the ark not united with the 'house of God'? Why, in other texts, does Mizpah appear to be the place where Israel meets Yahweh (20.1–2, cf. 11.11)? In what way are the Mosaic worship arrangements being cultivated, if at all?

---

18. In this text the temple is that of El-berith, presumably the same one as in 9.4, though the confusion of Baal and El is unusual.

19. Num. 35.1–8; Deut. 10.8–9; 18.1–8; Josh. 14.4; 21.

A corollary of these questions is a doubt about the very unity of Israel. The notion of a united Israel is sustained throughout the book (it is always 'Israel' that 'does evil', cries to Yahweh, is delivered). In what way can such a unity be maintained if the foundations of its existence as a people are undermined? Israelites are aware that they belong to Israel: Gideon's initial defensive response to the 'angel of the LORD' displays a similar concept of the people's composition – 'father's house', 'clan' (אֶלֶף), tribe – found in the fullest expression of this in Joshua 8 (Judg. 6.15). Israel *acts* as a united entity on a few occasions, as when 'the Israelites' offer Gideon the kingship (8.22), when they repent in the Ammonite crisis (10.10), and in the Benjaminite war. It is in the last of these instances, in the muster at Mizpah, that Israel comes closest to uniting as the assembly of Yahweh (20.1–2) in terms familiar from Deuteronomy and Joshua.[20] With this gathering of 'all the Israelites, from Dan to Beersheba, including the land of Gilead', the last stages of the book echo the same issue met in Joshua 22, namely the completeness and unity of the people in principle. The greatest hymn to the nation's unity is in the Song of Deborah (Judges 5, to which we return below).

But does this notional, ideal unity correspond to the reality of Israel as portrayed here? As is often observed, the action in the stories is often localized. Gideon operates in his home region around Oprah; it is the Shechemites who make Abimelech king (9.6), and the Gileadites who commission Jephthah (11.5–11). And Samson conducts low-level harassment of the Philistines in the area of Beth-Shemesh. In Judges, the ideal of unity struggles for realization.

The Judges and the Nature of Israel

Judges, no less than other parts of Genesis–Kings, has ultimately to be read from the perspective of the end, that is, from the standpoint of the fall of the kingdoms. It follows that reading Judges has a historical 'depth-dimension'. Most accounts of the book suppose that relatively early stories have been gradually assimilated into the developed theological work represented by the book as it is now known. It is the assimilated book, comprising story and theological reflection, that concerns us here. Stories of episodes in Israel's earliest time in the land have been made part of an account of the nature of Israel and its ongoing relationship with Yahweh.

The structure of Judges invites the reader to read the stories in the light of the preamble in 1.1–3.6, that is, as exhibiting the deliverances of Yahweh and the repeated apostasies of Israel. The editorial connections between preamble and stories are clear in the way in which they are in large measure subjected to the pattern announced in 2.16–19. Othniel supplies a parade example (3.7–11).[21] Preamble and stories also share the assumption that Israel is a unified people

---

20. The phrase וַתִּקָּהֵל הָעֵדָה כְּאִישׁ אֶחָד, 'the congregation assembled as one before the LORD', draws on the language of both P (עֵדָה) and D (קָהָל).

21. Barry Webb finds in Othniel 'the embodiment of an institution; all the key words assigned to judgeship in ch. 2 [vv. 16–19] are applied to Othniel here...there are no complicating details'; Webb, *The Book of the Judges: An Integrated Reading* (JSOTSup, 46; Sheffield: JSOT Press, 1987), p. 127.

made up of relatively independent tribes, and that their destiny is bound together and with Yahweh.

Our question is what view of Israel and its destiny is projected in the book. The answer to this scarcely lies on the surface of the stories of hero-deliverers that occupy the bulk of the book. True, here are figures who are in varying degrees admirable, and whom Yahweh calls to deliver Israel from enemies. Gideon's famous overcoming of the odds against the Midianites (Judges 7) is a classic example of the Divine Warrior theme. Even Samson, the least auspicious hero, is called before his birth '[to] begin to deliver Israel from the hand of the Philistines' (Judg. 13.5). The stories evince a sense that Yahweh's underlying purpose to secure the people of Israel in their land continues to go forward. Yet the portrayal of this Israel and these leaders is perplexing. Gideon's military success leads to a request by the Israelites that he rule them in the manner of a dynastic king (Judg. 8.22). He declines, citing the rulership of Yahweh, in conformity with the hesitations about human kingship expressed in Deuteronomy and (as we have seen) in Joshua. Yet the same Gideon immediately leads the people of his city to idolatry (8.24–27), adopts a lifestyle that looks regal (8.30–31, cf. 8.18), is also known as Jerubbaal (strives against Baal – or *for* him?[22]), and has a son, Abimelech, who attempts to rule Israel as a king (Judges 9).[23] When one considers the double-mindedness of Gideon-Jerubbaal, the ill-fated calculations of outsider Jephthah (Judges 11–12), and the bizarre exploits of Samson, the stories of the hero-figures in themselves do not add up to an ideal vision for Israel. Samson, indeed, in his blind helplessness, may be seen as a type of an Israel that no longer understands itself or its mission.[24]

4. *The Exercise of Power*

The question of Israel's nature and destiny lies close to one of the book's major themes, the type of human leadership that is appropriate for the people whose king is Yahweh. The immediate difficulty encountered in this connection is the book's ambivalence on the matter of kingship. It has passages which can be aligned on both sides of this debate. Gideon's ostensible refusal of dynastic rule, the debacle of Abimelech's attempt to rule as king (Judges 9), and Jotham's fable, embedded in the Abimelech narrative (9.7–15), all seem to speak against monarchic rule. Martin Buber called the fable 'the strongest anti-monarchical poem of world literature'.[25] On the other side, apparently, is the comment in Judg. 17.6; 21.25: 'In those days, there was no king in Israel; everyone did what

22. On the possible meanings of the name Jerubbaal see W. Bluedorn, *Yahweh versus Baalism: A Theological Reading of the Gideon–Abimelech Narrative* (JSOTSup, 329; Sheffield: Sheffield Academic Press, 2001), pp. 201–3.

23. The name Abimelech too (literally 'my father is king') may point an accusing finger at Gideon; see again Bluedorn, *Yahweh*, pp. 189–95.

24. Cf. Webb, *Judges*, p. 172.

25. M. Buber, *Kingship of God* (London: Allen & Unwin, 3rd edn, 1967), p. 75; also cited in David M. Gunn, *Judges* (Blackwell Bible Commentaries; Oxford: Blackwell, 2005), p. 128.

was right in his own eyes' (ESV), which becomes a recurring gloss on the chaotic conditions prevailing in the latter stages of the book (cf. 18.1; 19.1), and which is widely regarded as an appeal for monarchic rule.[26] If various passages in the book articulate opinions on either side of the question, is there a higher organizing voice which settles the matter one way or the other?

The commonest answer to this question, as with both Deuteronomy and Joshua, is that the book serves the royal Davidic programme of King Josiah.[27] The steep decline of Israel after Joshua, their persistent idolatry, their consequent failure to hold the land securely, are all attributed to the lack of consistent, strong leadership. Mark Brettler sees in the literary organization of Judges a gradual disclosure of the proposed solution, namely in the call for kingship implied in the latter chapters.[28] Yairah Amit thinks that 'the issue of leadership constitutes the central axis of the entire work'. She argues that the merely sporadic appearance of judges and their disappointing performance illustrate the need for permanency of leadership. Even the offer to Gideon and the brief reign of Abimelech express this necessity, and become part of the book's insistent message, 'that the people requires a continuous rule of centralized leadership capable of dealing with difficult political problems'.[29] The case of Abimelech illustrates what happens when rule is seized wrongly, and this is what Jotham opposes: the fable (or parable, in her terms) gives the reader tools 'to criticize the case of Abimelech, but does not serve as a principled anti-monarchist polemic'.[30] According to her view of the book's editing, therefore, even those parts traditionally ranged against monarchy are made to serve the pro-monarchic purpose.

But is it possible to subordinate the voices of Judges to a single programme in this way? There are important factors that suggest otherwise. It is curious that a book dedicated to an argument for Davidic monarchy should be silent on this in its most concentrated theological reflections (in 1.1–2.5). The difficulties of annexing Judges to 'deuteronomic' or 'Deuteronomistic' orthodoxy are well known.[31] Nor do the key passages really compel the issue one way or the other. Jotham's fable is by its nature elusive. Is the bramble-character of the king-figure inherent in the concept of kingship, as opposed to the productiveness of the noble trees who refuse to rule? Or is it a characteristic of Abimelech specifically, the

---

26. Yairah Amit, *The Book of Judges: the Art of Editing* (trans. Jonathan Chipman; BIS, 38; Leiden: E. J. Brill, 1999), p. 314.

27. One version of this approach, exemplified by F. Crüsemann, is the view that the pro-monarchical attitude properly characterizes the Deuteronomistic writer, while anti-monarchical voices simply diverge from that main line; Crüsemann, *Der Widerstand gegen das Königtum: die antiköniglichen Texte des Alten Testaments und der Kampf um den frühen israelitischen Staat* (WMANT, 49; Neukirchen–Vluyn: Neukirchener Verlag, 1978). More recent studies seek subtler formulations of editorial strategy.

28. Mark Zvi Brettler, *The Book of Judges* (Routledge: London and New York, 2002), pp. 80–91, 111–16. Brettler finds anti-Benjaminite (Saulide) polemic in the latter chapters of Judges, so that it pleads not merely for kingship, but specifically for Davidic kingship.

29. Amit, *Judges*, p. 118.

30. Amit, *Judges*, pp. 106–7. She is not alone in this understanding of Jotham's fable; see Bluedorn, *Yahweh*, pp. 210–29, for an account of interpretations.

31. See above, n. 3.

tragedy consisting precisely in the refusal of the noble to bear the responsibility of office? Or again, is the issue at stake one of kinship and not kingship?[32] Answers to these questions require a careful reading of texts in context. Even the refrain 'There was no king in Israel in those days; everyone did what was right in their own eyes' (chs 17–21) is somewhat opaque, not so obvious a plea for monarchical rule as is sometimes claimed. As Barry Webb has it, it is more of a drum-beat that signals what will be the next phase in the history of Israel with Yahweh, without evaluative commentary.[33] If Judges as narrative is taken seriously, it is difficult to hear the refrain as an unambiguous call for monarchy above the background noise of the complications of Gideon and Abimelech.[34] Moreover, it over-simplifies Judges to suppose that it can be understood merely as propaganda for one programme or another. The interpretation of Judges finds itself at times in false polarizations. The book is either pro-monarchical or anti-monarchical; or, in Amit's reading, it calls for a form of human rule that contrasts with 'the kingdom of God'.[35] These in different ways fail to explore adequately the way in which the issue of divine and human rule is pursued in Judges. In particular, they do not offer an answer to the problem identified in the opening chapters, namely the people's 'stubbornness of heart'. The issues in Judges go deeper than forms of leadership, and the argument of the book cannot be reduced to the advocacy of one sort or another.[36] It is only when the concerns of the book are conceived in a narrowly nationalistic sense that the answer to them can be thought of in such a way.[37] To the contrary, Dennis Olson believes, rightly in my view, that Judges shows the provisionality of all kinds of human rule:

> Kingship in Israel, like the judges, will in time be replaced by another form of human leadership, which will be necessary but also provisional and imperfect. The era of the judges thus becomes a paradigm of any human institution, mode of governance or ideology – necessary but provisional, helpful for a time, but eventually replaced by another.[38]

32. Gunn draws attention to these and other interpretations of the fable, in older as well as modern interpretation: *Judges*, pp. 127, 129.

33. Webb, *Judges*, pp. 202–3. See also Block, *Judges, Ruth*, p. 59.

34. R. Polzin finds the real contrast in Judg. 21.25 to be between 'Israelites doing what was right in their own eyes and Israelites having to do what was right in their king's eyes'; *David and the Deuteronomist* (Bloomington and Indianapolis: Indiana University Press, 1993), p. 75. And Block rightly cautions against Brettler's view that it 'not only minimizes the significance of several textual units that are critical of the monarchy but also disregards the critical stance towards Judah reflected in the book' (including its absence in the Song of Deborah); *Judges, Ruth*, p. 57.

35. For Amit, the period of the judges represents the pre-monarchical 'kingdom of God', while the advent of monarchy will embrace the practical necessity of human rule; *Judges*, p. 61, cf. p. 111.

36. David Jobling has rightly found a complex negotiation between the forms of leadership, without a definite preference for either. Writing on Judges and 1 Samuel 1–12, he says: '...the deuteronomic treatment of monarchy is a classic example of talking around a contradiction': *The Sense of Biblical Narrative: Structural Analyses in the Hebrew Bible II* (JSOTSup, 39; Sheffield: JSOT Press, 1986, 1987), p. 46. He welcomes Buber's idea of 'two antithetical parts (being) true simultaneously'; *Kingship of God*, p. 83.

37. Cf. the view of Amit, above (nn. 28–29).

38. Dennis T. Olson, 'The Book of Judges' (New Interpreter's Bible II; Nashville: Abingdon Press, 1998), pp. 721–888 (727).

Restraint on Human Power

Yet Judges does make a significant positive contribution to the topic of responsible leadership. Judges, like Deuteronomy, is deeply concerned with the relationship between divine and human power. This is evident in a number of ways. Most obviously, it consists in the prerogative of Yahweh to raise up judge-deliverers. The whole pattern of Israel's apostasy, foreign oppression, divine compassion, the appointment of deliverers, the limitation on Israel's land-possession, is expressly in the hands of Yahweh (Judg. 2.16–23). Here we see Yahweh acting in compassion, helping the judge, saving the people, judging the people, governing the affairs of both Israel and other nations. In the stories he is the divine warrior who turns events in Israel's favour against great odds (Judges 7), his spirit enables mighty deeds of victory (11.29), he discloses his plans to save in advance (Judges 13); conversely he brings a succession of enemies against his people, yet their sway too is limited.

The stories are also revealing about the manner of Yahweh's 'being with' the judge, or enabling by his spirit. Especially in the episodes involving Gideon, Jephthah and Samson, the personality of the individual leader is closely involved with the development of events. In Gideon may be found a deep hesitation between belief and unbelief, evidenced in his double test of Yahweh by means of a fleece (6.36–40), in his ready defection to Baal, even in his pursuit of the Midianite princes Zebah and Zalmunna, apparently in a personal vendetta the account of which says nothing about divine direction (Judges 8). Jephthah is the too-calculating political manoeuverer whose attempt to tie Yahweh into a deal has the unintended consequence of his daughter becoming the victim of his vow (11.34–40). Samson's military affairs are inextricably linked with his romantic affairs. Deeds and misdeeds are intertwined in this trial of what it means that Yahweh should work through human agents. The result is the paradox that Yahweh pursues his purpose for Israel (and others) in ways that bring with them the consequences of human foible. There are echoes of Jacob in this: one who is chosen, and subject to an overriding purpose which is in a sense irresistible, yet all the time pursuing personal agendas that have lasting effects on the contours of human relationship (with Laban, Esau, and indeed Leah and Rachel, a combination of vision and blindness that affects the very marrow of Israel). Judges offers penetrating reflection on the idea itself of divine and human power in concert.

It is in addition a story of the overcoming of tyrannical kings. The notion of kingship, and the concentration of the term 'king', is found most frequently in Judges in connection with the foreign rulers who are brought against Israel. There is more to these stories of oppression than the mere fact of the chastisement of disobedience; tyrannical kingship in itself is placed on stage here. The first oppressor, Cushan-Rishathaim, bears in his paradigmatic name (Cushan the 'doubly wicked') an emblem of monstrous rule (3.8–10). Eglon of Moab is cut down to size in his fat but vacuous pomp (3.15–23). Other significant figures are Jabin, king of Hazor, and Jephthah's adversary, the king of the Ammonites. In the stories concerning them, the word 'king' recurs repeatedly as if to draw attention to it as a theme (e.g. 4.24; 11.12–19). If Judges is in some sense about kingship, these texts play a crucial part. When Gideon falls prey to the temptations of power, the issue is whether the corruption of rule in the wider political environment will invade Israel. Gideon's pretensions are exhibited not only in his excessive lifestyle (8.29–31) but also in his pursuit of Zebah and Zalmunna, in which he displays a propensity for violence and cruelty (8.7–9, 16–17). It is from the hapless Midianite princes that we learn that Gideon has the appearance of a king (8.18). This Israelite 'deliverer' from oppression, the least in his insignificant family, has come to resemble, by dint of his realized power, the very model of tyranny. The potential of human rule to become monstrous is exhibited in Gideon–Abimelech, not only in the son but already in the father.

Kingship in Judges can hardly be adequately considered apart from the opposition of oppressive kings to Israel, nor the rise within Israel of rulers who exceed their God-given authority. In this sense the book continues the deprecation of tyranny that has been thematized since Exodus in the form of the Pharaoh, Deuteronomy's prohibition of having a foreigner as king (Deut. 17.15b), and the depiction of Joshua's enemies as the kings of Canaan (Joshua 12). If Judges is looking for order in the political sphere, it can only look apprehensively in the direction of kings. The phrase 'there was no king in Israel' can count among its possible connotations the notice that no foreign tyrant was currently present to oppress. It belongs in that case to the undercurrent of Judges in which Yahweh continues to safeguard the life of his people. If Israelite society finds in this relief from tyranny a freedom from all restraint, that is a measure of the difficulty of achieving a properly based order in human society.

There are, however, positive indications about the nature of human rule in Judges. We have noticed already the range of functions covered by the notion of 'judging' itself. It was an activity primarily of Yahweh, yet this had its counterpart in the whole complex of delivering, ruling and judging that was predicated variously of the leaders Yahweh raised up. In addition to the portrayal of such activity, however, the book offers a further perspective on non-tyrannical rule, in its concept of the unity and diversity of the people.

This perspective is found in the Song of Deborah, with its striking advocacy of limits and diversity in human power (Judges 5). Here leaders and people act concertedly in offering themselves to Yahweh's cause (5.1). The Song is a hymn to Yahweh, celebrating his march from Sinai (vv. 4–5) into the land of Canaan, and expressing the expectation of cohesive action on the part of the tribes in war against a common enemy. The singers' opening words record the willing offering of 'the people', Israel, and a call to bless Yahweh (5.2). Yahweh is the 'God of Israel' here (v. 5), and Israel the 'people of Yahweh' (v. 13). They go on to call 'kings' and 'princes' to witness his victory (5.3), in an echo of the appeal to the heavens and the earth in Deut. 32.1, and depict a war of Israel against the 'kings of Canaan' (v. 19, cf. again Joshua 12), Yahweh himself being the warrior (v. 23). As 'people of Yahweh', Israel unites in the face of a common foe. And the Song remembers his actions on Israel's behalf as the 'divine warrior' who came from Sinai. The 'triumphs of Yahweh' are memorialized here too, in a phrase which not only recalls victories but characterizes them as acts of 'justice', or 'righteous-ness' (*tsedaqah*), as we noticed above in the context of his universal rule.

However, while the accent is on Yahweh's action, it is particularly striking that the muster of the tribes against the enemy is described as coming to 'the help of Yahweh', a phrase that occurs twice in the passage in which Meroz is cas-tigated for failing to join the coalition (5.23), and nowhere else in the Old Testa-ment. It is a curious reversal of the more expected notion that Yahweh comes to the help of people (cf. 1 Chron. 12.18). This unusual angle on divine and human power is apparently a function of the willing offering of Israel in its several parts.

But the unity of Israel is not just military. Rather, certain ideals are expressed concerning its nature. The people (v. 1), and the 'commanders'[39] of Israel 'among the people' (v. 9), offer themselves willingly for united action. Not only leaders but the 'peasantry' of Israel (that is, village-dwellers) conduct this war (5.7, 11), indeed the 'triumphs of Yahweh' (v. 11) are in parallel with 'the triumphs of his peasantry'. It is the people in its full dimensions that belongs to Yahweh and joins in his cause. Several expressions in the Song express this. Ephraim follows Benja-min 'with your kin' (בעממיך, v. 14); the 'clans' of Reuben (פלגות ראובן) 'search their hearts' (v. 15). Leadership is tribal, but conforms to no particular pattern, a variety of terms being used throughout the Song.[40]

The Song presents the strongest advocacy anywhere of willing co-operation among the tribes. In this respect it provides a good continuation from the por-trayal of Israel in Joshua both as a unified people and as distributed tribes, finally without a supreme military or political leader. Its curiosity is that the picture of Israel is untidy when compared with the regularity of the twelve-tribe nation in the narrative up to Joshua. Familiar names of tribes, such as Dan, Asher, Zebulun, Naphtali, jostle with others known primarily as place-names (Machir, Gilead, Meroz) in this profile of pre-monarchical Israel, yet all representing agents capable of decision-making ('Gilead stayed beyond the Jordan', v. 17). Missing from the familiar twelve-tribe list are Manasseh, Gad, Simeon, Levi, and most strikingly, Judah. It may be that in some cases tribal names have been substituted by place-names of the territory they occupied (for example, Machir and Gilead are closely associated with Manasseh; Gen. 50.23; Num. 26.29). In any case, the untidiness of the poem's picture of Israel shows that it has not been subjected to a concern to display it in strict accordance with the preceding narratives.

In fact its haphazard portrayal by comparison with those is one factor in its widely agreed early date. In the wake of the ideal projections of twelve-tribe Israel in Genesis–Joshua, the Song affords a glimpse of an Israel in the actuality of a moment of time. It is hardly a complete image, since the omission of Judah

---

39. The word חקקים is unusual, and does not correspond to any office known elsewhere in Genesis–Kings. It varies to מחקקים in 5.14, which occurs elsewhere as 'governor', 'ruler' (Deut. 33.21; Isa. 33.22); because of affinities with חק, 'statute', the noun was taken as 'lawgiver' in KJV (cf. also Prov. 31.5).

40. The 'chiefs' of Issachar are שרים (שרי), v. 15. And cf. v. 14d, משכים בשבט ספר ('those who bear the marshal's staff', NRSV); אדירים, 'the noble' (v. 13a); and see preceding note.

would be hard to explain on such a view. The tribal muster was drawn from the northern regions, perhaps simply because that was where the threat lay. But the variations from Genesis–Joshua are not simply matters of omission. Rather there is adaptation and development here. This powerful evocation of a (mainly) faithful, cohesive Israel, reckons with the changes that are brought about by time and tide. There is, as we have observed already, a kind of 'dialectic' between the political vision of Genesis–Joshua and the realities of (any) contemporary life as in this case. If there are deficiencies in Israel by comparison with the vision in Deuteronomy, they are explained in part by the need to adapt, as illustrated in the Song.

While the Song offers material for reflection on the nature of rule in Israel, it sheds light at the same time on the nature of Israel itself. Co-operation, willing commitment, rallying to the cause of Yahweh are to the fore, rather than a strict accounting for genealogical integrity. Who belongs in reality to 'Israel'? As the Canaanite Rahab put down a marker on this in Joshua, so now Jael, wife of Heber the Kenite, does so in Judges. Jael strikes the decisive blow in the war against Sisera and Jabin. It is notoriously odd not only that the victory should be secured by a woman, but more importantly that the woman in question takes her identity from her husband, a 'Kenite'. While the theory of an early familial relationship between Israelites and Kenites has a long history, the designation in this context seems to point to someone natively external to Israel. The point is hard to evaluate, when major themes, such as unity, are presented ambivalently. Does the favourable report of Jael's act mean to advocate an 'open' Israel, as the book of Ruth (following shortly in the Christian canonical order) presumably does? The point gels with the tendency we have observed before about the constitution of Israel *not* strictly according to descent, but by acceptance of covenant and *torah*. While the topics of covenant and *torah* are not to the fore in Judges, it is at least worthy of comment that the strongest portrayal in it of a united Israel presents the outsider Jael in such favourable terms.

5. *Conclusion*

Judges can be read in the flow of Genesis to Kings as part of the account of Yahweh's purpose through Israel to establish his just rule in the world. It portrays Israel struggling with its ultimate loyalties, a struggle encapsulated in Gideon's alias 'Jerubbaal'. At stake in the contest between Yahweh and Baal for Israel's loyalty is the debate between slavery and the freedom of service, as in the Exodus narrative. In the unfolding story, which registers a tendency away from Yahweh and into religious-political decline, the themes of covenant, *torah* and justice-righteousness are muted. The possibility of establishing Yahweh's order in the world is asserted in his victories (a plural form of *tsedaqah*) over tyrannous kings, but also jeopardized by Israel's unfaithfulness.

However, the account of the victory over Jabin and Sisera, in its poetic form (Judges 5), offers a pattern for human power under Yahweh. It is a decentralized, co-operative model, in which Israel in its length and depth offers itself willingly in the struggle against tyranny. The Song of Deborah remains the Old Testament's great celebration of a form of political being that is by definition distinct from the idolatrous concentration of power. The decentralization of power proclaimed here corresponds to the resistance to tyranny that is the hallmark of the book. In the travails of judges, rulers, deliverers, Yahweh remains the Judge, Ruler, Deliverer (11.27). While the shape of Judges' prescription for political authority belongs to the particular context of tribal Israel among nations governed by tyrannical kings, the presiding genius of Yahweh's will to power with justice is visible through and beyond the imperfections of human government.

Israel itself, finally, is portrayed here in a pre-monarchical mode that some have taken to be its ideal form. While Judges provides no permanent template, Israel is depicted operating in unity and diversity, in a mode that is defined by its internal functioning. Its character is therefore essentially political, not ethnic, as is clear from its ready incorporation of Jael, like Ruth a zealot for Yahweh.

Chapter 8

MONARCHY: 1 AND 2 SAMUEL

The book of Samuel continues themes that are by now familiar: Yahweh's intention to exhibit through Israel his universal rule of justice-righteousness, the proper exercise of human power, and the nature of Israel itself. In this book, however, they are difficult to extricate from each other. Since the book's major focus is on the transition to kingship as the form of political power that will henceforth be recognized by Yahweh, the theme of the proper exercise of power is naturally to the fore. However, the book's thought on this topic is intricately bound up with its thought on the nature of Israel. The story of kingship as a form of rule under Yahweh tells at the same time of the envelopment of the people Israel in centralized statehood. By the same token the theme of Israel as witness to the divine purpose to exhibit his justice-righteousness to the nations is implicated in Israel's adoption of the political forms of its neighbours. But we turn first, in this instance, to the topic of the exercise of human rule.

1. *The Exercise of Power*

a. *Power: Human and Divine*
In the book of Judges, the complication of human rule in relation to divine appeared in the repeated threat to Israel from foreign tyrants as well as from the tendency within to serve foreign gods and so jeopardize the integrity of people and land. Judge-deliverers led and ruled with spasmodic but decreasing effectiveness, and the symbols of unity, the ark of the covenant and the central place of worship, dwelt in background shadow. The finale saw an uneasy peace without, a violent struggle for unity within, and the question posed as to whether a turn to kingship might not resolve Israel's problems. The book of Samuel[1] both continues the themes of Judges and introduces new dimensions. Samuel will track the advent of dynastic monarchy in Israel, but show with some force that such a move cannot in itself deal with the problem of corrupting power.

The centrality of human power in relation to the divine lies on the surface in Samuel. When the elders demand that the prophet Samuel appoint a king to lead them, Yahweh himself declares that in doing so they have rejected him as king

---

1. Samuel is best thought of as a single book, according to the oldest count of the Old Testament's canonical books. Together with Kings, it was subdivided in LXX; see Gordon, *I & II Samuel*, pp. 19–20.

over them (1 Sam. 8.7). There are shades of Gideon's refusal in this (Judg. 8.22–23). And as Judges began to disclose the potentially baneful consequences of monarchical rule, so Samuel develops the same theme in its microscopic scrutiny of dynasticism, not only in David, but in all the leadership contenders paraded in its opening chapters, Eli, Samuel himself, and Saul. The question posed to the reader here is not so much whether any particular form of rule is recommended, but in what way humans can bear the responsibilities of rule at all.

Critical study of Samuel often finds the background to its narratives in Israel's transition from tribal confederacy to centralized monarchical state. Pressure on the loosely connected tribes from the expansive Philistine city-states in the west led to Israel's mutation to a centralized kingdom that eventually proved able to overcome that danger.[2] The transition was inevitably controversial, with conservative resistance to monarchy reflected in those texts which see it as a challenge to Yahwism itself. On the basis of this presumed internal crisis, literary-critical analyses found opposing tendencies, respectively favourable and hostile to monarchy, embodied in literary layers that have come to compose the text in its finished form. In particular, 1 Samuel 8–12 could be analysed into components sympathetic to Saul's kingship and others that rejected it.[3] Interpreters tried to understand which of these voices came to prevail in the final form of the text, and how it then related to the tendency of the overarching Deuteronomistic History. Advocates could be found for the ultimate predominance of each viewpoint.[4]

However, as in Judges, the story of human power in Samuel cannot be reduced to the question whether or not monarchy is a good thing. Undoubtedly, the concept of kingship is intimated from the Song of Hannah on, when her hymn on Yahweh's raising of the weak culminates with:

> 'He will give strength to his king
> And exalt the power of his anointed (מְשִׁיחוֹ)' (1 Sam. 2.10).

As no king yet reigns in Israel at the time in question, this anticipatory affirmation is the more striking. It arcs forward to the 'last words of David', where David speaks of himself as 'the man whom God exalted'[5], and 'the anointed of the God of Jacob' (2 Sam. 23.1). This bracketing of the double book testifies to the significance of the figure of David in it. Even so, the concept of human rule is engaged subtly here.

b. *Power and Office*
At the beginning of Samuel, the ruling orders of Israel are in centre stage, but do not conform to a pre-set pattern. Rather, leadership roles are unexpected and

---

2.   Bruce C. Birch, 'The First and Second Books of Samuel', in *The New Interpreter's Bible II* (Nashville: Abingdon Press, 1998), pp. 949–1383 (953–4).

3.   The position was represented already by Wellhausen. A more recent form of it is offered by Crüsemann, *Der Widerstand gegen das Königtum*.

4.   As is the case for DtrH itself. Against Wellhausen, Crüsemann thought the anti-monarchical strains were earlier; so also Tomoo Ishida, *The Royal Dynasties in Ancient Israel* (BZAW, 142; Berlin: W. de Gruyter, 1977). Cf. Gordon, *I & II Samuel*, pp. 27–8.

5.   MT has 'the man who was raised on high'.

confused. Eli the priest presides at Shiloh, the place where Israelites come to worship Yahweh on annual pilgrimage. This seems at first like a welcome turn to order and stability following the anarchy of Judges 17–21. But such an impression is soon belied by Eli's failure to govern his own house, and the contempt of his sons Hophni and Phinehas for due order in worship at the central sanctuary (1 Sam. 2.12–17). Moreover, the degeneracy of Eli and his sons seems to stand for the state of governance in Israel. When the elders of Israel resolve to fetch 'the ark of the covenant of the LORD' to the battle-field against the Philistines, there is no record of his being involved in the decision, but only a note that the ark was accompanied by Hophni and Phinehas, whose disregard for it is already known (1 Sam. 4.3–4). When news of the ensuing defeat, death of his sons, and loss of the ark is brought to Eli, he immediately falls over dead (1 Sam. 4.18). But this report is followed by the surprising epitaph: 'he had judged Israel for forty years'.

The phrase unmistakably echoes the periods of rule by the 'judge-deliverers' in Judges, typically forty-year periods following acts of deliverance. Yet Eli is quite unlike such figures. First, he has patently not delivered Israel, quite the reverse. But second, he is a priest, holding a hereditary office, not raised up to deal with a crisis like the judge-deliverers. This 'judging', which as we have seen implies 'ruling', is predicated here of one who is already in a kind of dynastic office, while the story of 'judging' in Judges had precisely warned of the dangers of dynastic aspirations. In Eli, the dangers of dynasticism, foreshadowed in Judges, are vivid, and institutionalized in the heart of the people's life. His 'judging' of Israel is full of ominous irony: he has not ruled in an orderly way; he has not delivered Israel; indeed, his 'judging' only seems to elicit the response that there has been no one to deliver or rule in the way that such deliverance and rule formerly happened.

These deficiencies of Eli may be thought to have the effect of pointing to the need for a king (as some also read the failings of the judges). Against this, however, Eli has himself been perceived as a 'royal' figure. Polzin, finding connections in the poetics of Samuel between Eli, Saul, David and Absalom, thinks that the death of Eli symbolizes the ultimate passing of the kingship that the narrative is now moving inexorably towards. The death of Eli is the central event in 1 Samuel 1–7: '…in the fullness of time kingship in Israel would disappear'.[6] If this leans too heavily on the metaphorical character of 1 Sam. 4.18, it is true that Eli and his sons introduce the dangers of dynasticism as such, and place a shadow over the imminent acceptance of monarchy into Israel. A particularly telling parallel with David is found in the oracle against Eli's priestly house (1 Sam. 2.27–36), in which the promise once made to his ancestor (Aaron) that his family should serve as priests 'for ever' (v. 30), is now revoked, on the grounds that it has proved unworthy. The promise of a dynasty 'for ever' anticipates the promise that will in due course be made to David (2 Sam. 7.13). But the manner of the

---

6. R. Polzin, *Samuel and the Deuteronomist* (New York: Harper and Row, 1989), p. 64. See also p. 235 n. 3: 'Eli functions in these opening chapters as a royal figure'.

anticipation is a clear warning that a divine promise 'for ever' cannot be taken as an unconditional guarantee. When Yahweh declares, 'Those who honour me I will honour, but those who despise me shall be treated with contempt', the house of David is the ultimate target.

If Eli has 'judged' Israel for forty years and now lies dead, what follows next? The narrative gives different answers. The oracle declared to the old man by 'a man of God' points to a future successor of Eli in the office of priest (1 Sam. 2.35–36), an oracle that on the surface of the narrative finds fulfilment in Zadok, installed in the priestly office by Solomon (1 Kgs 2.35). Yet the sense of the immediate story is that Samuel himself succeeds Eli.[7] Raised in the Shiloh sanctuary he takes on a priestly role, as when he reserves to himself the right of sacrifice before Saul goes to battle (1 Sam. 10.8, cf. 9.13). But Samuel too cannot be contained within the confines of a single office. Not only a priestly figure, he is also said to have 'judged' Israel, in the sense that comprises both military victory and the regular administration of justice (1 Sam. 7.5–14, 15–17). And no less than these he acts as a prophet, in his role of declaring God's word and in anointing the newly chosen king. His prophetic status is underlined in a brief exchange between Saul and his servant, when it seems that the whole gamut of terms for prophet is applied to him (1 Sam. 9.5–10). There are, finally, hints in Hannah's vow that Samuel is a Nazirite.[8]

As priest, judge and prophet, Samuel's evident similarities to Moses may be taken as a recommendation, up to a point: here is indeed the 'man of God' who meets the crisis of the time. But just at the moment when he appears to fulfil all the qualities of leadership, in victory and administering justice, he is revealed as an aspiring dynast, who 'made his sons judges over Israel' (1 Sam. 8.1). Suddenly the similarities with Moses are severely qualified, for Moses was precisely not a dynast. When Samuel the judge delivers Israel *then* makes his sons judges, memories of the fatal flaw of Gideon overtake the memories of Moses. Samuel the dynast bespeaks eloquently a crisis in the constitution and leadership in Israel. Not surprisingly, perhaps, it is at this point that the elders of Israel demand a king (1 Sam. 8.5). The drumbeat comes to its critical moment.

Will kingship finally resolve Israel's need for good order? Saul will be chosen then rejected, in a further tilt at dynasticism (the heir-apparent, Jonathan, even taking the part of his father's rival). But how does the figure of Saul contribute to the struggle towards power properly exerted? Saul proves to be no less ambivalent than the other characters in the drama. In a curious incident he 'prophesies' in company with a band of ecstatic prophets, prompting the saying: 'Is Saul also among the prophets?' (1 Sam. 10.9–13). Impatient to get on with war against the Philistines, he usurps Samuel's priestly role in making the expected preparatory sacrifice (1 Sam. 13.8–9). When he first takes up his task of leading in battle, he

---

7. Cf. Polzin, *Samuel*, p. 60. L. Eslinger, following Buber, thinks that the oracle itself refers to Samuel, *Kingship of God in Crisis* (Sheffield: Almond Press, 1985), pp. 138–40; cf. David Firth, '"Play it Again, Sam": the Poetics of Narrative Repetition in 1 Samuel 1–7', *TynBul* 56.2 (2005), pp. 1–17 (8).

8. See Eslinger, *Kingship of God*, p. 92.

looks not so much like a king as one of the judge-deliverers familiar from Judges. In his action in 1 Samuel 11, which puts him in his best light, he is found plough- ing his fields, the spirit of God comes upon him, and he sends throughout Israel to gather the tribes together for war. The incident, revolving around Jabesh– Gilead and Gibeah, closely recalls the cause of war between Benjamin and the other tribes in Judges 19–21. Is the vacuum that existed in that place now met by a judge-deliverer, and does Saul's success in this capacity lead to the people's regret that they asked for a king?[9]

c. *Kingship and the King*
The most important reservation about Saul's role comes in the terminology used. Answering the demand for a 'king' (מֶלֶךְ, *melek*), Yahweh commands Samuel to anoint Saul 'prince' (נָגִיד, *nagid*) (9.16). Samuel then uses this term when he anoints Saul (10.1),[10] and later in relation to David (1 Sam. 13.14), only applying the word *melek* to Saul in such a way as to distance himself from it (1 Sam. 12.13–17, 25). In the view of both Yahweh and Samuel, the new role that is now initiated in Israel continues to be best represented by the term *nagid*, as we see when Samuel declares that Saul's rule will not continue, and that this office will pass to David (1 Sam. 13.14). The same designation recurs at key moments in the story of royal rule, as when David is acclaimed by 'all the tribes of Israel' (2 Sam. 5.2, cf. 6.21), in David's appointment of Solomon as his successor (1 Kgs 1.35),[11] and further in relation to Jeroboam, Jehu and Hezekiah. Most importantly, it is the expression chosen by Yahweh in his promise to David of dynastic rule (2 Sam. 7.8). While the term *melek* occurs in the narrative of this event as David's title, Yahweh avoids it in his words to David, recalling instead the time when David was preferred to Saul as 'prince'. Donald Murray has seen in the use of *nagid* here and throughout Samuel a deliberate ideological challenge to the idea of the king as *melek*. While the *melek* 'sees his power from Yahweh as susceptible to his own arbitrary manipulation', the *nagid* is 'no more than the willing subject of the divine monarch'.[12] Kings in Israel do not cease to be 'prince' (*nagid*) in Yahweh's eyes (1 Kgs 14.7; 16.2; 2 Kgs 20.5).[13] The characterization

---

9. So Polzin, *Samuel*, pp. 112–13. Cf. also E. M. Good, who described a double arc in the narrative of chs 8–12 in which Saul grew in confidence in his kingly role, while the people came to withdraw from their first enthusiasm; *Irony in the Old Testament* (London: SPCK, 1965), pp. 56– 80.

10. The designation of Saul as *nagid* and his resemblance initially to a judge-deliverer has led some to think that the narrative represents a real transition in a society that was not ready to assimi- late a full kingship model all at once; see Birch, 'Samuel', pp. 953–4; cf. P. K. McCarter, *I Samuel* (AB; New York: Doubleday, 1980), p. 206.

11. In this case David also employs the verb יַמְלִךְ, related to *melek*.

12. Donald F. Murray, *Divine Prerogative and Royal Pretension* (JSOTSup, 264; Sheffield: Sheffield Academic Press, 1998), p. 299.

13. It may be significant that these occurrences all come at significant junctures in Israel's life: the division of the kingdom, the appointment of Jehu to rid Israel of the Baal-worshipping dynasty of Ahab, and the period when Judah is about to stand alone, following the demise of the northern kingdom.

of the kings of Israel and Judah as *nagid* affirms their subordination to the rule of Yahweh. Saul proved unable to stay within the boundaries laid down. The second attempt in Israel to establish royal rule (after Abimelech) ends no more successfully than the first.[14]

It follows from these observations about the leading characters that 1 Samuel 1–12 presents no simple transition from 'judge' to 'king'. It is the activity of 'judging-ruling' that is in centre stage, while Eli, Samuel, (their sons), and Saul make their bids to take the reins of power. The sense of jostling for this privilege is conveyed by the lack of clear definition between the roles that the characters occupy. The overlap between them appears, for example, in the way in which the priest Eli can prefigure the king David (as we have seen), and even in the hint of confusion between Samuel and Saul in Hannah's declaration about her answered prayer (1 Sam. 2.27–28).[15] The rule exercised by the various leaders in 1 Samuel 1–12 can fulfil all the requirements of human responsibility, not least in the glimpse of Samuel's 'judgeship', in which he presides over Israel's defeat of the Philistines and administers justice to the whole people (1 Sam. 7.15–17). The thrice-repeated notice in these verses that he 'judged' Israel implies that the requirements of rule were satisfied in him. Even so, each character eventually proves wanting. In this portrayal of the human potential to rule justly, the possibility of such rule is accepted, but the danger of corruption lies waiting at the door. It is this cautionary beginning that prepares for the advent of the 'man after God's own heart', the youngest son of Jesse.

The story of David's rise to the throne of Israel is the single most important topic in the book of Samuel. But it is crucial to the treatment of it that it is prefaced by this extended exploration of human power in relation to the divine. The underlying assumption of the story is that kingship belongs properly to Yahweh, and human power is subject to his word. Samuel, though initially reluctant to nominate a king because of his own ambitions, represents in effect the supremacy of the prophetic word over the royal power. He anoints Saul, declares him in due course to have been found wanting (13.13), and perceives Yahweh's true choice for the role in the youngest son of Jesse (16.6–13). He also declares the 'law of the king' (*mishpat hammelek*, 8.11) and the 'law of the kingship' (*mishpat hammelukah*, 10.25). The term *mishpat* implies in this connection that the kingship is itself subject to governance, as is expressly brought out in the latter case.[16]

---

14. David Jobling, rightly identifying analogies between the stories of Abimelech and Saul, thinks the Abimelech story acts proleptically as a qualification of the favourable portrayal of Saul in 1 Samuel 8–12. It accords better with the development of the storyline in Judges and Samuel, however, if we suppose that the disaster of Abimelech, coming earlier in the narrative, works to cast a shadow over the story of Saul; with Polzin, *Samuel*, p. 241.

15. The play on the name 'Saul' occurs in Hannah's reference to her 'petition' (v. 27), and expressly in 'lent' (v. 28), which is precisely שָׁאוּל, Saul's name. McCarter thinks this shows that the Samuel birth-narrative has ousted one that originally referred to Saul; *I Samuel*, pp. 65–6. But given the capacity of this narrative to suggest meanings beyond the surface level, it is preferable to look for ways in which the birth of Samuel points to Saul. For suggestions on this, see Eslinger, *Kingship of God*, p. 94.

16. *Mishpat* can carry weaker senses, such as 'custom', which would be appropriate for 1 Sam.

That being so, Samuel's use of the former term is ironic, since the 'law of the king' turns out to be a picture of kingship as rigorous centralism turning to a tyranny that brings the people to cry in despair just as under the Pharaoh of the exodus (8.11–18). Samuel's vision may, no doubt, be affected at this point by his own displeasure at the people's request. Even so, the word proves to be prescient, finding its mark rather soon in the excesses of Solomon, already the implied target of the law of the king in Deut. 17.14–17,[17] and surpassed by the swaggering Rehoboam (1 Kgs 5.27–32[EVV 13–18]; 9.22; 12.1–11). Translations understandably look for alternatives to 'law' for *mishpat* here (e.g. 'the ways of the king', NRSV). But this misses the ironic echo that is heard between 8.11 and 10.25, and thus the point that a concept that implies regulation describes in fact the unbridled use of power.

With the 'law of the kingship' (10.25), the idea of due regulation emerges clearly.[18] After Saul has been anointed (*nagid*, by Samuel, 10.1) and acclaimed (*melek*, by the people, 10.24), Samuel writes this 'law' in a book and '[lays] it up before the LORD'. There are echoes here of the 'book of the law' that Moses commanded the Levites to keep with the ark of the covenant (Deut. 31.9, 25). Here are statutes governing the exercise of kingship, drawn up by prophetic sanction, and deposited in the place of worship as a witness that the exercise of this power must fall within the boundaries of Yahweh's covenant with Israel. What Samuel now writes is obviously different from what he declared would be 'the law of the king'. But because of the verbal echo of 8.11, we know that what is imposed upon the king as obligation has already had its overture in a prophecy that points towards the abuse of power.[19]

This discrepancy between the ideal and the actual finds further expression in the narrative. In the view of Samuel, the 'kingship' belongs within the covenant and under prophetic authority. This explains Samuel's instruction to king and people to 'renew the kingship' at Gilgal, and their '[making] Saul king' (11.14–15). The passage has often been thought to be out of place, since it comes so soon after Saul's confirmation as king in ch. 10.[20] However, it functions to locate the making of Saul king within the larger setting of an act of remembrance at Gilgal, the place where Israel had entered the land, with Yahweh as divine warrior (Josh. 4.19). Thus the conferring of kingship on Saul reminds that kingship properly belongs to Yahweh.[21] This indeed is the specific connotation of the

8.11 taken in isolation (cf. Polzin, *Samuel*, p. 86). However, its meaning emerges here by contrast with the similar phrase in 10.25.

17. While it is not necessary to suppose that Samuel actually refers to that law here, there is an unmistakable echo of it in a reading of Samuel after Deuteronomy.

18. Cf. Polzin, *Samuel*, p. 86.

19. Translations of 10.25 again try to spell out what is involved, as in NRSV's 'the rights and duties of the kingship'. While this is an accurate rendering of the immediate phrase, it risks distracting from the echo with 8.11.

20. This traditional critical approach is documented by R. Vannoy, *Covenant Renewal at Gilgal* (Cherry Hill, NJ; Mack, 1978), pp. 61–6.

21. Vannoy distinguished sharply between the kingship of Yahweh at this point and that of Saul, and saw the ceremony at Gilgal as a covenant-renewal; *Covenant Renewal at Gilgal*, pp. 67–91.

'kingship', the kind of kingly rule conceived according to Yahweh's purpose.[22] It is clear in the developing story, however, that Saul and his followers regard the 'kingship' as a thing to be possessed. This is manifested particularly in his fear that David will take it from him (18.8). And well after his death the Saulide Shimei reflects the same view when he taunts David that Yahweh will in turn take it from him to give it to Absalom (2 Sam. 16.8).[23]

d. *David as King*

David's rise and accession to the kingship can look like the culmination of hopes nurtured through earlier stages of the extended narrative. He has been categorically preferred over Saul (1 Sam. 13.14), and likelier contenders even from his own family (1 Samuel 16), and became the scourge of the Philistines in his victory over the seemingly invincible Goliath by virtue of his faith in Yahweh (1 Samuel 17). In Saul's jealous pursuit of him, David twice shows respect for 'the LORD's anointed' by refraining from laying violent hands on him, and is taught patience to wait for Yahweh's good time by the theologically articulate Abigail.[24] His sympathetic portrayal extends to the moving story of his friendship with Jonathan, and his grief over the death of both father and son (2 Sam. 1.19–27), such that the narrative has often been thought as intending to exonerate David from guilt for their deaths.[25] Furthermore, David succeeds where all others had failed. He leads a united Israel to a victory over the Philistines that enables him to recover the ark of the covenant from the place where it had remained in a kind of limbo for twenty years (1 Sam. 7.2), and brings it to Jerusalem (2 Samuel 6). With this unifying of the people, defeat of enemies, and restoration of Israel's chief religious symbol to the place of its own political control, it seems that a wholly new phase has arrived. And this is apparently confirmed by the language of 2 Sam. 7.1, where David is not only established as king, but has been granted 'rest from all his enemies around him', in an echo of Deut. 12.9–10. According to the typology of Deuteronomy, this 'rest from enemies' should be followed by

Eslinger in contrast thinks of an actual renewal of Saul's kingship, in which Saul and his detractors agree 'to act together under the auspices of the new monarchic constitution', *Kingship of God*, p. 378. He too, however, looks for a reconciliation of the human kingship with the divine prerogative.

22. Eslinger, *Kingship of God*, p. 378.

23. Besides המלוכה (11.14), three other terms for 'kingdom' appear, all related to *melek*: ממלכות (1 Sam. 15.28), מלכות (20.31), ממלכה (10.18). These are all descriptive terms, referring to the human kingdom (or kingdoms) as an established fact.

24. Robert Gordon has demonstrated the narrative analogies between the two incidents in which David has a potential advantage over Saul (1 Sam. 24 and 26, note 24.1–7; 26.6–12) and the intervening story of David, Nabal and Abigail, in which his sparing of Nabal for a failure to show hospitality becomes the occasion of a lesson from Abigail in trusting Yahweh to make him king in due course, without shedding blood (25.23–31); 'David's Rise and Saul's Demise: Narrative Analogy in 1 Samuel 24–26', *TynBul* 31 (1980), pp. 37–64. Abigail is no doubt politically as well as theologically astute, since she becomes in due course David's wife.

25. McCarter, *I Samuel*, p. 28. An original 'History of David's Rise' was postulated by L. Rost, *The Succession to the Throne of David* (trans. Michael D. Rutter and David M. Gunn; Sheffield: Almond Press, 1982; original 1926).

resort for worship to the place of Yahweh's choosing (Deut. 12.11). So in this respect too it seems that the typology finds its fulfilment when David turns his mind to building a temple for Yahweh in Jerusalem. Finally, after further victories, David administers 'justice and righteousness to all his people' (2 Sam. 8.15).

However, on closer examination the career of David gives less cause for celebration than first appears. While his behaviour in the flight from Saul can be given the benefit of the doubt, it can equally be read as displaying the tactics of one who is intent on taking power.[26] The story of his unification of Israel and establishment of a capital in Jerusalem, traditionally regarded as a masterstroke, is at the same time a record of civil war, in which the enmity between David and Saul has broken open an underlying rift between north and south in Israel (2 Samuel 2–4), reminiscent of the war against Benjamin in Judges 19–21. This internecine tendency in Israel is symptomized by the vendetta-like violence between leading figures on both sides: Saul's general Abner kills Asahel, to be avenged in time by Asahel's brothers Joab and Abishai, despite having defected to David; Saul's son Ishbaal (Ishbosheth), who had reigned briefly in Saul's stead, is murdered by Rechab and Baanah. As Polzin has observed, the murders in these chapters have fratricidal aspects,[27] which sit ill with the deuteronomic ideal of all Israel as 'brothers'. Once again there are moves to exonerate David. He mourns Abner as he had mourned Saul and Jonathan, and repudiates the violence of 'the sons of Zeruiah' (2 Sam. 3.27), and Rechab and Baanah meet a violent end in turn at his command (4.9–12). Yet David's grip on power has come about by means of such violence. And in his dying counsel to Solomon, he will recommend the political killing of his loyal general Joab, who in the conflict over the succession has sided with the loser Adonijah (1 Kgs 2.5–6, 28). The long transition into kingship carries with it the grim imperatives of statehood, as seen by the political class.

The ark's progress towards Jerusalem expresses at one level the end of the Philistine threat, but at another the ambiguities surrounding David's increasing hold on power. The death of Uzzah, and David's consequent anger, express Yahweh's refusal to be controlled and David's unease with this (2 Sam. 6.8).[28] And in the celebrations of its arrival, Michal's contempt for him is expressed in a form that plays on the ark-related concept of 'glory'; in her eyes David's 'honour/glory' is in reality his dishonour (2 Sam. 6.20).[29] The narrative casts doubt by implication on whether Yahweh has been glorified in David's march to the supreme political position in Israel.

---

26. This approach has been taken by Peter D. Miscall, who thinks David's character in many episodes is 'undecidable', but that some, such as 1 Samuel 25–30, suggest a negative reading more strongly than others; *1 Samuel: a Literary Reading* (Bloomington: Indiana University Press, 1986). p. 150. In the case of Goliath, David may see 'a perfect opportunity for personal fame and advancement', p. 120.

27. Polzin, *David*, pp. 47–51.

28. Donald Murray sees David's motive in respect of the ark the intention to bring all authority in Israel under his own sway, in what was effectively a challenge to the divine 'prerogative', *Divine Prerogative*, pp. 19–20, 247–8.

29. Polzin, *David*, p. 68, and cf. pp. 60–3.

The story of the promise to David of a dynastic house (2 Samuel 7) is similarly hedged about with reservations. The most obvious aspect of this is Yahweh's refusal of David's plan to build him a 'house' (meaning 'temple'). In doing so he declines to be subordinated to the ANE political-religious pattern according to which kings celebrate victories by building temples to the patron god.[30] Kings, claiming to be 'shepherds' of their peoples, would commemorate their roles as temple-builders by divine appointment.[31] Such claims are roundly rebuffed here. Not only is David not to build a temple, but also the language of kingship is questioned, for David has been taken from his 'shepherding' to be, not 'king' (*melek*), but 'prince' (*nagid*, v. 8). This is a pointed recollection of the struggle towards kingship under Saul, where the latter term had a definite limiting function.[32] Yahweh may speak of David's 'kingdom' here (ממלכה, v. 16), but not of David as 'king'. The concept of the Israelite king as *nagid* forms the most important single link between this narrative of the dynastic oracle and the story of Yahweh's first permission of kingship (1 Samuel 8–12).

Yahweh's manner of repudiating David's offer is to turn attention back to the origins of Israel at Sinai and after, when his presence had been symbolized in a tent-shrine (2 Sam. 7.5–7). In this way, the current position of Israel is carefully connected to the originating covenantal events, but the accent is on sharp contrast. The language of permanence is set against the language of mobility, recalling the movement of Yahweh with his people through wilderness to land.[33] Furthermore, as Polzin has pointed out, the phrase 'since the day I brought up the people of Israel from Egypt to this day' (v. 6), strongly recalls 1 Sam. 8.8, where Yahweh condemns the request for a king as a rejection of himself and an act of idolatry; similar phrases recur at other doom-laden moments in the larger narrative.[34] There is in addition an implication that David's intention is not according to the divine command (v. 7). To the superficial impression that David's political successes constitute a fulfilment of Deuteronomic command and promise, therefore, is a counterpoint that exposes David's own ambitions, and the implied conformity of his purposes to the very models of rule that the story of Israel's birth had set out to overcome.

Yahweh finally turns David's proposal to build him a 'house' into Yahweh's own contrary purpose to build a 'house' for David, namely a dynastic house. This wordplay becomes part of the rejection of the temple-project in principle, even though it would in time be realized, with Yahweh's permission, under Solomon. The idea of kingship had always carried with it the notion of succession, both in

---

30. Murray, *Divine Prerogative*, pp. 252–60. For example, he draws attention to inscriptions of Sargon II, concerning victories in battle followed by the building of a new capital city Dur-Sharrukin; pp. 252–3.

31. Murray, *Divine Prerogative*, p. 264–5.

32. Murray, *Divine Prerogative*, p. 266. *Nagid* is thus not only set against *melek*, but possibly also the Mesopotamian usage of 'shepherding' for kingly rule. If so, the 'shepherding' in v. 7 would negate the Mesopotamian usage in a different way, by predicating it of rulers who were not kings.

33. Murray, *Divine Prerogative*, p. 247.

34. Polzin, *David*, pp. 75–6. Cf. Judg. 19.30; 2 Kgs 21.15.

the law that governed it (Deut. 17.20), and in Israel's first request for it (Judg. 8.22–23). Moreover, had Saul's rule established itself, the succession would have carried with it the promise that it would be 'for ever' (1 Sam. 13.13–14). Now this promise comes to David, that his house will last 'for ever'. In a sense this is only to repeat what was in any case entailed in the dynastic idea. But the notion dominates the chapter in which the oracle is given. Three times Yahweh promises David that his kingdom and his son's would last 'for ever' (2 Sam. 7.7, 13, 16), and David then repeats it five times in his prayer in response (7.24–26, 29).[35] The appearance of unconditionality in the promise to David here is well known, and indeed was deeply rooted in Israel, as the perplexity of a psalm like Psalm 89 makes clear. Yet the very repetition of 'for ever' draws attention to the idea so strongly that the reader is bound to ask what is really implied in it, the more so, perhaps, as it is invoked more by David than by Yahweh. We have already before us the oracle to Eli in which a promise 'for ever' was rescinded because of the failure of his house to remain faithful to Yahweh (1 Sam. 2.30). And in the sequel to this oracle the relationship between the promise and the command that the Davidic kings actually remain faithful to Yahweh becomes a pressing topic. The conditionality of the dynastic promise gains expression in David's solemn charge to Solomon on his death-bed (1 Kgs 2.2–4). Yet in spite of this, a disparity emerges between Solomon's view of the divine assurance and Yahweh's: while Solomon sees the temple as a monument to Yahweh's perpetual presence, Yahweh himself continues to insist on obedience to his commands (1 Kgs 9.3–9). Eslinger has spoken of the 'surreptitious rhetoric' of Solomon in his prayers, seeing them as attempts to use the promise for his own ends. And indeed, his dedicatory prayer has travelled a long way from Yahweh's declaration that he has always dwelt in a tent (1 Kgs 8.12–13, cf. 2 Sam. 7.6–7).[36]

The portrayal of David as king is mixed. In a single verse, he is said to have 'administered justice and equity (*mishpat utsedaqah*) to all his people' (2 Sam. 8.15). He thus matches the kingly ideal as expressed in a psalm like Psalm 72, and briefly at least procures an order in Israel that has consistently been held out as desirable. Yet this glimpse of the righteous king is hedged about with reservation. Samuel too had 'administered justice to Israel' (1 Sam. 7.17), but as in his case the report of it was the immediate prelude to the trouble caused by his nepotism, so the story of David turns directly from this similar report to trouble in the area of sons and succession.[37] The notice that 'David's sons were priests'

---

35. The expression varies slightly in the last two cases from עֹד־עוֹלָם to לְעוֹלָם, but without significant change of meaning.

36. Lyle Eslinger, *Into the Hands of the Living God* (Sheffield: Almond Press, 1989), pp. 156–8. Eslinger's type of reading calls into question the approach to the text in which different interests are assigned to various editorial layers. In McCarter's view, for example, 2 Sam. 7.19, 22a, 27–28 (29bα) come from 'a Solomonic writer', whose purpose was 'to show that David's request for a dynasty was buttressed by a divine promise, and that the erection of the temple was an outgrowth of the arrival of the ark in Jerusalem', *II Samuel* (AB; New York: Doubleday, 1984, p. 240).

37. The story of David 's rule in 2 Samuel 9–20, 1 Kings 1–2 was long known as the 'Succession Narrative', following Rost, *Succession*. His belief that such an entity once had a separate existence from the surrounding material in Samuel is no longer widely held (see Gordon, *I and II*

(8.18) is an alert that the kingdom will revolve around the person and family of the king in ways that breach conventional lines of responsibility. Equally, the first intimations of state organization (8.16–18) show that dynasty will not mean succession only, but also the apparatus of centralism of which Samuel had warned.

The depiction of David's rule is a brilliant account of the conflict between the frailty of a human being and the exigencies of wielding power. Is it David's humanity that prevails in his warm treatment of Jonathan's son Mephibosheth (2 Samuel 9), or the dawning of that political ruthlessness that will flavour his later counsel to Solomon?[38] In his adultery with Bathsheba, human weakness is indulged by the use of royal power to procure the murder of her husband (2 Samuel 11). This sin elicits from the prophet Nathan a word of divine judgement on David, matching the promise of dynastic succession 'for ever' with another, that the 'sword shall not depart from your house *for ever*' (2 Sam. 12.10). Nathan elaborates, promising trouble 'from within your own house', and a punishment in kind for the violent possession of Bathsheba, when David's own wives would be publicly given over to another (2 Sam. 12.11–12). When David's son Amnon rapes his half-sister Tamar, in a perpetuation of his father's use of his power to possess a woman, the repercussions lead towards civil war, when Tamar's full brother Absalom murders Amnon in revenge (2 Samuel 13). The rumour goes up that Absalom has killed 'all the king's sons' (vv. 30–33), touching on the fear inherent in the situation that this act of revenge is also a bid for the throne. And indeed, Absalom's rage at his father for kid-glove treatment of Amnon leads in fact to such a bid, which temporarily drives David, together with the ark of the covenant, from Jerusalem (2 Samuel 15). David will in time return, though hardly in triumph. His imprisonment of the ten concubines he left to guard the palace, and with whom Absalom fulfilled Yahweh's word of judgement on him (16.20–23; 20.3), was a living reminder of his ignominy. But the climax of his tragedy occurs in the death of Absalom (2 Sam. 18.9–15), the son whom he dearly loved killed by the power of the state which David had constructed. In Joab's cold execution of the young man, and his contempt thereafter for the king's grief, lies all the logic of a centralizing power that alienates humanity itself (2 Sam. 18.3–19.8). Joab's appeal is based on a creed of loyalty to the state above all (19.5–6). There is deep irony in his accusation of David that he has 'made it clear today [by his display of grief] that commanders and officers are nothing to you' (v. 6). On the contrary, commanders and officers were the stuff of his ambition. But 'the man after God's own heart' is in the end deeply tormented by the kind of power that he has exercised. The deuteronomic law, with its self-effacing king (Deut. 17.14–20), stands over this desolate scene with a wisdom that David did not attain.

Samuel, pp. 41–2). The theme of 'succession' is part of the broader interest in issues of sons and dynasties in Samuel.

38. David shows suspicion towards Mephibosheth in 2 Sam. 16.1–4; 19.25, but his fears are apparently allayed (vv. 29–30). For his counsel to Solomon, see 1 Kgs 2.5–9.

The finale of the book of Samuel (2 Samuel 21–24) corresponds to the mixed picture of David that is painted by the book as a whole. Formerly considered an Appendix,[39] it is more accurately recognized as an artful ring-composition, formed from three pairs of discrete units from different times in the preceding story. The outermost panels are stories of judgement on David (21.1–14; 24.1–25); these are flanked by lists of David's warriors (21.15–22; 23.8–39); and at the centre stand two passages in David's own words, a psalm of thanksgiving for deliverance (22.1–51),[40] and the 'last words of David', in which he sings of the 'everlasting covenant' between God and his 'house' (23.1–7) – the book's only application of the term 'covenant' (ברית) to the relationship between Yahweh and David established by the dynastic promise (v. 5). The meaning of the Conclusion – and thus of the book of Samuel – is initially obscured by the structure of the composition itself. Are we compelled by the songs at the centre, in both of which David celebrates the commitment of Yahweh to him and his house 'for ever'? In the longer psalm this is the ground of his many victories (22.51); in the latter he applies to himself terms reminiscent of Hannah's Song ('anointed', 'exalted', 23.1, cf. 1 Sam. 2.10c), almost at the beginning of the book. The claim to justice and righteousness is entered in both songs (22.21; 23.3), and as this finds a corresponding note in the narrative (2 Sam. 8.15), it may be taken as a last expression of one of the themes of the book.

Or are we finally compelled by the stories of judgement? In the former (ch. 21) a famine is explained by bloodguilt on the house of Saul for a crime against the Gibeonites (not recorded in Samuel or elsewhere),[41] in violation of the ancient oath of Joshua protecting them (Joshua 9). The story hangs on the binding and lasting effect of oaths (David exempts Mephibosheth from the decimation in maintaining his own oath to Jonathan, v. 7). And it is oath-violation that falls foul of Yahweh's judgement here, pointing up a conflict between loyalty to Yahweh himself and the political expediency that presumably lay behind Saul's action.[42] In the latter episode, Saul has given way to David (as in the narrative). Yahweh's anger, in this case, is first said to be directed against Israel (24.1), without explanation, and the ensuing punishment, therefore, is not related primarily to

39. This was because of its disparate material and non-linear development. The interpretation of the Samuel Conclusion (as he calls it) has been well documented by H. H. Klement, *II Samuel 21–24. Context, Structure and Meaning in the Samuel Conclusion* (EUS XXIII/682; Frankfurt/M: Peter Lang, 2000), pp. 21–40. In particular, the status of the Conclusion in Samuel suffered from Rost's concept of the Succession Narrative, which jumped from 2 Samuel 20 to 1 Kings 1–2. For Klement's detailed analysis of the Conclusion, see pp. 164–240.

40. The psalm is virtually identical to Psalm 18.

41. See McCarter, *II Samuel*, p. 441, for a possible reference to the massacre at Nob, though McCarter himself thinks it best to suppose that the reference is simply to an otherwise unrecorded event.

42. The narrative signals that Saul's 'zeal for the people of Israel and Judah' (v. 2) is misplaced. It recalls his unwise flouting of Samuel's command in his anxiety to get on with the war against the Philistines (1 Sam. 13.8–10), and paradoxically with his laxness in prosecuting the 'devotion to destruction' of the Amalekites (1 Samuel 15). In all these cases Saul shows insensitivity to the real issues as interpreted by the prophetic word.

David's guilty census. Yet he too is implicated, presumably because of an illicit obsession with his growing power,[43] a danger perceived even by the pragmatic Joab (24.3). In these outer panels of the Conclusion, the progression from Saul to David recalls the same progression in the narrative, and the effect is to mitigate the strong distinction between the two kings. Power has blinded David to the true nature of his position just as it did Saul.[44] The memory of both Saul and David, furthermore, recalls the civil war between those two houses, which have continued to have their effects until well into David's reign (2 Sam. 16.5–8). Finally, the book is allowed to end with an account of a judgement in which 70,000 Israelites perish (24.17), and its sequel in the identification of the threshing-floor of Araunah as the place for the erecting of an altar, and implicitly therefore, of the temple.[45] The building of the temple, narrated in due course in Kings, therefore falls under the shadow not only of Yahweh's initial demurral in 2 Samuel 7, but also of this judgement-story.

The middle panels of the Conclusion consist of lists of David's powerful military hierarchy, interspersed with fragmentary war-reports (21.15–22; 23.8–39). These seem at first haphazard. But they draw attention to the military character of David's regime; they leave an impression of continuing war against the Philistines, raising a doubt about the picture of total victory sketched before (2 Sam. 7.1); and in a list of mute names, the last one of all speaks volumes, for it is none other than Uriah the Hittite (23.39), the noble-minded and courageous soldier whose death in battle David engineered so that he could dignify his own liaison with the man's wife with a formal legitimacy. The military machine so impressively documented here was not only put to the task of securing the borders of the kingdom, but to the king's private and nefarious uses.

The Conclusion therefore strongly qualifies the positive portrayal of David in the middle poetic sections. Both prophecies concerning David's house still stand by the end of the book, that 'the throne of his kingdom' will be established 'for ever' (2 Sam. 7.13), but that equally his house shall be subject to violence 'for ever'. Much of this violence, indeed, begins from within, and the schism between Judah and Benjamin is a harbinger of the lasting division between north and south that will result from Jeroboam's secession from Rehoboam's Judah (1 Kings 12). Brueggemann is right, therefore, when he sees the Conclusion as a 'deconstruction', finding that it aims 'to dismantle the high royal theology which has been enacted elsewhere in the narrative, and historically in the Jerusalem establishment'.[46] Commenting on the divine anger with Israel in 24.1, Polzin sees its ultimate reason in Israel's demand for a king in the first place. For him, 'declarations of divine will concerning royal succession need always to be balanced by the Deuteronomist's continuing view of kingship, David's included,

---

43. Cf. Polzin, *David*, p. 213.
44. Cf. Klement, *II Samuel 21–24*, p. 179.
45. It is taken thus at least in 1 Chron. 21.28–22.1.
46. CF. W. Brueggemann, '2 Samuel 21–24: an Appendix of Deconstruction?', *CBQ* 50 (1988), pp. 383–97 (385).

as idolatry'.[47] Both of these assessments judge the Conclusion to be carefully integrated into the book's theology, and let its accent fall on the reservations about monarchical power that are expressed from the beginning, in spite of the conferral of divine favour on David entailed in the dynastic promise.

2. *Israel*

The story of Israel in Samuel is a function of the story of David. His advent occasions at one level the completion of the final instalment of the gift of the land. David wrests from non-Israelite peoples the last enclaves that Joshua's Israel could not, including Jerusalem. The land has rest, the people have sought and found the place that Yahweh would choose to signal his ownership of the land, and as the place of worship for all the tribes. As we have observed, the promise-command of Deut. 12.5–12 is at last fulfilled to the letter according to the terms of 2 Sam. 7.1 in the immediate prelude to the dynastic promise.

Yet the same story has also evolved out of Israel's choice to ask for a king, which is portrayed as a rejection of Yahweh. And in the dynastic promise itself, the proposal to build a temple is also characterized as a misunderstanding of the nature of Israel's God. The final occupation of Canaan occurs in the midst of a transformation in Israel, from tribal confederacy to centralized state. As Samuel foresaw, the balances between the central and the local are upset, as the development of mechanisms of state puts people at the service of the centre. And the story of David has shown how this transformation now puts Israel in the grip of the unstoppable logic of centralized power. The person of the king, and the state itself, must be preserved at all costs and by all means. The spirit of the new Israel is expressed perfectly in the ruthlessness of Joab, its alienation and inhumanity symbolized in the helplessness of David as the logic of statehood eliminates his best-loved son.

Forced unity, finally, proves to be weak at its core. The tribes had co-existed in their diversity, and this could even amount to enmity, as in the Benjaminite war. Yet Israel was able to respond to that crisis and regroup. In a time of centralized power, division may be more serious and permanent. The signs are already there in David's Israel that the adoption of Jerusalem as his capital, putatively his political masterstroke, could not force the disparate parts of Israel into rigid unity. The very attempt to unify creates the conditions for definitive breach. Israel is divided, just at the point of conflict opened up by the struggle for royal power, thus anticipating two Israels and two kings.

3. *Kingship and Yahweh's Universal Rule*

Having examined the view of kingship in Samuel, it remains to consider the cosmic dimension of the book's politics. As I have been proposing, the context of human rule in Israel has been set since Genesis in the created order, Yahweh of

---

47. Polzin, *David*, p. 52, cf. p. 212. For Polzin 'the Deuteronomist' is the ultimate authoritative voice in the books from Deuteronomy to Kings.

Israel being also the creator God. David's partial achievement of just and righteous rule is thus a partial realization of Israel's role as witness before the nations
to the true nature of the creator and the creation. The ultimate allegiance of the
rulers and the ruled to this universal Yahweh is symbolized in Samuel, more than
in any other book since Exodus, by the presence of the ark of the covenant.

As the book opens, the ark is found at Shiloh, at the centre of Israel's worship.
This establishes a link with Josh. 18.1, where the tribes assembled at Shiloh to
express the unity of Israel before Yahweh; and further back to themes of tabernacle, with its echo of the heavenly throne (Exodus), and chosen place (Deuteronomy). The exodus is conspicuously invoked in the first confrontation with
the Philistines. In fear of defeat, Israel produces the ark on the field of battle,
recalling its function in the route from Egypt to the promised land, when it symbolized Yahweh's march before the people as divine warrior (1 Sam. 4.3–4; cf.
Num. 10.35–36). The architecture of the divine presence in the tabernacle is
recalled in the epithet 'enthroned on the cherubim' (4.4, cf. Exod. 25.22). It is the
Philistines, however, who give voice to the theology of Israel's liberation, rather
as Balaam had once done (Numbers 22–24), and later Rahab (Josh. 2.8–11). They
testify to the power of God ('these mighty gods', in their perception), to the
plagues wrought on Egypt (4.8), and even to the issue of liberation and enslavement itself, which they rightly see to be at the heart of Israel's story (4.9). There
are fulfilments of the Song of the Sea here, not only because of the line 'pangs
seized the inhabitants of Philistia' (Exod 15.14), but also because of their acknowledgement of a uniqueness about Yahweh's intervention (1 Sam. 4.7b–8), echoing
the Song's 'Who is like you, O LORD, among the gods?' (Exod. 15.11).[48]

The recognition of Yahweh's power by the Philistines, however, puts a critical
light on Israel's own handling of the ark. It is wrested from its place at Shiloh in
a way that seems to show a lack of due care (1 Sam. 4.3). The bare statement that
its guardians Hophni and Phinehas, whose self-regarding time-serving we already
know, 'were there with the ark of the covenant of God' (v. 4b) reinforces the
impression. Eli himself does not appear until we see him waiting in dread for
news (4.13a). At a moment when divine support is sought the house of Eli has
nothing to say. There is no gathering of the tribes 'before the LORD' in preparation for battle (as they did even in the Benjaminite war, Judg. 20.1), but instead
hasty desperation which makes of the ark a talisman. It is no surprise then,
though starkly ironic after the Philistines' recognition of Yahweh's power, that
Israel now crashes to further defeat, and the ark is lost (4.10–11). The house of
Eli begins to meet its judgement in the deaths of Hophni and Phinehas, followed
by Eli's own death, which bears the marks of a judgement on himself as well as a
judgement of God (4.12–18).[49] Israel's failure to seek God is symbolized in this
departure of the ark, expressed in the naming of Phinehas' new-born son Ichabod,
'the glory (כבוד, *kabod*) has departed from Israel' (4.22).

---

48. See also Brueggemann, *Theology*, p. 177, for these links.

49. Polzin sees Eli's death as symbolic: 'The crashing death of Eli in 4.18 foreshadows and
embodies the Deuteronomist's graphic evaluation of the institution that Israel at first thought would
bring good news and glad tidings…'; *Samuel*, p. 61. The institution he means is that of kingship.

The sequel demonstrates how first Philistines then Israelites come to show due deference to the God whose presence the ark symbolizes (chs 5–6). The ark is received again by Israel, but in a situation that is makeshift, temporary, and a cause of lamentation (7.1–2). In narrative terms, it remains thus unsettled until David brings it to Jerusalem, only after a further setback when the holiness of God kills Uzzah for his unauthorized handling of it (2 Sam. 6.6–7). The ark's trajectory in Samuel poses the question of true recognition of Yahweh. 'Who is able to stand before the LORD, this holy God?', ask the people of Bethshemesh (1 Sam. 6.20), and on the death of Uzzah David himself asks, 'How can the ark of the LORD come into my care?' (2 Sam. 6.9)? It comes at last to Jerusalem on a note of rejoicing and blessing (2 Sam. 6.12–15, 17–19). Yet even this is not triumphant finality. The ark is carried out of Jerusalem again during the civil war with Absalom (2 Sam. 15.24–29), only to be ordered back by David, who sees in this critical moment that the presence of God might not after all be attached irreversibly to himself. And a final resting-place for it is not identified until (by implication) the last verses of the book, and then in the context of further judgement (2 Sam. 24.18–25).

The effect of the narrative concerning the ark is to ensure a focus on the reality of faithfulness to Yahweh that underlies the political issues being played out. The ensconcement of David in his capital with royal power is not lightly given. In his response to Yahweh's gift of the kingdom he turns to the theme of the uniqueness of Israel's God, in a claim to his universal power that echoes Deuteronomy's link between the redemption of Israel and the creation (2 Sam. 7.22–23, cf. Deut. 4.32–40). In this confession, an Israelite king recognizes, if transiently, that his own kingship is subordinate to the higher purposes of God for all creation. The development of the narrative will eventually sever the two.

4. *Conclusion*

After Deuteronomy, the book of Samuel airs most penetratingly the issues involved in the relation between divine and human power. The topic of the proper exercise of human power is to the fore here, and the necessity of maintaining it is demonstrated forcefully by means of this subtle and powerful narrative. While King David briefly succeeds in realizing justice and righteousness in Israel, the dominant tendency is to show the discrepancy between the divine will to establish such rule on earth and the performance of Israel in these early stages of the monarchy. In the book of Judges, God the Judge (Judg. 11.27) was represented by 'judges' of variable quality in character and performance; in Samuel, God the King is represented by a king who was 'a man after his own heart', but who in time was bedazzled by power. The course of the divine rule on earth does not run smooth.

Alongside the topic of constraint on human power are, once again, the provisionality of power structures, the role of Israel, and the cosmic dimension of the political realm. The provisionality of monarchy as a means of realizing the divine rule on earth is expressed paradoxically in Samuel, since the establishment of

David as king comes with the sanction of a promise that his throne would last 'for ever'. As we have seen, however, this guarantee is not the same as a confirmation that Davidic rule is the ultimate and best; on the contrary the narrative tends in the opposite direction. The permanency of the Davidic house is belied by the reluctance on principle of Yahweh's initial acceptance of monarchy, by the salutary example of the demise of the house of Eli, and by the ephemeral nature of David's sound rule. The concept that the Davidic house should last 'for ever' becomes fixed in the king's mind as a point of no return, but is belied by his moral shortcomings, and his entrapment by the blandishments and exigencies of power. The real tendency of the narrative is to hint at the inevitability of the end of the story as told in Kings, of the fall of both the kingdoms that trace their origins to David.[50] As for Israel, it has begun already here to fall apart under the strain of a centralizing monarchy whose very strength lay ostensibly in its power to unite. The story of this disintegration will be prominent in the book of Kings. Finally, the cosmic dimension of Yahweh's rule is expressed in the story of the ark, which sheds its own light on the fragility and contingency of the royal power. The project of divine rule on earth continues in spite of the fragility of David, and is greater than the power struggles that beset Israel.

---

50. Cf. Polzin, *David*, p. 125, 130.

Chapter 9

WHAT IS ISRAEL? 1 AND 2 KINGS

1. *Back to Babel-Egypt*

With the book of Kings, the story that began in Genesis comes full circle. The trajectory that led towards a people descended from Abraham possessing the land of Canaan culminates in that people's expulsion from the same land (2 Kings 25). The remnant of Abraham's line returns to the place of his own origins, 'Beyond the Euphrates' (Josh. 24.2). The disengagement from 'Babel' in Genesis, embodied not only in the story of the Tower (Gen. 11.1–9), but also in the accounts of creation and flood, meets its ironic counterpart in the kingdom of Judah's subjugation to Nebuchadnezzar's Babylon. Return to Babylon is also return to 'Egypt', in the sense that the latter stands symbolically for Israel's enslavement. In the covenantal formulations, return to Egypt is both prohibition and threat (Deut. 17.16; 28.68). The prohibition is flouted already by Solomon through marriage and commerce, and the strangely expressed threat ('the LORD will bring you back in ships to Egypt') is fulfilled in the forced march eastward.[1] Everything that the kings of Israel and Judah had laboriously put together – temple, administration, military apparatus and subjugation of neighbouring powers – is now thoroughly put asunder, with little prospect of relief. The coda to the book, in which the exiled King Jehoiachin is released from his Babylonian jail to take an honoured place at the royal table (2 Kgs 25.29), is only a paltry mitigation of the deluge that has engulfed the chosen people.

Where does such an outcome leave the mission once given to Abraham? If Israel was to be the bearer of the message of God's creative purposes to the world, how is that message to be borne in the absence of a visible Israel? That is the key question presented by the narrative of Kings, and thus the topic of Israel itself will chiefly occupy us here. We will attend, however, to each of our recurring topics: the exercise of human power, the nature of Israel, the provisionality of particular institutions, and the universality of Yahweh's rule.

---

1. See R. E. Friedman, 'From Egypt to Egypt: Dtr[1] and Dtr[2]', in B. Halpern and J. D. Levenson (eds.) *Traditions in Transformation: Turning Points in Biblical Faith* (Festschrift F. M. Cross; Winona Lake; Eisenbrauns, 1981), pp. 167–92. The symbolic interchange of imperial names is known otherwise in the Hebrew Bible, e.g. Ezra 6.22, where 'Assyria' stands for Persia.

2. *The Exercise of Human Power: Solomon to Josiah*

Everything essential about the limitations placed on monarchic power has been settled by the book of Samuel. There already the potential for dynastic kingship to become tyrannous was declared and manifested. The picture in Kings extends and confirms such fears. David's dying charge to Solomon is two-sided. While he makes explicit the need for the king to keep the terms of the Mosaic covenant (1 Kgs 2.2–4), only implicit in the dynastic oracle (2 Samuel 7), he immediately follows this by commending the executions of Joab, the commander who had helped secure his kingdom, and Shimei, the Benjaminite whom he had formerly pardoned (1 Kgs 2.5–9). These 'last words of David' evoke disturbingly those 'last words' recorded in 2 Sam. 23.1–7: the David who there claimed to rule justly and proclaimed the punishment of the wicked now plans the punishment of those who threaten the security of the kingdom, or who have merely offended the king. That he urges Solomon to take such measures by his 'wisdom' (2.6, 9) casts a shadow in advance over Solomon's prayer for wisdom in the sequel (ch. 3).[2] Solomon's rule, born in palace intrigue and power play (ch. 1), is then secured by the murders of Adonijah, Joab, and Shimei (ch. 2). The 'establishment' of Solomon's kingdom (2.46b) is in express fulfilment of the dynastic promise (2 Sam. 7.13). But the manner of it recalls, or exceeds, Samuel's fears (1 Sam. 8.10–18).

The course of Solomon's reign has often been read as falling into two distinct parts, a period of wise rule followed by apostasy in the end.[3] Closer study shows, however, that it is from the beginning an unravelling of Yahweh's mission for Israel.[4] Solomon's 'twelve officials over all Israel', drawn from the regions of the land (4.7–19a), carry an echo of the twelve tribes, but demonstrate that the king thinks of Israel in a quite different way from its former tribal composition. The division of Israel is now administrative, and organized around the needs of the royal household. Curiously, Judah is omitted from the count of twelve, though the single unnamed officer, mentioned as an afterthought in 4.19b, may have been placed over it.[5] Solomon's administrative revolution, therefore, not only

---

2. I take 1 Kings 1–2 to be the proper introduction to the Solomon narrative, rather than the conclusion to the so-called Succession Narrative. See Gillian Keys, *The Wages of Sin: A Reappraisal of the 'Succession Narrative'* (JSOTSup, 221; Sheffield: Sheffield Academic Press, 1996).

3. See, for example, Sweeney, *King Josiah of Judah*, pp. 98–9.

4. The suggestion that Solomon shows Machiavellian tendencies from the beginning, and that his prayer of dedication of the temple focuses too much on himself, is well made by J. T. Walsh, *1 Kings* (Berit Olam; Collegeville: Liturgical Press, 1996), e.g. pp. 76–7, 113–14.

5. The name 'Judah' is absent from 1 Kgs 4.19 MT, but found in LXX. LXX is often preferred in translations (as NRSV) because MT's 'in the land' seems to lack something. It could have fallen out by haplography since 'Judah' is the first word in 4.20, or indeed, if it originally occurred only once, it might have been at the end of v. 19; M. Cogan, *1 Kings* (AB; New York: Doubleday, 2000), p. 211. Some think v. 19c secondary (e.g. James Linville, *Israel in the Book of Kings: the Past as a Project of Social Identity* (JSOTSup, 272; Sheffield: Sheffield Academic Press, 1998), p. 128, and P. S. Ash, 'Solomon's? District? List', *JSOT* 67 (1995), pp. 67–86.

reveals his systematic centralism, but by the same token signals a division between Israel and Judah. The king's disposition to repressive rule is further marked by his levy of 'forced labour out of all Israel' (5.27 [EVV 5.13], cf. 4.6b; but see 9.15–22).

The nuanced discourse of 1 Kings 1–11 proclaims at one level a fulfilment of promise in relation to Israel. Solomon is given wisdom to rule the people (3.3–14); they become numerous and dwell content (4.20–21, 25). Jerusalem, identified as the place chosen by Yahweh for the nation's worship, is graced with a magnificent temple. Yet what is given in one rhetorical flourish is taken away by another. The wealth that Israel enjoys goes hand in hand with the amassing of a military machine, in defiance of the deuteronomic command (4.26; 10.26–29, cf. Deut. 17.16). His possession of the land has some appearance of an empire, rather than the strict observation of bounded territory (4.21, cf. Deut. 2.1–25). Conversely, it also betrays a curious dependence on the goodwill of the Egyptian pharaoh, in a relationship cultivated by Solomon through diplomatic marriage (9.16, cf. 3.1).

The picture of a numerous and contented Israel, therefore, an apparent realization of the Abrahamic promise (Gen. 15.5, cf. Deut. 1.10), is mocked by a range of factors: the application of 'wisdom' to the murder of enemies, the construction of a military machine, the securing of power by means of alliance, national wealth in the service of the king's own grandeur at the expense of the citizens' freedom of action, and a 'chosen place' intended for communal worship by the tribes of Israel now becomes the capital of a centralized and self-protecting state. The culmination of Solomon's reign in flagrant assimilation of non-Yahweh cults and the outrageous trappings of despotic power is prepared for in the trends within the story, and it is no surprise to find the incipient dismantling of the land hard won by David (1 Kgs 11.1–25). The rejection of Rehoboam by the people of Israel upon his declaration that he will exceed his father in harshness (1 Kings 12) confirms the picture sketched in chs 1–11. The irrevocable disintegration of Israel into two parts is sanctioned in advance by Yahweh in the formal transfer of much of the territory of Israel to Jeroboam, in a prophetic word to Jeroboam which is at the same time a word of judgement on Solomon (11.26–40).[6]

The potential of kingship to become tyrannical is exhibited in numerous ways in the story of the monarchies. King Ahab of the northern kingdom typifies self-serving rule as much as any, notably in his conflict with his neighbour Naboth over a piece of Naboth's ancestral land (1 Kings 21). Naboth's defence of his 'ancestral inheritance' (21.3) bespeaks the traditional view of Israel, in which each Israelite had a stake by right in the land given by Yahweh (Deut 4:21; 15:4; Joshua 13–22). The land is gift of Yahweh, and held by Israel as people. Ahab's view in contrast, supported by his ruthless Phoenician wife Jezebel, is that land rights are at the disposal of kings. Naboth pays the price of this ideological con-

---

6. For readings of 1 Kings 1–11 that portray Solomon as tyrannical from the outset, see J. J. Kang, *The Persuasive Portrayal of Solomon in 1 Kings 1–11* (EUS, XXIII/760; Bern: Peter Lang, 2003); cf. the present writer's 'Narrative and Meaning in the Books of Kings', *Biblica* 70 (1989), pp. 31–49.

flict, and is murdered. The nature of Ahab's Israel is all too evident in the sordid intrigue, in which due process is corrupted and the assassination is performed by the sort of people who are ready to live off tyrants and outside law or morality. The Israel that is ruled from Samaria is a mockery of the Israel delivered in the beginning from tyranny. These are kings who fall in readily with the norms of the surrounding political culture. The kingdom of Judah, with important exceptions, follows suit. King Ahaz, famous recipient of Isaiah's Immanuel oracle urging non-submission to the imperial power (Isaiah 7), follows a deliberate Assyrianizing policy (2 Kings 16).

Throughout the story of Israel and Judah a dissident, Yahwistic strain is present, as when the priest Jehoiada leads in the overthrow of Queen Athaliah, a scion of Ahab who has burgeoned murderously in Judah (2 Kings 11). The prophetic resistance is spearheaded by Elijah (1 Kings 17–2 Kings 2), and the prophets as a body are said to have declared Yahweh's word throughout the period, only to go unheeded (2 Kgs 17.13–14). In Judah, eight kings are judged to have 'done right' in Yahweh's eyes, though mostly with reservations concerning their tolerance of the 'high places', regarded by the authors as non-Yahwistic.[7] The supreme achievements are those of Hezekiah and Josiah. Josiah's rediscovery of the Mosaic 'book of the law', his consequent repentance and reinstitution of the celebration of Passover, and his eradication of worship-centres outside Jerusalem, are the most rigorous attempts by a king to accept the rule of law and obedience to Yahweh (2 Kings 22–23). It is not for nothing that the programmes of Deuteronomy and Josiah have been closely linked by critical scholarship since the early nineteenth century.[8] In modern scholarship that advocates an edition of Deuteronomy–Kings supporting Josiah, it is held that hopes were placed in him for the revival of a Davidic kingdom. In Kings as we have it, however, the die is cast before Josiah even comes to the throne, because of the sins of Manasseh (2 Kgs 21.10–15, 23.26–27). There is no apparent connection between Josiah's righteousness and his unexpected end in a vain attempt to resist the advancing Pharaoh Neco. The prophecy of Huldah, that he would die 'in peace' and not see the evil Yahweh had determined for the land (22.20) is barely fulfilled here. Josiah is unlike David at least in this, that Yahweh is finally not with him whenever he goes out against his enemies.

By means of the judgement on Manasseh, the portrait of Josiah in Kings finds a way of leaving his reputation intact while accounting for his failure in battle and the rapid decline of Judah following his death. The game is up before the discovery of the 'book of the law' and the measures taken as a result. Josiah's righteous acts cannot affect the course of events now in train. In his ill-starred sortie against Neco, he has simply misread the times. Judah's borders can no more be defended. The power plays in the region will henceforth involve only the great powers. It is highly significant for the politics of Kings that the reduc-

---

7.   Asa, Jehoshaphat, Jehoash, Amaziah, Azariah, Jotham, Hezekiah, Josiah.
8.   The seminal work was W. M. L. de Wette, *Dissertatio Critica* (Jena, 1805). In recent scholarship a Josianic edition of Deuteronomy–Kings has been widely advocated, e.g. in Knoppers, *Two Nations Under God*.

tion of Judah is signalled precisely in the reign of Josiah. As at the close of Judges a drumbeat heralded the end of an era and the imminent experiment with monarchy, so the helplessness of righteous Josiah portends the return of the land of Israel to the grip of powers that are not Israel, and the return of Israel to the hands of foreign kings. Josiah remains in memory the most excellent successor of David, the only king expressly said to have placed his rule under the *torah*, and to have taken the symbolic steps necessary to re-establish the worship of Yahweh alone. These things the writer affirms, exonerating Josiah himself, while carrying the story nonetheless to its conclusion in the demise of Israel as monarchy.[9]

The subordination of royal power to Yahweh is nowhere better illustrated, as Jacques Ellul has shown, than in the Elisha cycle, and especially in the story of Naaman, the commander of the Syrian king's armies. Seeking a cure for his leprosy he is advised by a little Israelite servant-girl that the prophet in Samaria could cure him (2 Kgs 5.3). Naaman, wishing to tap this source of power, consults his royal master who takes it to be a matter that can be settled between kings, and demands that the king of Israel cure Naaman (5.5–6). The king of Israel knows he cannot do this (v. 7), and the healing is performed by the prophet with a deliberate repudiation of the pomp and fanfare of state. Naaman, at first outraged by this lack of regard for his high standing, accepts the humble way and is restored (5.10–14). The healing of Naaman, together with his subsequent acknowledgement of Yahweh though intending pragmatically to sustain his master's political-religious power base in the cult of Rimmon, sharply illustrates that 'the politics of God' has its own logic and is by no means constrained by the delusions of human power.[10]

Provisionality of Political Structures

The story of Israel has borne witness hitherto to the provisionality of particular structures of power. The story of kings expresses this as decisively as anywhere. As rule by judge-deliverers gave way to rule by kings, so now rule by kings of Israel and Judah passes into history. Here indeed the transience of institutions is affirmed emphatically. No political structures remain apart from those imposed from outside by a foreign power. The deuteronomic synthesis of people, law and land is fully dismantled. The detachment of the people from the land is the most trenchant aspect of this. Regardless of the historical factuality of the depopulation of Judah,[11] for the writer of Kings the tenure of Canaan by Israel is in

---

9.   Linville writes of the kings: 'The monarchy is not seen to be the ultimate answer to the problems of Israelite politics, and its loss is not fatal to Israel as Yahweh's people. Rather, hope may be had in those who fulfil the obligations of the *nagid* who represents Yahweh on earth. It is interesting that the title occurs mostly in the context of the origins of the monarchy and its early history, and that few of these figures live up to their roles'; *Israel in the Book of Kings*, p. 149.

10.   See Jacques Ellul, *The Politics of God and the Politics of Man* (Grand Rapids: Eerdmans, 1972), pp. 23–40.

11.   How far Judah was in fact depopulated as a result of the Babylonian campaigns is disputed. Those who think a large proportion of the population remained in Judah include Hans Barstad, *The Myth of the Empty Land: a Study of the History and Archaeology of Judah During the Exile Period*

principle over. Correspondingly, the *torah*, so recently recovered, no longer has its place as the 'law of the land' (*lex terrae*), its borders, given and defined by Yahweh, have no standing. The ruined temple poignantly testifies to these things.

Is this then the end of everything? Despite the indeterminate ending of Kings, there are reasons to think not. The removal of king and temple is, after all, merely to undo measures that were originally unwelcome to Yahweh. In the divine accommodation to Israel's will, king and temple did bear responsibility for leadership and worship in Israel during their time, even if such obligations were mostly honoured in the breach. The designation of Hezekiah as 'prince' (*nagid*) testifies to the persistence of Yahweh's perspective that kings were charged with a responsibility delegated from him (2 Kgs 20.5). Kingship became Yahweh's provision for the time being. With its demise, however, the question comes back to the nature of Israel itself. Without land, worship-centre or political structures, is there another mode of existence it can assume as the people chosen by Yahweh to be witnesses in his world? A preliminary signal comes already in Solomon's prayer, anticipating exile, invoking Israel's 'cause' (*mishpat*) in such a way as to suggest the continuance of covenant in some form, and asking Yahweh that her captors might have compassion on them in their exile (1 Kgs 8.46–51). There is no stipulation of return to land here, and thus no assumption that Israel's existence is fundamentally predicated upon it. What is assumed is that Israel will continue in some form, but it is left entirely open what that form might be.

3. *Israel in Kings*

The name 'Israel' bears several distinct meanings in the biblical narrative. It refers first to the renamed patriarch Jacob (Gen 32.28; 35.10), then variously to the people of Yahweh that came up out of Egypt and into Canaan ('my people', Exod. 5.1), the territory they occupied, the united kingdom of David and Solomon, the northern kingdom 'Israel' as distinct from Judah, Judah itself after the fall of the north (e.g. 2 Kgs 19.15),[12] and the post-exilic community, no longer a kingdom, and predominantly based on old Judah (Ezra 2.70 = Neh. 7.73; Isa. 63.16).[13] Studies of the Old Testament have sometimes identified one form of Israel or another as the most essential or typical.[14] But this capacity of 'Israel' to

(Oslo: Scandinavian University Press, 1996); Joseph Blenkinsopp, 'The Bible, Archaeology and Politics; or the Empty Land Revisited', *JSOT* 27 (2002), pp. 169–87. Ephraim Stern, however, argues that the population was severely depleted: *Archaeology of the Land of the Bible. II. The Assyrian, Babylonian and Persian Periods (732–332 B.C.E.)* (ABRL; New York: Doubleday, 2001), and 'The Babylonian Gap: the Archaeological Reality', *JSOT* 28 (2004), pp. 273–7.

12. The distinction between Israel and Judah is largely maintained in 2 Kings 18–25, however. The identification of Judah with 'Israel' is implied in designations of Yahweh as 'God of Israel' in oracles to Judah.

13. Further nuances may be discerned; see Linville, *Israel in the Book of Kings*, pp. 43–4; cf. Davies, *'Ancient Israel'*, p. 50.

14. In the view attributed in modern 'revisionist' history-writing to W. F. Albright, John Bright, Martin Noth and others, 'the defining moment of Israelite history' is the rise of the Israelite state and in particular the Davidic monarchy (see Whitelam, *Invention*, p. 128). For N. K. Gottwald, on

adapt to new situations and adopt new nuances cannot be overlooked, and the quest for what is truly 'Israel' may not finish by identifying it with any particular period of its existence. Indeed, in our study so far I have tried to show that the meaning of Israel is to be found in the extent to which it fulfils its destiny as witness to the nations of the divine government of the world.

Kings is perhaps the most significant Old Testament treatise on the nature of Israel after Deuteronomy. Its concern with the topic is stamped on the storyline. It is this book that records the key: from one kingdom to two, thence back to one, 'Israel' at each stage having a different referent. With the exile comes the loss of all marks of statehood, and the people's claim to be 'Israel' is thereby put in doubt. Thus, while the subject of the story is Israel, the events pose the question of what Israel is. The ambiguity surrounding it suffuses the whole book, as is apparent in a wide range of texts.

Solomon is installed as king over all Israel, yet from the start the ambiguity over Israel appears, recalling the deep division that David, with only partial success, had sought to heal.[15] When David pronounces that Solomon shall rule in his place he first instructs Nathan to anoint him 'king over Israel' (meaning all Israel), but follows with 'I have appointed him to be king over Israel and Judah' (1 Kgs 1.34–35), showing that Israel and Judah are at one level considered to be separate entities.[16] In some texts the term 'all Israel' is used to make it clear that on these occasions Israel is meant in its broader sense and that Judah is included (e.g. 1.20; 2.15; cf. 3.28; 11.16).

This inherent duality comes to a head in the account of Solomon's apostasy and Yahweh's removal of the kingdom from him. The terms of Yahweh's first words of judgement to Solomon are categorical: 'I will surely tear the kingdom from you and give it to your servant' (1 Kgs 11.11 – the exact undoing of 1 Kgs 2.46). According to this word and the ensuing appointment of Jeroboam, there is a sense in which what was once given to David is now passed to Jeroboam. He, like David, receives a prophetic commission to be 'king over Israel' (1 Kgs 11.37), and Yahweh's promise that he will 'build him a sure house' has express Davidic echoes (v. 38). Finally, in Yahweh's words 'I will give Israel to you', Jeroboam is made to succeed not only Solomon, but also David.

Does 'Israel' truly continue in the northern kingdom, therefore, which Jeroboam proceeds to establish with a capital (initially) in Shechem, the old Israelite covenant centre (12.25), and state shrines in Bethel and Dan? He certainly claims continuity from the Israel of old, with his appeal to Yahweh's deliverance from Egypt (12.28 – note 'O Israel').

the other hand, it was the tribal league; *The Tribes of Yahweh: A Sociology of the Religion of Liberated Israel* (Maryknoll, NY: Orbis Books, 1979), cf. C. J. H. Wright, *God's People in God's Land: Family and Property in the Old Testament* (Grand Rapids: Eerdmans, 1990).

15. 1 Sam. 11.8; 15.4; 17.52; 18.16; 2 Sam. 2.1–4; 20.1. In 2 Samuel 24 Israel and Judah are numbered separately (24.1). The division is presented as between two pretenders to be king of Israel, but apparently this hides a deeper rift; cf. Linville, *Israel in the Book of Kings*, pp. 116–17.

16. Cogan regards them as 'the two constituent political components of David's kingdom', *I Kings*, p. 162, referring to 2 Sam. 5.5; 24.9; 1 Kgs 4.20. Cf. also 1.9.

Yet Yahweh plans to leave 'one tribe' to Solomon's son 'for the sake of David my servant and for the sake of Jerusalem which I have chosen' (11.13, cf. v. 36). Furthermore, the gift of Israel to Jeroboam, described as an affliction of David, will not be 'for all the days' (כל־הימים, 11.39, curiously not עד־עולם, 'for ever'). On this point clear water is put between the promises to David and to Jeroboam. The chastisement of David's house has a time limit, and the promise to Jeroboam lacks the aspect of perpetuity (i.e. Jeroboam's inheritance takes on a temporary aspect). Meantime, David is to have a 'lamp' (ניר) in Jerusalem 'all the days' (v. 36). So is the continuance of 'Israel' after all in Jerusalem, David's capital and ostensibly the 'chosen place' of worship, now graced by the splendid temple that Yahweh allowed Solomon to build? Each scenario has its plausibility, yet the answer will not lie ultimately with either of these entities. Each and both will function for a time as 'Israel', but neither will fully embody its meaning.

a. *The Northern Kingdom of Israel*
The tone for the north is set from the start by its ambivalence at best about its ultimate loyalty. Jeroboam I founded worship-centres at Dan and Bethel, and made an appeal to the northern tribes which played on the memory of their tribal past, but which, in echoing the idolatry of the Golden Calf places the northern kingdom at odds with its true inheritance at the outset (1 Kgs 12.28–30, cf. Exod. 32.4). The sin of 'Jeroboam the son of Nebat' resounds throughout the narrative as a comment on the pervasive idolatry of the kings.

However, the story of the northern kingdom is in its way the story of Israel. This is well illustrated by the conflict between King Ahab and the prophet Elijah over the drought invoked by Elijah. King and prophet accuse each other of having 'troubled' Israel (1 Kgs 18.17–20). In the prophet's view, the troubling of Israel lies deep, in the loyalty of the king to Baal. Elijah calls for a great gathering to the showdown he plans on Mt. Carmel. The contest turns on which god the people shall serve, but it goes deeper to the notion of Israel itself. It is 'all Israel' that is summoned by Elijah (vv. 19–20), harking back to the days of a united people. His call is for nothing less than the Mosaic 'assembly' before Yahweh, a realization of Israel that radically undercuts the pretensions of this Baalist king, and relativizes the rump 'Israel' over which he reigns. In the contest itself memories of historic Israel are awakened by the twelve stones with which the prophet rebuilds the altar of Yahweh on Carmel, one for each of the historic sons of Jacob. And in the same breath Elijah recalls Jacob's struggle with the mysterious 'man' at the River Jabbok, when his name was changed to Israel (18.30–32, cf. Gen. 32.22–32). Elijah himself has evident affinities with Moses throughout the narrative, especially in his witness before Israel as to the true character of its God, whom, like Moses, he invokes as 'the God of Abraham, Isaac, and Israel/Jacob' (18.36, cf. Exod. 3.13–15). The Mosaic analogy is pressed by the narrative as far as Elijah's flight to Horeb (Sinai), the scene of the covenant that first constituted Israel as the people of God (19.11–18). The conflict, therefore, goes further than an exposure of Ahab's false allegiances, to a vivid re-enactment of the true nature of Israel by reference to its origins.

Ahab is nevertheless repeatedly designated 'king of Israel', especially in the account of his wars with Syria (1 Kgs 20.4, 7, 11, 22; and throughout 1 Kings 22). In the narrative's preference for this title for Ahab over his name (in ch. 22), in contrast to Jehoshaphat of Judah who is named regularly, it seems that attention is being drawn to Ahab's official status. But there is an ironic twist. What can the claim to be 'king of Israel' mean, given the presence of another king in 'Israel', namely Jehoshaphat of Judah? And can this man really match any reasonable claim to bear the title? The same feature is visible in another story, this time involving Jehoshaphat and Ahab's son Jehoram (2 Kings 3 – Jehoram is designated only as 'king of Israel' from v. 9). The aimless wilderness circuits of the alliance led by Jehoram seem somehow parabolic of the lack of direction in Israel (2 Kgs 3.9). However, while it is Jehoram who bears the title 'king of Israel', it is Jehoshaphat who constrains Elisha to offer a word of God (2 Kgs 3.14).

The Ahab-Elijah narratives imply that 'Israel' is in some sense mediated by the northern kingdom. Yet the destiny of Israel continues to be played out in the divided kingdoms. Israel, therefore, is too big to be contained within the northern kingdom. In Ahab's appeal to Jehoshaphat, and the latter's co-operation, lies a nostalgia for unity. Israel is 'troubled' not only by Ahab, but in a sense also by Jehoshaphat. Here is an Israel neither quite united nor quite divided, but its halting unity and its underlying doubt about its true allegiance, are mocked by the prophetic dramatization of its truest unity, allegiance and destiny.

The status of the northern kingdom is also illustrated by the reign of Jehu. Jehu is appointed king by Yahweh's word to the prophet Elijah during Elijah's withdrawal to Horeb in the aftermath of his conflict with Ahab's prophets of Baal (1 Kgs 19.16). His reign is therefore uniquely auspicious, originating from the mount of the covenant and Israel's most Moses-like prophet. In due course he is anointed king by one of the prophets under Elisha,[17] and enjoined by Yahweh to eradicate the house of Ahab (2 Kgs 9.4–9). The reign of Jehu, therefore, enjoys the sanction of Yahweh in a way which is not true of any other northern king. For his zeal in destroying the house of Ahab, and with it the worship of Baal, he expressly gains Yahweh's approval, and the promise of a dynasty, albeit of limited duration (2 Kgs 10.28, 30). The story of Jehu is spliced into that of Elijah, as part of the rejection of Baal-worship in the northern kingdom.

Most importantly, the mission of Jehu affirms the status of the north as intrinsically Yahweh's Israel. In Yahweh's command to Elijah, he is to be anointed 'king over Israel' (1 Kgs 19.16), and the prophet who carries it out elaborates this to 'king over the people of Yahweh, over Israel' (2 Kgs 9.6). The covenantal 'people of Yahweh' evokes the concept of greater Israel, and thus a kinship is affirmed between the kingdom and the historic people. For a time it looks as if Jehu might become king over all Israel, since in his war on Ahab's son Joram he finds himself also pitched against Ahaziah, king of Judah, who has joined him. Is

---

17. He is the only king apart from Saul and David (1 Sam. 9.16; 16.3) who is commanded by Yahweh to be anointed. Solomon is anointed by the command of David (1 Kgs 1.33–34).

Yahweh's scourge sent to make war on both kingdoms? When he kills both kings (2 Kgs 9.21–28) he is set fair to be the only legitimate monarch in greater Israel. But it is Athaliah who succeeds in Judah, with more bloodshed, and her reign, not dignified with legitimacy by the writer, leads to the reassertion of Davidic kingship with Jehoiada and Joash.

Jehu's legacy is mixed, therefore. In the pattern of regular judgements on kings he is like all other northern kings in failing to walk in Yahweh's ways, and especially to turn back the idolatry of Jeroboam I (2 Kgs 10.29, 31; 13.2). Because of this, Yahweh brings enemies against Israel, reducing their territory as in the days of Solomon (13.3). In this very failure, however, is an important clue. For in answer to a prayer of Jehoahaz, Jehu's son, Yahweh raises a 'saviour' (*moshia'*), as in the days of the judges (13.4–5). As Linville has it, 'this recovery is due not to a divine promise to a dynasty, but to a more basic association between Yahweh and Israel, an association that transcends monarchy completely and so grants the north even more legitimacy'.[18]

b. *The Kingdom of Judah*

Judah's claim to represent the mission and destiny of Israel lies on the surface in its possession of Jerusalem and in its continuity from David. As to its character, it both resembles and differs from the north, having a number of kings judged to have remained loyal, and a strain that stands against the influence of Ahab in Judah as attested in the overthrow of Athaliah by the zealous Yahwistic priest Jehoiada. The enthronement of the young Joash affirms the allegiance of Judah to the ancient covenant with Yahweh more emphatically than anywhere else in the narrative prior to Josiah's reform (2 Kgs 11.17).

The narrative's view of Judah as representative of Israel comes to the fore when the northern kingdom falls. The first glimpse of this comes when Judah is included by anticipation in the summary condemnation of the north (2 Kgs 17.18–21). In vv. 18–19 Judah and Israel are distinguished, according to this book's usual view, and the term Israel refers again to the north in v. 21. But who are 'all the descendants of Israel' in v. 20? In Provan's words 'The phrase "all the people of Israel" in verse 20 is, indeed, highly ambiguous. Does it refer only to the "Israel" of verses 18 and 21 (the northern kingdom)? Or does it reach forward in the story to embrace Judah...?'[19] The phrase 'all the seed of Israel' favours an inclusive reading, as it harks back to the patriarch Jacob–Israel (cf. 1 Kgs 18.31). At this point, then (as also in v. 34), the larger view of Israel, always in the background in Kings, asserts itself again, in a judgement which embraces Judah as well as the northern kingdom.[20] This book's final report on the

18. Linville, *Israel in the Book of Kings*, p. 197.
19. Iain W. Provan, *1 and 2 Kings* (NIBC; Peabody, MA: Hendrickson, 1995), p. 249. For him the answer is provided in the sequel. Elsewhere he took the view that v. 20 included Judah and had to be seen from an exilic perspective: *Hezekiah and the Book of Kings* (BZAW, 172; Berlin; W. de Gruyter, 1988), p. 70, n. 35; cf. R. D. Nelson, *The Double Redaction of the Deuteronomistic History* (JSOTSup, 18; Sheffield: Sheffield Academic Press, 1981), p. 56.
20. Not all accept this. Marvin Sweeney thinks that only the northern kingdom is in view in

north, therefore, points once again to the historic destiny of Israel. In doing so it involves Judah in the failure to fulfil that destiny, even though the story of Judah has not yet been fully told. Judah stands alone for over a century after the fall of the north to Assyria, and its story occupies seven more chapters of Kings. What is its status during this time?

Even though the demise of Judah is signalled already in 2 Kings 17, its potential to be 'Israel' in truth is aired in chs 18–25. Here the question is raised anew whether the Davidic kings can conform to the model of kingship permitted by Yahweh when he originally acceded to the people's request. When 'King Hezekiah of Judah' (2 Kgs 18.14), becomes ill, Yahweh sends the prophet Isaiah to him, calling him 'the prince (*nagid*) of my people' (2 Kgs 20.5). As we have seen above,[21] this title represents Yahweh's own view of the authority of the kings, namely that it derived from Yahweh, who was himself the true king of Israel. The effect of applying the title to Hezekiah is both to instal him in the same privileges granted then to David and to place him under the same constraints.[22] Just as important, however, is the point that he is '(*nagid*) *of my people*'. This term, applied in practice to Judah, has the force of the historic covenant people Israel. This historic people now has its visible existence in the small remnant of the original twelve-tribe Israel centred on Jerusalem and Judah. The famous defence of Jerusalem from the invasion of Sennacherib, which occupies a large part of the ensuing narrative of Judah alone, reinforces the notion of Yahweh's faithfulness to his ancient covenants with Israel now manifest on behalf of Judah. By his own testimony, Yahweh's old exemption of Judah from his decision to remove the kingdom from Solomon operates in this new act of salvation (19.34).

There are a number of further indications that Hezekiah's Judah represents historic Israel, not least in his trust in 'the God of Israel' (19.15), and the typically Isaianic 'holy one of Israel' (19.22). The Assyrian Rabshakeh's verbal assault on the besieged populace of Jerusalem contributes to the point by mimicking deuteronomic language on the gift of the land, which recalls the constitution of Israel in

---

v. 20, holding that ch. 17 takes in only the horizon of that kingdom and Assyria, the anticipation of Judah's exile entering the story only with Manasseh in ch. 21. Behind Sweeney's argument is his view that the present form of 2 Kings 17 is part of a major Josianic redaction; *King Josiah of Judah*, pp. 85–92. He agrees, however, that 'When read in relation to the exilic edition of the DtrH and its concern for Judah's exile, it can point forward to that reality as well, but it does not seem to have been written for that purpose' (p. 86).

21. See the preceding chapter.

22. Linville's take on this is, 'The monarchy becomes a cover for a theocracy', *Israel in the Book of Kings*, p. 143. This is oddly dismissive of the seriousness with which the respective powers of Yahweh and king are explored in Samuel–Kings. He cites in support Eslinger, *Kingship of God*, pp. 307–9. As Linville points out, the term *nagid* is applied to several kings between David and Hezekiah, namely Solomon, Jeroboam and Baasha (1 Kgs 1.35; 14.7; 16.2). The chief characteristic of its use is that, with the exception of Solomon, it occurs in a speech of Yahweh given through a prophet. The status of kings as *negidim* is thus portrayed as Yahweh's view. In the exceptional case, David appoints Solomon to be both king and *nagid* (1 Kgs 1.35). But as we have seen, this passage testifies to the tendency of the later David to interpret the kingdom as belonging inalienably to himself, and to convey this perspective to Solomon.

its original extent (18.31–33, cf. Deut. 4.34). It follows from this depiction of Hezekiah and Judah that what is at stake fundamentally is the continuance of Israel itself.[23]

The story of the last years of Judah is at the same time the story of the last days of Israel under the kings. When Manasseh introduces altars to Baal and Asherah in the temple, Yahweh's promise to David and Solomon is recalled thus:

> 'In this house, and in Jerusalem, which I have chosen out of all the tribes of Israel, I will put my name for ever; I will not cause the feet of Israel to wander any more out of the land that I gave to their ancestors, if only they will be careful to do all that I have commanded them, and according to all the law that Moses my servant commanded them' (2 Kgs 21.7b–8).[24]

This vista takes in not only the first kings of greater Israel but also Moses and the law given at Sinai. It recalls a promise 'for ever', in the act of rescinding it (in the manner of the word of judgement against Eli, 1 Sam. 2.27–36). But further, it shows that Jerusalem never became merely the capital of Judah in the eyes of God, but remained the place that he had chosen out of all the tribes, in a promise that pertained to the historic land in its totality.

The all-Israel perspective is maintained in the account of King Josiah. Josiah is the nemesis of the idolatrous cult of Jeroboam I, proclaimed as such in a prophecy to Jeroboam himself (1 Kgs 13.2), which is expressly recalled in the account of Josiah's desecration of the altar at Bethel (2 Kgs 23.15–18). He recognizes no borders between north and south here.[25] His actions in entering the territory of the former northern kingdom and purging it of the relics of non-Yahwistic worship from the time of Solomon reassert the rights and identity of historic Israel beyond the limits of the southern kingdom. The discovery of the 'book of the law', the name used in Deuteronomy for the words of Moses recorded there (22.8, cf. Deut. 28.61; 31.26), the renewal of the covenant (23.1–3) and the celebration of a Passover the like of which had not been kept since the days of the judges (23.21–23)[26] all place the reform in the context of the whole stretch of Israel's history since Moses. Conversely, the destruction of the temple by the invading Babylonians writes *finis*, symbolically, to the story of the united kingdom, the temple being carefully designated as that which Solomon had built (24.13).

Judah, in the end, fails to stand permanently in its function as the visible manifestation of historic Israel. Its fate is as that of the north, because in spite of

---

23. Linville, referring to the application of *nagid* to Hezekiah in 2 Kgs 20.5, says: 'That Judah had lost and then regained the symbolic leadership of Yahweh's people seems implicit with the inclusion of the title [Davidic] in the Hezekiah oracle'; *Israel in the Book of Kings*, p. 146.

24. The words attributed to Yahweh do not correspond exactly to any previous word of his. They bring together elements in the deuteronomic command regarding the single altar (Deut.12.5), the promise to David of a perpetual dynasty and the building of 'a house for my name' (2 Sam. 7.13–16), and the specific application of this to the Jerusalem temple expressed in Solomon's dedicatory prayer (1 Kgs 8.16).

25. Cf. Linville, *Israel in the Book of Kings*, pp. 190–1.

26. The reference may be to Joshua's Passover, the first celebrated upon entry to the land (Josh. 5.10–12).

some successes, its cumulative record did not fulfil the prerequisites of the mission of Yahweh in the world.

c. *'Israel' in Exile?*

What then is the entity that goes eventually into exile, shorn of trappings that might qualify it as either 'Israel' or 'Judah'? This is perhaps the acutest question for the first audience of the book. The clearest answer comes in Solomon's dedicatory prayer, in which he envisages that a disobedient Israel might one day go into exile. In that event, he prays that God would hear their prayer and *maintain their cause* (Hebrew *mishpat*, 1 Kgs 8.49), that is, a legal right that presupposes their relationship with Yahweh continues. And they are then explicitly equated with 'your people, your inheritance, which you brought out of Egypt, from the midst of the iron furnace' (1 Kgs 8.51, cf. Deut. 4.20). Kings is unlike Deuteronomy and Jeremiah in not envisaging a return to land, and so to a form of political life resembling that which had been lost. Here the outward appearance and constitution of the future people is an unresolved question. But this is an important statement in itself. The true nature of Israel depends, not on institutions, not even on possession of land, but on loyalty to Yahweh, and this as manifested in commitments to justice as exemplified by the case of Naboth.

This analysis is distinct from two others that may be noticed here, and close to a third. In Marvin Sweeney's view, the book of Kings went through Hezekian, Josianic and exilic editions, these all postdating the fall of the northern kingdom. He supposes throughout a southern perspective in which the north is considered apostate, and in which the view is that it should return to the south, and thus obedience to the Jerusalem temple.[27] In this context, he consistently prefers to take 'Israel' to refer to the northern kingdom: 'Once the northern tribes revolted from Rehoboam and turned to Solomon, the DtrH stresses that they were lost as every monarch followed in the paths of Jeroboam and caused Israel (the northern kingdom) to sin.'[28] Sweeney has this in common with the widely held thesis of a Josianic edition which vested much hope in that king's reform. In our view there is no difference ultimately between north and south; while Josiah behaved in an exemplary way, neither kingdom fulfils the destiny of Israel.

In contrast to Sweeney, E. T. Mullen reads Kings as a unitary composition. As part of DtrH, it arose from the exiled community's 'redressive' phase, in which it looked to rebuild its identity after the trauma inflicted by the destruction of its fundamental symbols in 587 BC.[29] Its leading concern consequently, was 'to provide a set of boundaries for the community for which it was produced'.[30] And its method was to insist upon continuity with the past. The Athaliah episode, for example, was 'a piece of propaganda supporting the unbroken dynastic line of

---

27. Sweeney, *King Josiah of Judah* (e.g. p. 102 n. 12, on 1 Kings 8.25–26, 46–51).

28. Sweeney, *King Josiah of Judah*, p. 101. This explains why he interprets ambiguous passages such as 1 Kgs 9.7; 2 Kgs 17.20 to refer to the northern kingdom. See above, n. 20.

29. E. T. Mullen., *Narrative History and Ethnic Boundaries* (SBLSS; Atlanta: Scholars Press, 1993), p. 43, cf. pp. 38–9. He follows V. Turner's idea of 'social dramas'.

30. Mullen, *Narrative History*, p. 14.

David in Judah'.[31] In the identity which Mullen thinks is asserted by the narrative for the community, ethnicity plays a crucial part: 'a significant aspect of ethnicity, especially in regard to its religious function, is the denial of such changes [viz. the cultural and historical situation of the group] and the insistence upon an absolute continuity with the past'.[32] As for Josiah, his actions are interpreted in connection with a messianic understanding of Deut. 17.14–20, and taken to 'enforce the group identity formulated in the deuteronomic corpus'.[33] Josiah fails, but the narrative retains a function, proclaiming that an obedient Israel could yet take the land.[34] Mullen's analysis is unlike Sweeney's in important respects, yet shares the latter's favourable account of the portrayal of Josiah and thus of hope attached to the monarchic institutions of Judah. Again however, our own analysis differs because of its thesis about the provisionality of all particular modes of rule in Israel.

More promising, in my view, is Linville's account. Like Mullen, he treats Kings as a unity and shares his belief that it addresses the identity of a people that has lost its ideological moorings. However, Linville shares with the present essay a scepticism about the alleged permanency of the institutions of Israel, and a sense that no model of leadership is absolutized, but all held up for scrutiny.[35] Rather, he finds in the narrative 'a sense of entropy' that is true of both kingdoms, and a 'depiction of Judah and Israel as two rival microcosms of the collective, neither one able to claim full legitimacy'.[36] While each of these manifestations of 'Israel' in its way embodies the reality, neither is complete. But most importantly, Kings appears to hold out no expectation of a new Davidic era and reconstitution of Israel as a singular whole.[37]

Of the interpretations mentioned here, Linville's is closest in my view to capturing the portrayal of Israel in Kings. For him, the construction of an identity for Israel is an unfinished task that confronts the exilic community, or rather communities, for he is sensitive to the incipient pluralism of post-exilic Judaism. He is commendably cautious, however, about the precise way in which Kings relates to social debates of the writer's day.[38]

I think one may offer more directly theological reasons why Israel is left such an elusive, enigmatic entity in Kings. These have to do with the attempt to understand how the God of Israel (the God who is 'One') might still be in covenant with the people who bore his ancient promises, in the new situation of loss of political independence, and after the destruction of the temple, and the failure of

31. Mullen, *Narrative History*, p. 32.

32. Mullen, *Narrative History*, p. 37.

33. Mullen, *Narrative History*, pp. 47, 77.

34. Mullen, *Narrative History*, pp. 79–80.

35. See for example his criticism of Mullen's idea of a Davidic Golden Age, *Israel in the Book of Kings*, pp. 83–91, and his recognition of the pervasive critique of Solomon in 1 Kings 1–11, pp. 135–7. For the scrutiny of all types of leadership, see pp. 103–4.

36. Linville, *Israel in the Book of Kings*, p. 23.

37. Linville, *Israel in the Book of Kings*, pp. 162–3.

38. Linville, *Israel in the Book of Kings*, p. 301.

the Davidic monarchy. Kings is essentially open, a little puzzled perhaps. But it knows that when it speaks of the 'God of Israel' that is more vocational than descriptive of any particular type of national or institutional arrangements.

4. *Creation and Universality*

If the ending of the book of Kings poses a question about the particular role of Israel, it returns us by the same token to the matter of Yahweh's universal rule. Israel's story began in political impotence, in a foreign land under foreign rule, though that rule proved to be subject to Yahweh's. So in the end, land and people are returned to servitude under a foreign king. The question at the end of Kings, however, is not just about Israel's survival, but about how Yahweh will rule in the world. This is implicit not only in the agenda that we found to underlie Genesis and Exodus, which still affects our reading of the end of this long narrative treatise, but also in traits in the book of Kings itself.

Solomon's rule is set firmly within the context of the whole creation. His wisdom surpasses that of all the sages of the east, of Egypt, and indeed 'all human beings' (*'adam*),[39] and his reputation for it reaches 'all the surrounding nations' (1 Kgs 5.10–11 [4.30–31 EVV]). This characterization of Solomon as wise makes wisdom itself a universal phenomenon and a function of creation (as it is in the biblical wisdom literature). Since it is an answer to Solomon's prayer for wisdom to rule, it makes human rule too, even in the special case of the Davidide king in Jerusalem, subordinate to the God of creation. The substance of Solomon's wisdom also speaks of the creation, with its 'animals, birds, reptiles and fish' recalling the orders of Genesis 1.

This location of Solomon's rule within God's creative reach continues into the narrative of temple construction. Cedars of Lebanon are no longer merely a topic of the king's wisdom (5.13 [4.33]), but are now put to use as timber for the house of Yahweh (5.20 [5.6]). The temple as symbol of Yahweh's rule in heaven is appropriately constructed from materials from the best that the earth can offer. The co-operation of Hiram of Tyre, and his actual words of praise to Yahweh (5.21 [5.7]), further confirm that the temple of Yahweh in Jerusalem is the focus of his worship in all the world.

The story of Israel in Kings is also that of Yahweh's sovereign control over world affairs. Along with Jehu and Elisha, Elijah is instructed to anoint Hazael king of Syria (1 Kgs 19.15), thus bringing even this foreign rule within the ambit of Yahweh's prophet. Yahweh's sway over non-Israelite nations is then substantiated in the Elisha cycle, and the wars of the northern kingdom with its neighbour Syria. Not only the king of Israel is subject to Yahweh's word by Elisha, but the king of Syria too knows that the same word stands in the way of his own ambitions, and so he attempts to capture the prophet (2 Kgs 6.8–14). Such plans prove useless, however, because the Syrians fail to perceive the true source and nature

---

39. NRSV's 'anyone else' in 4.31 [EVV] is pale. The reference to *'adam* points to the creation of humanity. RSV's 'all men' fails the inclusive language test, but is more accurate.

of power (6.15–23). Syrian impotence continues throughout the cycle, even when the odds seem stacked in their favour, a miraculous deliverance of Samaria foreshadowing the Assyrian fiasco at Jerusalem some generations later (2 Kgs 6.24–7.20, cf. 19.35–37). Most telling, however, is again the Naaman episode, when the Syrian commander, cured of his leprosy, declares: 'Now I know that there is no God in all the earth except in Israel' (2 Kgs 5.15), and plans, if crudely, to worship Yahweh in the land of Syria (vv. 17–19).

If Israel is favoured in Elisha's day, the ultimate undoing of the two kingdoms is also presented as a function of Yahweh's rule in the world. Assyria is brought against the northern kingdom, but shown conversely to be impotent against Yahweh's decree when it comes against Jerusalem (2 Kings 18–19, cf. Isa. 10.5–19). Babylon becomes in its turn Yahweh's agent against Judah, and also the subject of Solomon's prayer that they should have compassion on the exiles (1 Kgs 8.50). In all these turns of international affairs Yahweh is seen to carry his purposes forward. The unanswered question about Israel's future at the end of the book is at the same time an unanswered question about the future of human rule in the world. But it is clear that whatever transpires it will be at the behest of Yahweh. The prohibition on Assyria from taking Jerusalem is a central token of this. Two things emerge therefore from the political currents revealed by Kings: that all human rule is subject to Yahweh, and that his rule in the world continues to be asserted apart from political Israel–Judah.

5. *Conclusion*

The book of Kings, like those that precede it, has for its subject the rule of God in the world. The story is predicated throughout on the confession of Yahweh as the one and only God. As David asserted the uniqueness of both God and Israel (2 Sam. 7.22–23) in a manner reminiscent of Deuteronomy (Deut. 4.7–8, 34), so the confession recurs in 1 Kgs 8.60, in Solomon's dedicatory prayer, in one of its strongest forms in the Old Testament. It is at the heart of Elijah's conflict with the prophets of Baal (1 Kgs 18.21, 37, 39), and taken on the lips of the Syrian Naaman (2 Kgs 5.15). It is the foundation of the miraculous deliverance of Jerusalem from the Assyrians (2 Kgs 19.15), and the assumption behind events that have befallen the Babylonian exiles (1 Kgs 8.50b–53). This sovereignty of God in human affairs is set against the fickleness of human rule, its tendency to tyranny, its self-deluding pretentiousness.

Moreover, the kings of Kings are not those of Israel and Judah only, but also of Syria, Edom, Moab, Assyria and Babylon. All wield their power according to an estimate of it that is belied by the prophetic vision which sees and mocks its limitations. The kings of Syria take their cue from the prophet of Israel even as their weakness is exposed by him, as in the case of Naaman. Kings misread the nature of power. Hazael is shown by the word of Elisha that he will be king, but grasps at power by murdering his sick father (2 Kgs 8.7–15). For him, power consists in force, the strength of the human arm. Yet that is precisely the view that the Elisha cycle undermines. In the most exquisite ironic twist, the Assyrian

Rabshakeh uses 'deuteronomic' language to deride the claims of Yahweh to give land, deliverance and security, asserting instead the power of the Assyrian king to do these things (2 Kgs 18.28–35). Yet he is finally mocked by his own words, when the Assyrians are humiliated at the gates of Jerusalem.

Despite royal pretensions, life remains the gift of God. The little captive Israelite girl knows this better than kings and commanders. Elisha provides food, heals the sick and raises to life by the prophetic word (2 Kings 4).

These are the grounds for hope bequeathed by the book of Kings. The prophetic cycles show how best to evaluate even the reform of a righteous king or the release of a captive king from his Babylonian jail. Such are not the straws in the wind that give ultimate hope to the people of God. Rather it is because royal power is transitory and subject to the divine will that the exiles in Babylon, and those left in the land, may yet hope for the kingdom of God to be realized among them.

Chapter 10

CONCLUSION: AN OLD TESTAMENT POLITICAL THEOLOGY

1. *The Divine Order in Political Life*

My aim in the present volume has been to explore the understanding of the relationship of God to the political order presented in the Old Testament's primary history (Genesis–Kings). This was conceived in response to a number of related factors: the modern tendency to make a sharp division between theology and politics; the claim that the Old Testament was formed as a mechanism of social and political control; and the view that appeals to God in politics lead inevitably to exclusiveness and even tyranny.[1] I have tried to show, on the contrary, that the biblical picture demonstrates a vision for political life on the broadest canvas as a function of the creative purpose to bless humanity. The story of Israel leads out of tyranny and into freedom, in a vision that is universal.

The issue is both theological and hermeneutical. In what ways may the 'Old Testament' or 'Hebrew Bible' speak about politics (or indeed about any topic)? Approaches to the subject are involved necessarily in choices about how to read the material: do the texts speak with one voice? Are some parts weightier than others? How may various voices be heard in relation to each other?

The critical hermeneutical decision made here was the choice of Genesis–Kings as the text for discussion. It affected the argument in a number of ways. First, it located the material concerning Israel's polity in a narrative that begins with creation and a vision of the divine purpose for all humanity. Second, it sought to place Deuteronomy in particular in a context in which it is both a culmination and a beginning. This is in contrast to the prevalent tendency to endow Deuteronomy with a separate identity, in the sense that all things 'deuteronomic' (and derivatively, 'Deuteronomistic') belong within a movement or 'school' distinct from other theological movements in the Old Testament. This construct of Deuteronomy as the manifesto of a distinctive movement lies deep within historical criticism, which has used the lens of Josiah's reform to read it. Deuteronomy is thus put at odds with the priestly theology of P, which roots Israel's story in creation, and in general with those parts of the Old Testament held to be universal in their scope. The reading offered here, in contrast, subordinates the programme of Deuteronomy to the larger purpose that opens up in Genesis. Third, the voice of Deuteronomy is heard according to this place-

---

1. E.g. Blenkinsopp, Davies, Chapter 1 above; Assmann, Brueggemann; Chapter 2 above.

ment, in such a way, for example, that the language of 'land' carries connotations of 'earth', and thus the gift of land to Israel has eschatological and universal implications.

The decision to take Genesis–Kings as subject may be justified along canonical or narrative lines, or both, and these need no further elaboration here. Since no attempt has been made to account for the historical development of the literature, this study cannot by definition rule out the construal of its parts by means which occupy the vantage-points of historical criticism. However, the interpretation offered here resists the notion that the meaning of the parts of the OT must first be established by such criticism before constructive interpretation of the texts may proceed. Our study calls for an appraisal of the material, especially of Deuteronomy, according to the interrelationships of its parts in the form in which it has been received. And this has important corollaries for the interpretation of Old Testament politics.

The choice of Genesis as the starting-point of the study not only draws on narrative and canonical interpretation, but also corresponds to the now well-established rediscovery of the so-called creation-horizon in Biblical Theology. The chief implication of according primacy to the category of creation in the biblical literature is, as explained in Ch. 3, its embedding of justice-righteousness in the created order, derived from the character of God, and inscribed in the laws of Israel. This has the corollary that the entire story proceeds under the influence of that vision and invites critique in terms of it.[2] Crucially affected is the way in which texts are heard to enunciate political ideas. Do the texts promote a 'primordial' view of nationhood through Israel's story, or in contrast, one that exhibits more universal themes? In response to this question Grosby puts texts in Genesis–Kings at odds with each other, when he asks:

> Does the meaning of our existence revolve around those primordial beliefs about the significance of the objects of [the origin and transmission of life itself] – descendants and land – conveyed unambiguously by the so-called unconditional covenant in Gen 17:7, 28:15, and especially 2 Samuel 7; or are such beliefs and the existence of the collectivities that bear them – the family and that bounded territorial collectivity of nativity, the nation – subordinate to a meaning of righteousness that transcends, hence conditions, vitality and its transmission as stated in Deuteronomy 30.[3]

The method I have adopted proceeds differently with the interaction of such texts. The argument construed the differences between 2 Samuel 7 and Deuteronomy in terms of an ongoing critical dialogue between Israel's vocation and its performance. The witness to the created order in Israel is contingent on its faithfulness to its covenant with Yahweh, and its institutions are always provisional. All its political forms are subjected to the rigorous scrutiny of the primary history's own standard of *torah*, not least the Davidic dynastic monarchy. This is why the conceptualization of what is 'deuteronomic' should not be framed according to the interests of the monarchy, still less the Josianic reform programme.[4]

2. In Knierim's terms, history is subordinate to cosmos; see above, Chapter 3.
3. Grosby, *Biblical Ideas of Nationality*, p. 5.
4. Deuteronomic/-istic influence is often precipitately claimed on superficial grounds, often

In a similar vein, the rediscovery of the creation horizon in Old Testament Theology has also enabled a fresh comparison between the Old Testament's primary history and that of the Mesopotamian narrative that proceeds from creation to established political institutions.[5] Unlike it, however, its purpose is not to vindicate and justify the institutional arrangements which came to fruition under the kings in Jerusalem, arrangements which have unravelled by the end of the story. The centrality of covenant and law in the account of Israel's origins stands against institutional permanency. The critical nature of the primary history is, in my view, crucial to an understanding of the Old Testament's political theology. Its prescriptions for political life are partly fulfilled in Israel's history and institutions, but those institutions are carefully prevented from taking on permanent or absolute significance. This tension between the law and the performance is an important aspect of the argument presented here.

It follows that Genesis–Kings is not merely oblique evidence of an ancient dispute over primordial or universal conceptions of nationhood, but rather that it constitutes an argument for the latter. Israel, in its laws and in its self-understanding according to its own literature, testifies to what it might mean to be a people that lives in obedience to norms of justice-righteousness that transcend its own life and become universal.

Before proceeding to recall the argument more fully, it is in place to orientate it to O'Donovan's bid to reclaim the biblical story of Israel for political theology, which was an important incentive to my own. O'Donovan found in Israel's history the revelation of God's purpose for the political order, expressed in the triad of victory (or salvation), judgement (*tsedeq/tsedaqah*) and possession.[6] The echoes of his work in the present study were conspicuous in Ch. 5, where I attempted to elucidate the political themes of Deuteronomy. I have differed from him, first, in adopting the approach described above, and thus the claim that there are aspects of social ordering which are rooted in the divine creative ordering. There lies in this a different construal of the force of *tsedaqah* and *mishpat*, for in his analysis these closely related concepts are understood as acts of 'judgement', which are essentially corrective and do not presuppose an antecedent order.[7] In contrast, the effect of beginning with creation is that justice-righteousness is

---

simply linguistic. Linville makes important critical points on this: *Israel in the Book of Kings*, pp. 66–9.

5.   The 'Epic of Creation', or Enuma Elish, relates the victory of Marduk over the primaeval forces of Chaos and his enthronement as lord of Babylon; see Dalley, *Myths*, pp. 228–77.

6.   See Chapter 5, above, nn. 22–35; O'Donovan, *Desire of the Nations*, p. 36.

7.   O'Donovan, *Desire of the Nations*, pp. 38–9. See also O'Donovan's response to Jonathan Chaplin in *A Royal Priesthood?*, pp. 309–13. In that place he reaffirms his view that justice is essentially 'negative' (p. 309, cf. in the same place, 'Injustice has epistemological priority over justice'), and 'a train of corrective reasoning' (p. 313). O'Donovan does find a transition from individual performances of judgement to a lasting validity of Yahweh's judgements as a function of the close relationship between law and history in Israel, and the growth of a 'law-culture' out of the salvation-history emphases of older Israelite religion; *Desire of the Nations*, p. 39. The argument thus rests on a particular reconstruction of Israel's history, and imparts authority to that history, in a way that I have tried to avoid here.

located prior to history, in the character of God, thence inscribed on the creation, and so expressed in the laws of Israel. It is for this reason that I have preferred to express what is involved in *tsedaqah* and *mishpat* as 'justice-righteousness' rather than O'Donovan's 'judgement'.[8]

2. *The Order Unfolded in the Primary History*

The specifically political question faced by the primary history is how the just rule of the one God Yahweh in the world might be implemented initially in the political life of a people. Here humanity stands before the one universal God, created in his image, yet possessed of a drive for power (to be 'like God', Gen. 3.5) in a fragile and dangerous world that is no longer a protected paradise. The story is not written on a *tabula rasa*, but against the background of the religio-politics of the Ancient Near East. Can there be a recipe for mature political life, nurturing the creation intention to bless humanity, the dignity of humanity as such, and the divine will to righteousness in the world? In what way can *Israel* fulfil the divine intention that righteousness should be realized concretely on earth? Must it not succumb to dangers of nationalism and power itself?

The answer to these questions lay in the lineaments of the story, which stages an encounter between the ideal and the real, the eschatological and the pragmatic, these being inseparable. The key concepts of the thesis are established in Genesis. Here the goal of righteousness is set for all humanity in its predication of Noah. Placed as a special obligation upon Abraham and his descendants, it remains broader than these alone, as is clear in Abraham's own prayer over Sodom (Genesis 18), and his encounter with Abimelech of Gerar (Genesis 20). The deep-lying conflict engendered by the divine purpose emerges powerfully in the arc that spans Egypt to Moab (Exodus–Numbers). Yahweh's claim upon Israel meets the unyielding resistance of Pharaoh's demand to subject everything to himself. Freedom in service to Yahweh can only be achieved by a victory over all-encompassing, enslaving, 'chaotic' human power, in alliance with the moral influence of Egypt on Israel itself. The deliverance from tyranny has its express purpose in Israel's worship of Yahweh in the wilderness, and in that connection the representative role of Israel within a universal concept stands out. For in the architecture and rituals of the tabernacle appears the possibility of *humanity* standing before God (in spite of the loss of the divine presence that comes from the dawn of life itself) and realizing its creation status as 'image' with its mandate to 'rule' over the earth. Finally, in the giving of law, though law codes are in themselves transitory and provisional, justice-righteousness is made the norm of political life in contrast to self-serving power.

With Deuteronomy, the biblical *politeia* reaches its centre and summit. Here Israel in its God-given land is once again a surrogate for humanity on the earth

---

8. On this I am rather in agreement with Jonathan Chaplin, who in his nuanced critique of O'Donovan speaks of 'a perdurable order of social justice', which he illustrates from the Jubilee laws; 'Political Eschatology and Responsible Government: Oliver O'Donovan's "Christian Liberalism"', in Bartholomew, *et al.* (eds.), *A Royal Priesthood?*, pp. 265–308, especially pp. 290–1.

('earth' and 'land' being readily interchangeable since each is variously *'erets* and *'adamah*). The installation of Israel in bounded land is therefore not only an episode in history and geopolitics but also a partial realization of the creative purpose for humanity. In its promulgation of *torah*, its vision for the life of a people in legitimate possession of bounded territory, lies a charter for nationhood as distinct from nationalism, universal in its conception rather than primordial. 'Natural' entitlements are expressly eschewed here: the people is neither great nor good, and the land is given and may be taken away. On the contrary, in the institutions envisaged for Israel are established the parameters of rightly grounded political life, with concepts of responsible citizenship, the sovereignty of the people under God and law, and corresponding constraints upon monarchical power.

The constituents of nationhood, people, land, law, memory and worship,[9] reach their full expression here. The deuteronomic institutions are fully intelligible against the backcloth of the hierarchically dominating forms of power in Israel's political environment, and conceived as measures against the possibility of tyranny. Part of the force of Deuteronomy's provisions is that, in this context, it mandates the construction of beneficial institutions as part of its programme for political life. The argument with Mesopotamian politics is at the same time an argument with its religion, each political vision being founded ultimately on a concept of god and creation. Institutions themselves are historically contingent and subject to change, as our analysis has shown. And Deuteronomy knows that institutional forms are not enough in themselves to fulfil the divine mandate, without the commitment of those who bear responsibility within them to seek 'justice and only justice' (Deut. 16.20).[10] Yet there is a creative energy between the changing institutions of Israel and the mandates in Deuteronomy, in which lies the possibility for reform and regeneration. The deuteronomic programme also fights shy of the concentration of power in an individual or a centralized state, as its law of the king shows, where the king is strictly supernumerary, and his power in any case emphatically subjected to *torah*. The subjection of institutional power to law (or the lack of it) consequently became one of the running themes of Joshua–Kings.[11]

The narrative in Joshua–Kings shows Israel partly conforming and partly not conforming to its vocation. Its encounter with the kings of Canaan behind Yahweh the divine warrior is in reality a conflict with the forces of Chaos, in

---

9.   This shorthand account of the elements of nationhood was intended to embrace O'Donovan's four elements of deliverance, judgement, community-possession and praise, and Smith's more general definition; see above, Chapter 5, at n. 29.

10.   Such commitment is in effect the quality of *eusebeia* advocated by Josephus; cf. above. Chapter 5, n. 52. While I have reservations about O'Donovan's insistence upon the primacy of 'the political act' over political institutions (*Desire of the Nations*, p. 20, cf. my Law and Monarchy'. p. 80), it is clear that right judging and acting is essential to the proper functioning of institutions.

11.   See Chaplin's defence of the concept of 'separation of powers' as biblical, again in critical dialogue with O'Donovan's concept of a unitary agency of authority; *A Royal Priesthood?*, pp. 293–5, and n. 116.

parallel with the earlier conflict with the pharaoh of the exodus. Israel's assembly around the tent of meeting at Shiloh (Josh. 18.1) is an earnest of the eschatological fulfilment of the primaeval mandate to 'rule' over the creation. Correspondingly, Israel edges towards a mode of being that is based on the constitutional programme of Deuteronomy, with due regard for *torah*, and political authority exercised by a range of leaders on behalf of the people. Joshua himself has a limited role which is effective for the duration of the period of the occupation only. With the inclusion of Rahab and her descendants, Israel exhibits a move towards a strictly political (not ethnic-primordial) conception, in spite of ambiguities concerning its conduct towards her. The covenant at Shechem prepares the reader for the discrepancy between ideal and performance that will characterize its further history (Josh. 24.19), and shows that even in Joshua the concept of a righteous nation prevails over a primordial one.

After Joshua, Israel attempts to exercise its responsibility to govern itself justly between the constraints of law-covenant, the religious-political pressures from the environment, and its own propensity to 'primordial' Baalism.[12] The conflict with Chaos is thus perpetuated into the ongoing life of Israel. In this context, the relationship between divine and human power is played out. Yahweh the Judge (Judg. 11.27) raises 'judge-deliverers' for a series of crises, in repeated recurrence of the theme of salvation-victory. Yahweh the King permits dynastic kingship and the Canaanite symbolism of a fixed temple, but only with critical retrospect on their essential inappropriateness in covenantal Israel. While there are moments of sound rule, the political life of Israel never conforms to the pattern anticipated in Deuteronomy. Rather, the temptations of power infect all classes of religious and political leadership, and affect not only the forms of political life but its ethics (as is clear in the collision between Elijah, prophet of Yahweh, and Ahab, king in thrall to Baal). The lapse of Israel from its vocation to realize Yahweh's intention of just rule may be expressed as a failure in the realm of memory, in terms of the analysis of Deuteronomy 8. Israel does not effectively nurture those memories and traditions that form its distinctive covenantal heritage.[13] All five aspects of soundly-based nationhood are infringed: the *people* of Israel itself lacks definition; the *land* is fragmented and finally forfeited; the *law* is marginalized in favour of rule by force; the specific covenantal *memory* of Israel is lost, until symbolically but belatedly recovered in the discovery of the 'book of the law;' and *worship* is directed towards Baal and the gods of Assyria in place of the God of deliverance and freedom, Yahweh.

Israel therefore progressively takes forms which place it at a distance from the creation mandate, the Abrahamic purpose and the Mosaic ideal. The conclusion of Israel's story poses a question as to the mode in which it can continue to exist, if at all. The issue identified at the beginning – in what way can there be righteousness on earth? – is there at the end, and set in the context of a world of

---

12. In the Old Testament's perspective, Baalism combines a political conservatism that sustains minor potentates and their bureaucracies, and a form of religion that postulates connections between peoples and land that may be classed as primordial.

13. This is to refer again to the terms of Smith, *Chosen Peoples*, pp. 24–5.

empires. The Old Testament's story from creation to politics differs from the ANE precisely in this respect, that its interpretation of origins is at the service neither of the idea of one nation's intrinsic right to predominate, nor of a given political *status quo*. There was a positive side to the story in that it illustrated Yahweh's readiness to allow his rule to find correspondences in a variety of actual political forms. However, it ends in an absence of institutions, and only eschatological pointers. We traced this downward trajectory from Joshua to Kings in terms of the creation perspective, the exercise of human power, and the nature of Israel. As Judah is subjected to Babylonian rule, Yahweh's intention for just rule in the world is intact; a role of 'Israel' is not necessarily exhausted, but the question as to its future mode of existence, as nation and political entity, is open. Even so, Solomon's prayer makes clear that any future life of Israel will depend on the formative events of the past, and on a 'right' (*mishpat*) of Israel that derives from them (1 Kgs 8.49, 51).

3. *The Old Testament in Political Interpretation*

At the beginning of the present study I proposed to consider Genesis–Kings at three levels of interpretation, the worlds 'behind', 'of' and 'in front of' the text. In locating the biblical narrative and laws in their broad ANE context ('behind' the text) I have tried to show their radical character in advocating a mediation of political authority that directly challenged the hierarchical systems of its world. In offering a consecutive reading of Genesis–Kings ('world of the text'), I have suggested that the many interconnections of the text played a vital part in its meaning. Most importantly, the story of Israel's political life is subordinated to the larger purpose of God in creation. But in addition, the high points of Israel's political achievement (arguably David and Josiah) are qualified by many nuanced reservations, and by the conclusion of the story itself. And we began to consider the appropriation of the political ideas 'in front of the text', when we observed how modern interpreters, often referring initially to Josephus, adopt concepts from political history (such as 'constitution', 'democracy') in order to assess the full impact of the ideas they find, especially in Deuteronomy. This was intended, in part, to respond to the idea that the meaning of the texts was governed by the interests and intentions of those who composed them.[14]

It is beyond our present scope to offer a political reception-history of the parts of the Old Testament reviewed here.[15] An account of it would undoubtedly show that Scripture can be called in aid of quite diverse causes. However, it is clear from a glance at a few instances that that strand of the Old Testament which some have convicted of fostering violence, oppression and exclusivism[16] has at times had more productive and liberating applications. The Puritan John Milton, contending against what he saw as the tyranny of the Stuart monarchy, mounted a fully fledged argument for 'commonwealth', or 'democracy', as conforming to

14. See above, Ch. 1, at nn. 18–21, on Rowland and Mosala.
15. For a helpful introduction to this, see McBride, 'Deuteronomy'.
16. See Chapter 2 above, at nn. 13–27, for documentation of this claim.

the biblical pattern.[17] 1 Samuel 8 is foregrounded, and Deut. 17.14–20 underlies. Here is expounded the sovereignty of the people, delegated to an elected assembly,[18] individual liberty, civil rights, advancement according to merit, and even small government.[19] To turn back to kings 'after this light' would be to 'return to Egypt'.[20] Milton's concept of individual liberty would no doubt suffer modern strictures. But it is a passionate use of the 'deuteronomic' political texts under conviction of their liberative power. It is a salutary perspective in view of other more 'nationalist' Puritan appropriations, for example of Cromwell and Cotton Mather.[21]

Modern appropriations of the deuteronomic law are as committed in their own ways as these examples from the past. Two examples will make the point. First, Thanzauva and R. L. Hnuni, in Mark Brett's collection on ethnicity and the Bible, see a connection between the 'aliens' (גרים) in Deuteronomy and tribal Indian Christians. The deuteronomic legislation, which they set against the background of the social system that followed the rise of the monarchy, aims to protect precisely such groups from oppression by the aristocratic layers of society.[22]

Second, T. J. Gorringe adopts Deuteronomy in his critique of global capitalism. Here too a link is made between the origin of the law code and its contemporary appropriation. Characterizing Deuteronomy as the document of 'utopian realists' in the time of King Manasseh, he sees it as resisting the 'alien norms' imbibed from the wider cultural environment, namely slavery, prostitution and taxation for the purpose of maintaining a standing army.[23] With this adoption of the category of idolatry, the 'religious' aspect of Deuteronomy is fully accepted as part of the deuteronomic message. The ultimate beliefs upon which a society is based constitute its 'worship'.[24]

In order to ground his use of Deuteronomy in an ethical argument he makes use of a version of 'natural law', in which law is part of human tradition;[25] the ethical sense is 'primordial', rooted in relationships and the need to preserve the continuance of the race.[26] Gorringe draws on Deuteronomy to establish an argu-

17. *The Ready and Easy Way to Establish a Free Commonwealth, and the Excellence Thereof Compared with the Inconveniences and Dangers of Readmitting Kingship in This Land*, in Stephen Orgel and Jonathan Goldberg (eds.), *John Milton: The Major Works* (Oxford World Classics; Oxford: Oxford Univerity Press, 2003), pp. 330–53.

18. Milton, *Ready and Easy Way*, p. 339.

19. Milton, *Ready and Easy Way*, p. 350.

20. Milton, *Ready and Easy Way*, p. 352.

21. See above, Chapter 2, n. 12.

22. Thanzauva and R. L. Hnuni, 'Ethnicity, Identity and Hermeneutics: An Indian Tribal Perspective', in Mark G. Brett (ed.), *Ethnicity and the Bible* (BIS, 19; Leiden: E.J Brill, 2002), pp. 343–57, especially pp. 355–7.

23. T. J. Gorringe, *Capital and Kingdom: Theological Ethics and Economic Order* (London: SPCK, 1994), p. vii.

24. Gorringe, *Capital and Kingdom*, pp. 25–6.

25. Gorringe, *Capital and Kingdom*, pp. 5–6.

26. Gorringe, *Capital and Kingdom*, p. 11. The use of the term 'primordial' here is, of course, in a different context from that in which we have met it above (Chapter 5), where it described a certain view of ethnicity.

ment about human equality as intimately connected with justice.[27] He thinks the deep divisions within humanity, attested biblically in Genesis 3, are mitigated by the law of the king, which aims to proscribe forms of government that lead to tyranny.[28] He goes beyond equality to notions of solidarity and resistance, and finds warrant in his use of the biblical law to criticize structural injustices undergirding capitalist economics. His use of Deuteronomy leans heavily on its orientation towards the life of all members of the community as the supreme good, to which all policy must be subordinated. The proper justification of any development towards democracy in non-democratic countries is the return of power and resources to the people of those countries.

Some modern interpretations of Deuteronomy, therefore, take it in the direction of 'resistance', as at least one seventeenth-century strand also did. Both those cited understand the deuteronomic law to be critical of the concentration of power in a monarchy or privileged class. They also share a belief that the law has a prophetic spirit which has the capacity to challenge corruption and oppression in the quite different societies to which they are addressed.

3. Conclusion

Our study has placed the 'deuteronomic' texts of the Old Testament in their context in the primary history of Genesis–Kings, and broadly in their ANE context. I have argued that the dichotomy often found to exist between the deuteronomic and the inclusive, universal prophetic strands is false. On the contrary, both are necessary. It is the former that shows the merely relative status of all specific political arrangements, and the derived nature and proper limitations of all earthly power, yet at the same time offers a vision for both righteousness and liberation in the political realm, and sanctions political activity as such. In the affirmation of the need for politics and citizenly participation together with a belief in the contingency and provisionality of all specific institutional forms, policy and eschatology are linked. It is the eschatological perspective of the biblical narrative, together with its attribution of ultimate authority to 'the Judge of all the earth [who does] right', and its insistence that he alone is worthy of ultimate loyalty, that stands as a bulwark against tyranny.

27. Gorringe, *Capital and Kingdom*, p. 52.
28. Gorringe, *Capital and Kingdom*, pp. 62–3.

BIBLIOGRAPHY

Abbot, Wilbur Cortez, *The Writings and Speeches of Oliver Cromwell Vol. III* (Cambridge, Mass.; Harvard University Press, 1945).

Aichele, George, *The Control of Biblical Meaning: Canon as Semiotic Mechanism* (Harrisburg: Trinity Press International, 2001).

Alt, A., 'The Origins of Israelite Law', in *Essays on Old Testament History and Religion* (Sheffield: JSOT Press, 1989).

Alter, Robert, *The Art of Biblical Narrative* (New York: Basic Books, 1981).

Amir, Yehoshua, 'Josephus on the Mosaic "Constitution"', in H. Graf Reventlow, Yair Hoffmann and Benjamin Uffenheimer (eds.), *Politics and Theopolitics in the Bible and Postbiblical Literature* (JSOTSup, 171; Sheffield: JSOT Press, 1994), pp. 13–27.

Amir, Y., 'θεοκρατία as a Concept of Political Philosophy: Josephus' Presentation of Moses' πολιτεία', *SCI* 8–9 (1985/88), pp. 13–27.

Amit, Yairah, *The Book of Judges: the Art of Editing* (trans. Jonathan Chipman; BIS, 38; Leiden: E. J. Brill, 1999).

Anderson, Benedict, *Imagined Communities: Reflections on the Origin and Spread of Nationalism* (London: Verso, 1983).

Arnold, Bill T., 'Religion in Ancient Israel', in David W. Baker and Bill T. Arnold (eds.), *The Face of Old Testament Studies* (Grand Rapids: Baker/Leicester: Apollos, 1999), pp. 391–420.

Ash, P. S., 'Solomon's? District? List', *JSOT* 67 (1995), pp. 67–86.

Assmann, Jan, 'Monotheismus und Ikonoklasmus als politische Theologie', in E. Otto (ed.), *Mose: Ägypten und das Alte Testament* (Stuttgarter Bibelstudien, 189; Stuttgart: Katholisches Bibelwerk, 2000), pp. 121–39.

—*Moses the Egyptian: the Memory of Egypt in Western Monotheism* (Cambridge, Mass.; Harvard University Press, 1997).

Bal, Mieke, *Death and Dissymmetry: The Politics of Coherence in the Book of Judges* (Chicago: University of Chicago Press, 1988).

Barstad, Hans, *The Myth of the Empty Land: A Study of the History and Archaeology of Judah During the Exile Period* (Oslo: Scandinavian University Press, 1996).

Bartholomew, Craig, Jonathan Chaplin, Robert Song and Al Wolters (eds.), *A Royal Priesthood? The Use of the Bible Ethically and Politically* (SHS, 3; Grand Rapids: Zondervan/ Carlisle: Paternoster Press, 2002).

Bartholomew, Craig, Colin Greene and Karl Möller (eds.), *After Pentecost: Language and Biblical Interpretation* (SHS, 2; Carlisle: Paternoster Press/Grand Rapids: Zondervan, 2001).

Bartholomew, Craig, Mary Healey, Karl Möller and Robin Parry (eds.), *Out of Egypt: Biblical Theology and Biblical Interpretation* (SHS, 5; Carlisle: Paternoster Press/Grand Rapids: Zondervan, 2004).

Barton, John, 'Canon and Old Testament Interpretation', in Edward Ball (ed.), *In Search of True Wisdom: Essays in Old Testament Interpretation in Honour of Ronald E. Clements* (JSOTSup, 300; Sheffield: Sheffield Academic Press, 1999), pp. 37–52.

Barton, John, and Michael Wolter (eds.), *Die Einheit der Schrift und die Vielfalt des Kanons* (Berlin and New York: W. de Gruyter, 2003).

Bauckham, R. J., 'Biblical Theology and the Problems of Monotheism,', in Bartholomew *et al.* (eds.), *Out of Egypt*, pp. 187–232.
—*The Bible in Politics* (London: SPCK, 1989).
Beale, Gregory K., *The Temple and the Church's Mission: A Biblical Theology of the Dwelling-Place of God* (Leicester: Apollos/Downers Grove, IL; IVP, 2004).
Berghe van den, P. L., *The Ethnic Phenomenon* (New York, Elsevier, 1981).
Birch, Bruce C., 'The First and Second Books of Samuel', in *The New Interpreter's Bible II* (Nashville: Abingdon Press, 1998).
Blenkinsopp, J., *Prophecy and Canon: A Contribution to the Study of Jewish Origins* (Notre Dame: University of Notre Dame Press, 1977).
—'The Bible, Archaeology and Politics; or the Empty Land Revisited', *JSOT* 27 (2002), pp. 169–87.
—'The Structure of P', *CBQ* 38 (1976), pp. 275–92.
Block, Daniel I., *Judges, Ruth* (NAC; Nashville: Broadman and Holman, 1999).
Bluedorn, W., *Yahweh versus Baalism: A Theological Reading of the Gideon-Abimelech Narrative* (JSOTSup, 329; Sheffield: Sheffield Academic Press, 2001).
Blum, E., *Studien zur Komposition des Pentateuch* (BZAW, 189; Berlin: W. de Gruyter, 1990).
Boling, Robert G., *Judges* (AB; New York: Doubleday, 1975).
Braulik, G. (ed.), *Bundesdokument und Gesetz: Studien zum Deuteronomium* (HBS, 4; Freiburg: Herder, 1995), pp. 65–78.
Brettler, Mark Zvi, *The Book of Judges* (Routledge: London and New York, 2002).
Bruckner, James K., *Implied Law in the Abraham Narrative: a Literary and Theological Analysis* (JSOTSup, 335; Sheffield: Sheffield Academic Press, 2001).
Brueggemann, W., '2 Samuel 21–24: An Appendix of Deconstruction?', *CBQ* 50 (1988), pp. 383–97.
—*Theology of the Old Testament; Testimony, Dispute, Advocacy* (Minneapolis: Fortress, 1997).
Buber, M., *Kingship of God* (London: Allen & Unwin, 3rd edn, 1967).
Burleigh, Michael, *Earthly Powers* (London: HarperCollins, 2005).
Carrière, J.-M., *La théorie du politique dans le Deutéronome* (ÖBS, 18; Frankfurt: Peter Lang, 1997).
Carroll, R. P., 'Textual Strategies and Ideology in the Second Temple Period', in Davies (ed.), *Second Temple Studies I*, pp. 108–24.
Chaplin, Jonathan, 'Political Eschatology and Responsible Government: Oliver O'Donovan's "Christian Liberalism"', in Bartholomew *et al.* (eds.), *A Royal Priesthood?*, pp. 265–308.
Childs, B. S., *Introduction to the Old Testament as Scripture* (London: SCM Press, 1979).
Clements, R. E., *God and Temple* (Oxford: Blackwell, 1965).
Clines, D. J. A., *The Theme of the Pentateuch* (JSOTSup, 10; Sheffield; JSOT Press, 1978).
Cogan, M., *I Kings* (AB; New York: Doubleday, 2000).
Cross, F. M., *Canaanite Myth and Hebrew Epic* (trans. Allan W. Mahnke; Cambridge, Mass.: Harvard University Press, 1973).
Crüsemann, Frank, *Der Widerstand gegen das Königtum: Die antiköniglichen Texte des Alten Testaments und der Kampf um den frühen israelitischen Staat* (WMANT, 49; Neukirchen–Vluyn: Neukirchener Verlag, 1978).
—*The Torah: Theology and Social History of Old Testament Law* (Minneapolis: Fortress, 1996).
Dalley, Stephanie, *Myths from Mesopotamia* (Oxford; Oxford University Press, 1991).
Davies, P. R., *In Search of 'Ancient Israel'* (JSOTSup, 148; Sheffield: Sheffield Academic Press, 1992, repr. 1995).
—'Scenes from the Early History of Judaism', in Diana Vikander Edelman (ed.), *The Triumph of Elohim: From Yahwisms to Judaisms* (Grand Rapids: Eerdmans, 1995), pp. 145–82.
Davies, P. R. (ed.), *Second Temple Studies I: Persian Period* (JSOTSup, 117; Sheffield: JSOT Press, 1991).

Day, John (ed.), *In Search of Pre-Exilic Israel: Proceedings of the Oxford Old Testament Seminar* (JSOTSup, 406; London: T&T Clark, 2004).

—*Yahweh and the Gods and Goddesses of Canaan* (JSOTSup, 265; Sheffield: Sheffield Academic Press, 2000).

Deist, F., 'The Dangers of Deuteronomy: A Page from the Reception History of the Book', in F. García Martínez *et al.* (eds.), *Studies in Deuteronomy in Honour of C.J. Labuschagne on the Occasion of His 65th Birthday* (*VTSup, 53*; Leiden: E. J. Brill, 1994), pp. 13–29.

Dietrich, W., 'History and Law. Deuteronomistic Historiography and Deuteronomic Law Exemplified in the Passage from the Period of the Judges to the Monarchical Period', in A. de Pury, Thomas Römer and Jean-Daniel Macchi (eds.), *Israel Constructs its History: Deuteronomistic Historiography in Recent Research* (JSOTSup, 306; Sheffield. Sheffield Academic Press, English language edn, 2000), pp. 315–42.

Dion, P., 'The Suppression of Alien Religious Propaganda in Israel during the Late Monarchical Era', in B. Halpern and D. Hobson (eds.), *Law and Ideology in Monarchic Israel* (JSOTSup, 124; Sheffield: Sheffield Academic Press), pp. 147–216.

Driver, S. R., *Introduction to the Literature of the Old Testament* (Edinburgh: T&T Clark, 3rd edn, 1892).

—*The Book of Genesis* (London: Methuen, 1904).

Dutcher-Walls, P., 'The Social Location of the Deuteronomists: A Sociological Study of Factional Politics in Late Pre-Exilic Judah', *JSOT* 52 (1991), pp. 77–94.

Eco, Umberto, '*Intentio Lectoris*: the State of the Art', in Eco, *The Limits of Interpretation* (Bloomington and Indianapolis: Indiana University Press, 1990), pp. 44–63.

Ellis, Marc H., *Israel and Palestine: Out of the Ashes; the Search for Jewish Identity in the Twenty-First Century* (London and Sterling VA: Pluto Press, 2002).

Ellul, Jacques, *The Politics of God and the Politics of Man* (Grand Rapids: Eerdmans, 1972).

Eslinger, L., *Into the Hands of the Living God* (Sheffield: Almond Press, 1989).

—*Kingship of God in Crisis* (Sheffield: Almond Press, 1985).

Finkelstein, I., *The Archaeology of the Israelite Settlement* (Jerusalem: Israel Exploration Society, 1988).

Firth, David, '"Play it Again, Sam": The Poetics of Narrative Repetition in 1 Samuel 1–7', *TynBul* 56.2 (2005), pp.1–17.

Fishbane. M., *Biblical Interpretation in Ancient Israel* (Oxford: Clarendon Press, 1985).

Fleming, Daniel E., *Democracy's Ancient Ancestors: Mari and Early Collective Governance* (Cambridge: Cambridge University Press, 2004).

Freedman, D. N., 'Canon of the Old Testament' (IDBSup; New York and Nashville: Abingdon Press, 1975), pp. 130–6.

—'The Law and the Prophets' (VTSup, 9; Leiden: E.J. Brill, 1963), pp. 250–65.

Fretheim, T. E., *Exodus* (Interpretation; Louisville, KY: John Knox, 1991).

—'Numbers', in John Barton and John Muddiman (eds.), *Oxford Bible Commentary* (Oxford: Oxford University Press, 2001), pp. 110–34.

Friedman, R. E., 'From Egypt to Egypt: Dtr[1] and Dtr[2]', in B. Halpern and J. D. Levenson (eds.), *Traditions in Transformation: Turning Points in Biblical Faith* (Festschrift F. M. Cross; Winona Lake; Eisenbrauns, 1981), pp. 167–92.

Gadamer, H. G., *Truth and Method* (trans. J. Weinsheimer and D. G. Marshall; New York: Crossroad, rev. edn, 1991).

Garbini, G., *History and Ideology in Ancient Israel* (New York: Crossroad, 1988).

Gerstenberger, E. S., *Theologien im Alten Testament: Pluralität und Synkretismus alttestamentlichen Gottesglaubens* (Stuttgart: W. Kohlhammer, 2001).

Gnuse, R., *No Other Gods: Emergent Monotheism in Israel* (JSOTSup, 241; Sheffield: Sheffield Academic Press, 1997).

Good, E. M., *Irony in the Old Testament* (London: SPCK, 1965).

Gordon, R. P., *1 and 2 Samuel* (Exeter: Paternoster Press, 1986).

—'David's Rise and Saul's Demise: Narrative Analogy in 1 Samuel 24–26', *TynBul* 31 (1980), pp. 37–64.

Gorringe, T. J., *Capital and Kingdom: Theological Ethics and Economic Order* (London: SPCK, 1994).

Gottwald, N. K., *The Tribes of Yahweh: A Sociology of the Religion of Liberated Israel* (Maryknoll, NY: Orbis Books, 1979).

Grabbe, Lester L., 'Reconstructing History from the Book of Ezra', in Davies (ed.), *Second Temple Studies I*, pp. 98–106.

Grosby, Steven, *Biblical Ideas of Nationality Ancient and Modern* (Winona Lake, IN: Eisenbrauns, 2002).

Guillaume, P., *Waiting for Josiah: the Judges* (JSOTSup, 385; London: T&T Clark, 2004).

Gunn, David M., *Judges* (Blackwell Bible Commentaries; Oxford: Blackwell, 2005).

Gunn, David M., and Danna Nolan Fewell, *Narrative in the Hebrew Bible* (Oxford: Oxford University Press, 1993).

Hallo, W. W., and K. Lawson Younger (eds.), *The Context of Scripture I: Canonical Compositions from the Biblical World* (Leiden: E. J. Brill, 1997).

Halpern, B., *The Constitution of the Monarchy in Ancient Israel* (HSM, 25; Chico, CA; Scholars Press, 1981).

Handy, Lowell K., *Among the Host of Heaven: the Syro-Palestinian Pantheon as Bureaucracy* (Winona Lake, IN: Eisenbrauns, 1994).

Hartley, John E., *Leviticus* (WBC, 4; Dallas: Word Books, 1992).

Hastings, Adrian, *The Construction of Nationhood: Ethnicity, Religion and Nationalism* (Cambridge: Cambridge University Press, 1997).

Hawk, Daniel, *Joshua* (Berit Olam; Collegeville, MN; Liturgical Press, 2000).

Heard, R. C., *The Dynamics of Diselection: Ambiguity in Genesis 12–26 and Ethnic Boundaries in Post-Exilic Judah* (SBL Semeia Studies, 39; Atlanta: SBL, 2001).

Hill, Christopher, *Milton and the English Revolution* (London: Faber and Faber, 1977).

Hobsbawm, Eric, *Nations and Nationalism Since 1780* (Cambridge: Cambridge University Press, 1990).

Iser, Wolfgang, *The Act of Reading: A Theory of Aesthetic Response* (Baltimore: The Johns Hopkins University Press, 1978).

Ishida, Tomoo, *The Royal Dynasties in Ancient Israel* (BZAW, 142; Berlin: W. de Gruyter, 1977).

Janowski, B., *Gottes Gegenwart* (BTAT, 1; Neukirchen–Vluyn: Neukirchener Verlag, 1993).

—*Sühne als Heilsgeschehen: Studien zur Sühnetheologie der Priesterschrift und zur Wurzel KPR im Alten Orient und im Alten Testament* (WMANT, 55; Neukirchen–Vluyn: Neukirchener Verlag, 1982).

Japhet, Sara, *I and II Chronicles* (OTL; Louisville, KY: WJK, 1993).

—*Ideology of the Books of Chronicles and Its Place in Biblical Thought* (trans. Anna Barber; BEATaJ, 9; Frankfurt/M: Lang, 1989).

Jenson, P., *Graded Holiness* (JSOTSup, 106; Sheffield: JSOT Press, 1992).

Jewett, Robert, and John Shelton Laurence, *Captain America and the Crusade Against Evil* (Grand Rapids: Eerdmans, 2003).

Jobling, David, *The Sense of Biblical Narrative: Structural Analyses in the Hebrew Bible II* (JSOTSup, 39; Sheffield: JSOT Press, 1986, 1987).

Kang, J. J., *The Persuasive Portrayal of Solomon in 1 Kings 1–11* (EUS, XXIII/760; Bern: Peter Lang, 2003).

Keys, Gillian, *The Wages of Sin: a Reappraisal of the 'Succession Narrative'* (JSOTSup, 221; Sheffield: Sheffield Academic Press, 1996).

Klement, H. H., *II Samuel 21–24. Context, Structure and Meaning in the Samuel Conclusion* (EUS XXIII/682; Frankfurt/M: Peter Lang, 2000).

Klein, R. W., *1 Samuel* (WBC; Waco, TX: Word Books, 1983).

Knierim, Rolf, *The Task of Old Testament Theology: Substance, Method and Cases* (Grand Rapids: Eerdmans, 1995).

Knight, D. A., 'Political Rights and Powers in Monarchic Israel', in Knight (ed.), *Ethics and Politics in the Hebrew Bible* (*Semeia* 66; Atlanta: Scholars Press, 1995), pp. 93–117.

Knoppers, G. N., *Two Nations Under God: The Deuteronomistic History of Solomon and the Dual Monarchies* (HSM, 52-53; 2 vols.; Atlanta: Scholars Press, 1993–94).

Kuschel, Karl-Josef, *Abraham: a Symbol of Hope for Jews, Christians and Muslims* (trans. John Bowden; London: SCM Press, 1995).

Launderville, Dale, *Piety and Politics: The Dynamics of Royal Authority in Homeric Greece, Biblical Israel, and Old Babylonian Mesopotamia* (Grand Rapids: Eerdmans, 2003).

Levenson, Jon D., *Creation and the Persistence of Evil: The Jewish Drama of Divine Omnipotence* (San Francisco: Harpercollins, 1988).

—*Sinai and Zion: An Entry into the Jewish Bible* (Minneapolis: Winston, 1985).

—'The Temple and the World', *JR* 64 (1984), pp. 275–98.

Levinson, B. M., *Deuteronomy and the Hermeneutics of Legal Innovation* (New York: Oxford University Press, 1998).

Lichtheim, Miriam, *Ancient Egyptian Literature I: The Old and Middle Kingdoms* (Berkeley: University of California Press, 1975).

Linville, James, *Israel in the Book of Kings: The Past as a Project of Social Identity* (JSOTSup, 272; Sheffield: Sheffield Academic Press, 1998).

Lohfink, N., 'Die Bedeutungen von hebr. jrš qal und hif', *BZ* 27 (1983), pp. 14–33.

—'Die Sicherung der Wirksamkeit des Gotteswortes durch das Prinzip der Schriftlichkeit der Torah und durch das Prinzip der Gewaltenteilung nach den Ämtergesetzen des Buches Deuteronomium (Dt 16,18–18,22)', in H. Wolter (ed.), *Testimonium Veritati* (FS W. Kempf; Frankfurt: Knecht, 1971), pp. 143–55; English edn, 'Distribution of the Functions of Power: The Laws Concerning Public Offices in Deuteronomy 16:18–18:22', in D. L. Christensen (ed.), *A Song of Power and the Power of Song* (SBTS, 3; Winona Lake: Eisenbrauns, 1993), pp. 336–52.

—'Gewalt und Monotheismus: Beispiel Altes Testament', *ThPQ* 153,2 (2005), pp. 149–62.

—'Macht Euch die Erde untertan', in *Studien zum Pentateuch* (SBAB, 4; Stuttgart, Verlag Katholisches Bibelwerk, 1988), pp. 11–28.

—'The Cult-Reform of Josiah of Judah: II Kings 22–23 as a Source for the History of Israelite Religion', in P. D. Hanson (ed.), *Ancient Israelite Religion: Essays in Honor of Frank Moore Cross* (Philadelphia: Fortress, 1987), pp. 459–75.

—*Theology of the Pentateuch: Themes of the Priestly Narrative and Deuteronomy* (trans. Linda M. Maloney; Edinburgh: T&T Clark, 1994).

—'Zur Fabel des Deuteronomiums', in Braulik (ed.), *Bundesdokument und Gesetz*, pp. 65–78.

Lyons, William John, *Canon and Exegesis: Canonical Praxis and the Sodom Narrative* (JSOTSup, 352; Sheffield: Sheffield Academic Press, 2002).

MacDonald, Nathan, *Deuteronomy and the Meaning of "Monotheism"* (FAT 2/1; Tübingen: Mohr-Siebeck, 2003).

Mayes, A. D. H., 'On Describing the Purpose of Deuteronomy', *JSOT* 58 (1993), pp. 13–33.

McBride, S. Dean, 'Deuteronomy', in John H. Hayes (ed.), *Dictionary of Biblical Interpretation A-J* (Nashville: Abingdon Press, 1999), pp. 273–94.

—'Polity of the Covenant People: the Book of Deuteronomy', *Interpretation* 41 (1987), pp. 229–44, repr. in Christensen (ed.), *A Song of Power*, pp. 62–77.

McCarter, P. K., *I Samuel* (AB; New York: Doubleday, 1980).

—*II Samuel* (AB; New York: Doubleday, 1984).

McCarthy, D. J., 'The Inauguration of Monarchy in Ancient Israel: A Form-Critical Study of
     I Samuel 1–12', *Interpretation* 27 (1973), pp. 401–12.
McConville, J. G., *Deuteronomy* (AOTC, 5; Leicester; Apollos, 2002).
—'Deuteronomy's Unification of Passover and Massot', *JBL* 119 (2000), pp. 47–58.
— 'King and Messiah in Deuteronomy and the Deuteronomistic History', in John Day (ed.),
     King and Messiah in the Old Testament (JSOTSup, 270; Sheffield: Sheffield Academic
     Press, 1998), pp. 271–95.
—'Law and Monarchy in Deuteronomy', in Bartholomew *et al.* (eds.), *A Royal Priesthood?* pp.
     69–88.
—'Narrative and Meaning in the Books of Kings', *Biblica* 70 (1989), pp. 31–49.
—'Singular Address in the Deuteronomic Law and the Politics of Legal Administration', *JSOT*
     97 (2002), pp. 19–36.
McConville, J. G., and J. G. Millar, *Time and Place in Deuteronomy* (JSOTSup, 179; Sheffield:
     Sheffield Academic Press, 1994).
Mettinger, T., *The Dethronement of Sabaoth: Studies in the Shem and Kabod Theologies*
     (ConBot, 18; Lund: C. W. K. Gleerup, 1982).
Milton, John, *The Tenure of Kings and Magistrates*, in Stephen Orgel and Jonathan Goldberg
     (eds.), *John Milton: The Major Works* (Oxford World Classics; Oxford: Oxford Univer-
     sity Press, 2003).
Miscall, Peter D., *1 Samuel: A Literary Reading* (Bloomington: Indiana University Press, 1986).
Mitchell, G., *Together in the Land: A Reading of the Book of Joshua* (JSOTSup, 134; Sheffield;
     Sheffield Academic Press, 1993).
Moberly, R. W. L., *At the Mountain of God: Story and Theology in Exodus 32–34* (JSOTSup,
     22; Sheffield: JSOT Press, 1983).
—*The Old Testament of the Old Testament: Patriarchal Narratives and Mosaic Yahwism* (OBT;
     2; Minneapolis: Fortress Press, 1992; repr. Eugene, Oregon: Wipf and Stock, 2001).
—'Toward an Interpretation of the Shema', in C. Seitz and K. Greene-McCreight (eds.),
     Theological Exegesis in Honor of Brevard S. Childs (Grand Rapids; Eerdmans, 1999),
     pp. 124–44.
Moberly, R. W. L., R. D. Nelson and G. Braulik, 'The Destruction of the Nations and the
     Promise of Return: Hermeneutical Observations on the Book of Deuteronomy', *Verbum
     et Ecclesia* 25.1 (2004), pp. 46–65.
Moran, W. L., 'The Ancient Near Eastern Background of the Love of God in Deuteronomy',
     CBQ 25 (1963), pp. 77–87.
Mosala, Itumeleng, *Biblical Hermeneutics and Black Theology in South Africa* (Grand Rapids:
     Eerdmans, 1989).
Mullen, E. T., *Ethnic Myths and Pentateuchal Foundations: a New Approach to the Formation
     of the Pentateuch* (Atlanta: Scholars Press, 1997).
—*Narrative History and Ethnic Boundaries* (SBL Semeia Studies; Atlanta: Scholars Press,
     1993).
Murray, Donald F., *Divine Prerogative and Royal Pretension* (JSOTSup, 264; Sheffield: Shef-
     field Academic Press, 1998).
Nelson, R. D., *Joshua* (OTL; Louisville, KY: WJK, 1997).
—'Josiah in the Book of Joshua', *JBL* 100 (1981), pp. 531–40.
—*The Double Redaction of the Deuteronomistic History* (JSOTSup, 18; Sheffield: Sheffield
     Academic Press, 1981).
Nicholson, E. W., *Deuteronomy and Tradition* (Oxford: Blackwell, 1967).
Nissinen, M., C. L. Seow and Robert K. Ritner, *Prophets and Prophecy in the Ancient Near
     East* (Writings from the Ancient World, 12; Atlanta; SBL, 2003).
Noth, M., *Das Buch Josua* (HAT, I/7; Tübingen: Mohr-Siebeck, 1953).
O'Donovan, Oliver, *Desire of the Nations: Rediscovering the Roots of Political Theology*
     (Cambridge: Cambridge University Press, 1996).

Olson, Dennis T., 'The Book of Judges' (New Interpreter's Bible II; Nashville: Abingdon Press, 1998), pp. 721–888.

Otto, E., *Krieg und Frieden in der Hebräischen Bibel und im Alten Orient* (Stuttgart: W. Kohlhammer, 1999).

—'Rechtsreformen in Deuteronomium XII–XXVI und im Mittelassyrischen Kodex der Tafel A (KAV 1)' (VTSup, 61; Leiden: E. J. Brill, 1995), pp. 239–73.

—*Wandel der Rechtsbegründungen in der Gesellschaftsgeschichte des antiken Israel: eine Rechtsgeschichte des "Bundesbuches" Ex XX 22—XXIII 13* (StudBib, 3; Leiden: E. J. Brill, 1988).

Perlitt, L., 'Der Staatsgedanke im Deuteronomium', in S. E. Balentine and J. Barton (eds.), *Language, Theology and the Bible: Essays in Honour of James Barr* (Oxford: Oxford University Press, 1994), pp. 182–98.

Person, Raymond F., *The Deuteronomic School: History, Social Setting, and Literature* (Studies in Biblical Literature, 2; Leiden: E. J. Brill, 2002).

Pixley, George V., *On Exodus: A Liberation Perspective* (Maryknoll, NY: Orbis Books, 1987).

Polzin, R., *David and the Deuteronomist* (Bloomington and Indianapolis: Indiana University Press, 1993).

—*Samuel and the Deuteronomist* (New York: Harper& Row, 1989).

Provan, Iain W., *1 and 2 Kings* (NIBC; Peabody, MA: Hendrickson, 1995).

—*Hezekiah and the Book of Kings* (BZAW, 172; Berlin: W. de Gruyter, 1988).

Rad, G. von, *Das Gottesvolk im Deuteronomium* (BWANT, 47; Stuttgart: W. Kohlhammer, 1929).

—'Faith Reckoned as Righteousness', in von Rad, *The Problem of the Hexateuch and Other Essays* (trans. E. W. Trueman Dicken; London: Oliver and Boyd, 1966), pp. 125–30.

—*Old Testament Theology I* (trans. D. G. M. Stalker; Edinburgh and London: Oliver and Boyd, 1962).

—'The Problem of the Hexateuch', in *The Problem of the Hexateuch*, pp. 1–78.

—'The Theological Problem of the Old Testament Doctrine of Creation', in *The Problem of the Hexateuch*, pp. 131–43.

—*Wisdom in Israel* (trans. James D. Martin; London: SCM Press, 1972).

Richter, Sandra L., *The Deuteronomistic History and the Name Theology: l°šakkēn š°mô šām in the Bible and the Ancient Near East* (BZAW, 318; Berlin/New York: W. de Gruyter, 2002).

Richter, W., *Die Bearbeitungen des 'Retterbuches', in der deuteronomischen Epoche* (BBB, 21; Bonn: Peter Hanstein, 1964).

Ricoeur, Paul, *Interpretation Theory* (Fort Worth: T.C.U. Press, 1976).

—'Metaphor and the Central Problem of Hermeneutics', in J. B. Thompson (ed.), *Hermeneutics and the Human Sciences: Essays on Language, Action, and Interpretation* (Cambridge: Cambridge University Press, 1981), pp. 165–81.

Rivers, Julian, 'Nationhood', in Michael Schluter and John Ashcroft (eds.), *Jubilee Manifesto* (Leicester: IVP, 2005), pp. 122–37.

Rost, L., *The Succession to the Throne of David* (trans. Michael D. Rutter and David M. Gunn; Sheffield; Almond Press, 1982; original 1926).

Rowland, Christopher, 'In This Place: the Center and the Margins in Theology', in Fernando F. Segovia and Mary Ann Tolbert (eds.), *Reading from this Place: Social Location and Biblical Interpretation in Global Perspective* (Minneapolis: Augsburg Fortress, 1995), pp. 177–82.

Rüterswörden, U., *Von der politischen Gemeinschaft zur Gemeinde. Studien zu Dt 16,18–18,22* (BBB, 65: Frankfurt: Athenäum, 1987).

Said, Edward, *Culture and Imperialism* (London: Chatto and Windus, 1993).

Schäfer-Lichtenberger, C., 'Der deuteronomische Verfassungsentwurf: Theologische Vorgaben als Gestaltungsprinzipien sozialer Realität', in Braulik (ed.), *Bundesdokument und Gesetz*, pp. 104–18.

—*Josua und Salomo: eine Studie zu Autorität und Legitimität des Nachfolgers im Alten Testament* (VTSup, 58; Leiden: E. J. Brill, 1995).

Schmid, H. H., 'Creation, Righteousness and Salvation: "Creation Theology" as the Broad Horizon of Biblical Theology', in B. W. Anderson (ed.), *Creation in the Old Testament* (Philadelphia: Fortress, 1984), pp. 102–17.

—*Gerechtigkeit als Weltordnung: Hintergrund und Geschichte des alttestamentlichen Gerechtigkeitsbegriffes* (BHT, 40; Tübingen: Mohr-Siebeck, 1968).

Schmid, Konrad, *Erzväter und Exodus: Untersuchungen zur doppelten Begründung der Ursprünge Israels innerhalb der Geschichtsbücher des Alten Testaments* (WMANT, 81; Neukirchen–Vluyn: Neukirchener Verlag, 1999).

Schmitt, R., *Zelt und Lade als Thema alttestamentlicher Wissenschaft: eine kritische forschungsgeschichtliche Darstellung* (Gütersloh: Mohn, 1972).

Schüle, Andreas, 'Made in the "Image of God": The Concepts of Divine Images in Gen 1–3', *ZAW* 117 (2005), pp. 1–20.

Schwartz, Regina M., *The Curse of Cain: The Violent Legacy of Monotheism* (Chicago and London: University of Chicago Press, 1997).

Seitz, G., *Redaktionsgeschichtliche Studien zum Deuteronomium* (BWANT, 93; Stuttgart: W. Kohlhammer, 1971).

Shils, Edward, *Center and Periphery: Essays in Macrosociology* (New York: St. Martin's, 1975).

Ska, Jean-Louis, 'Biblical Law and the Origins of Democracy', in William P. Brown (ed.), *The Ten Commandments: The Reciprocity of Faithfulness* (Louisville, KY: WJK, 2004), pp. 146–58.

Smend, R., 'Das Gesetz und die Völker: ein Beitrag zur deuteronomistischen Redaktionsgeschichte', in H. W. Wolff (ed.), *Probleme biblischer Theologie: Festschrift Gerhard von Rad* (Munich: Chr. Kaiser, 1971), pp. 494–509, translated as 'The Law and the Nations: a Contribution to Deuteronomistic Tradition History', in G. N. Knoppers and J. G. McConville (eds.), *Reconsidering Israel and Judah* (SBTS; Winona Lake: Eisenbrauns, 2002), pp. 95–110.

—*Yahweh War and Tribal Confedaration* (New York and Nashville: Abingdon Press, 1970).

Smith, A. D., *Chosen Peoples* (Oxford and New York: Oxford University Press, 2003).

Smith, Mark S., *The Early History of God; Yahweh and the Other Deities in Ancient Israel* (San Francisco; Harper & Row, 1990).

Smith, Morton, *Palestinian Parties and Politics That Shaped the Old Testament* (New York: Columbia University Press, 1971; London: SCM Press, 2nd edn, 1987).

Smith-Christopher, Daniel L., 'The Mixed Marriage Crisis in Ezra 9–10 and Nehemiah 13: A Study of the Sociology of the Post-Exilic Judaean Community', in Tamara C. Eskenazi and Kent H. Richards (eds.), *Second Temple Studies, 2: Temple Community in the Persian Period* (JSOTSup, 175; Sheffield: JSOT Press, 1994), pp. 243–65.

Sonnet, J.-P., *The Book Within the Book: Writing in Deuteronomy* (Biblical Interpretation Series, 14; Leiden: E. J. Brill, 1997).

Sparks, Kenton L., *Ethnicity and Identity in Ancient Israel* (Winona Lake: Eisenbrauns, 1998).

Stern Ephraim, *Archaeology of the Land of the Bible. II. The Assyrian, Babylonian and Persian Periods (732–332 B.C.E.)* (ABRL; New York: Doubleday, 2001).

—'The Babylonian Gap: the Archaeological Reality', *JSOT* 28 (2004), pp. 273–7.

Steymans, U., *Deuteronomium 28 und die adê zur Thronfolgeregelung Asarhaddons: Segen und Fluch im Alten Orient und in Israel* (OBO, 145; Göttingen: Vandenhoeck & Ruprecht, 1995).

Stiver, Dan, 'Ricoeur, Speech-act Theory, and the Gospels as History', in Bartholomew *et al.* (eds.), *After Pentecost*, pp. 50–72.

Stulman, Louis, *Order Amid Chaos: Jeremiah as Symbolic Tapestry* (Biblical Seminar, 57; Sheffield: Sheffield Academic Press, 1998).

Sweeney, Marvin A., *King Josiah of Judah: the Lost Messiah of Israel* (Oxford: Oxford University Press, 2001).

Tate, W. R., *Biblical Interpretation: An Integrated Approach* (Peabody, Mass.: Hendrickson, 1991).

Thanzauva and R. L. Hnuni, 'Ethnicity, Identity and Hermeneutics: An Indian Tribal Perspective', in Mark G. Brett (ed.), *Ethnicity and the Bible* (Leiden: E. J. Brill, 2002), pp. 343–57.

Thiselton, A. C., '"Behind" and "In Front of" the Text: Language, Reference and Indeterminacy', in Bartholomew *et al.* (eds.), *After Pentecost*, pp. 97–120.

Tsumura, D., *The Earth and the Waters in Genesis 1 and 2: A Linguistic Investigation* (JSOTSup, 83; Sheffield: Sheffield Academic Press, 1989).

Vanhoozer, K., *Is There a Meaning in This Text? The Bible, the Reader, and the Morality of Literary Knowledge* (Grand Rapids: Zondervan, 1998).

Vannoy, R., *Covenant Renewal at Gilgal* (Cherry Hill, NJ; Mack, 1978).

Van Seters, John, *Prologue to History: the Yahwist as Historian in Genesis* (Louisville, KY: WJK, 1992).

Vogt, Peter, *Deuteronomic Theology and the Significance of Torah: A Reappraisal* (Winona Lake: Eisenbrauns, 2006).

Walsh, J. T., *1 Kings* (Berit Olam; Collegeville: Liturgical Press, 1996).

Webb, Barry, *The Book of the Judges: An Integrated Reading* (JSOTSup, 46; Sheffield: JSOT Press, 1987).

Weinfeld, M., *Deuteronomy 1–11* (AB; New York, Doubleday, 1991).

—*Deuteronomy and the Deuteronomic School* (Oxford; Clarendon Press, 1972).

—'Sabbath, Temple and the Enthronement of the Lord: The Problem of the *Sitz im Leben* of Genesis 1:1–2:3', in A. Caquot and M. Decor (eds.), *Mélanges bibliques et orientaux en l'honneur de M. Henri Cazelles* (AOAT, 212; Kevelaer/Neukirchen–Vluyn, 1981), pp. 501–12.

Wenham, G. J., *Genesis 1–15* (WBC, 1; Waco, TX; Word Books, 1987).

—*Genesis 16–50* (WBC, 2; Dallas: Word Books, 1994).

—'Sanctuary Symbolism in the Garden of Eden Story', in *Proceedings of the Ninth Congress of Jewish Studies* (Jerusalem: World Union of Jewish Studies, 1986), pp. 19–25.

Westermann, C., *Blessing in the Bible and the Life of the Church* (trans. Keith Crim; OBT, 3; Philadelphia: Fortress, 1978).

—*Die Geschichtsbücher des Alten Testaments: Gab es ein deuteronomistisches Geschichtswerk?* (TBü, 87; Gütersloh: Kaiser, 1994).

—*Genesis 1–11* (trans. John J. Scullion; Minneapolis; Augsburg,/London: SPCK, 1984).

—*Genesis 12–36* (trans. John J. Scullion; Minneapolis: Augsburg,/London: SPCK, 1985).

Wette de, W. M. L., *Dissertatio Critica* (Jena, 1805).

Whitelam, Keith W., *The Invention of Ancient Israel: The Silencing of Palestinian History* (London: Routledge, 1996).

Williamson, H. G. M., *Israel in the Books of Chronicles* (Cambridge: Cambridge University Press, 1977).

Wolter, Michael, 'Die Vielfalt der Schrift und die Einheit des Kanons', in John Barton and Wolter (eds.), *Die Einheit der Schrift und die Vielfalt des Kanons* (Berlin and New York: W. de Gruyter, 2003), pp. 45–68.

Wright, C. J. H., *God's People in God's Land: Family and Property in the Old Testament* (Grand Rapids: Eerdmans, 1990).

Younger, K. Lawson, 'Ancient Conquest Accounts: a Study in Ancient Near Eastern and Biblical Historiography' (JSOTSup, 98; Sheffield: JSOT Press, 1990).

INDEX OF REFERENCES

OLD TESTAMENT

INDEX OF SUBJECTS

The following short index omits certain terms which recur repeatedly throughout the book such as justice-righteousness, or are localized in the discussion, such as Naboth's vineyard. Alternatively, as in the case of 'land', it indicates a key discussion only. In any case, key discussions are indicated in bold type.